UNIVERSITY OF CALIFORNIA
PUBLICATIONS IN HISTORY

VOLUME L

EDITORS
J. S. GALBRAITH
R. N. BURR
BRAINERD DYER

THE
SOUTHERN CLAIMS
COMMISSION

BY

FRANK W. KLINGBERG

OCTAGON BOOKS

A DIVISION OF FARRAR, STRAUS AND GIROUX

New York   1978

Originally published by the
University of California Press in 1955

Reprinted 1978
by special arrangement with the University of California Press

OCTAGON BOOKS
A DIVISION OF FARRAR, STRAUS & GIROUX, INC.
19 Union Square West
New York, N.Y. 10003

Library of Congress Cataloging in Publication Data

Klingberg, Frank Wysor.
    The Southern Claims Commission.

    Reprint of the 1955 ed. published by the University of California
Press, Berkeley, which was issued as v. 50 of the University of
California publications in history.
    Based on the author's thesis, University of California at Los
Angeles.
    Bibliography: p.
    1. United States. Commissioners of Claims.   2. United States—
History—Civil War, 1861-1865—Claims.   3. United States—
History—Civil War, 1861-1865—Finance, Commerce, Confisca-
tions, etc.   I. Title.   II. Series; California, University, Univer-
sity of California publications in history; v. 50.
[E480.K58   1978]   973.7'14   77-18510
ISBN 0-374-94594-2

Manufactured by Braun-Brumfield, Inc.
Ann Arbor, Michigan
Printed in the United States of America

TO

MY MOTHER AND FATHER

PREFACE

THE RECORD of Southern Unionism which prevailed after Fort Sumter was supposedly preserved only in family history, letters, diaries, and folklore. Unknown, uncatalogued, and unexamined were the voluminous manuscripts of the Southern Claims Commission, scattered through Federal agencies in Washington. The commission was created by act of Congress, March 3, 1871. During the decade of its activity, 22,298 petitions, claiming $60,258,150.44 for quartermaster and commissary supplies furnished the Federal armies, were filed by professed Unionists. A probable 220,000 witnesses for the claimant or the government testified.

The guide to the sources of the National Archives listed miscellaneous records of the commissioners of claims, but these entries led only to a skeleton collection of ledgers, entry journals, account books, and letters. The actual cases were not to be found in the Archives, the Library of Congress, or the usual depositories. When the obvious means of uncovering their whereabouts had been exhausted, a round of interviews traced the prescribed path of a claim lodged against the government. To Congress (petition for redress), the Committee on Claims (preliminary recommendation), the attorney general (ruling on admissibility), the Justice Department (investigation), the Court of Claims (judicial decision), the Treasury Department (payment), the comptroller general (custodian of governmental records in active use), and the General Accounting Office files (storage of disbursement records) went the investigation.

The Accounting Office files, scattered in warehouses in Virginia, contain the fiscal records of the United States government, including claims ranging from the time of the Revolutionary War to the Second World War. For the Civil War period the indices are slender, but gradually the allowed cases of the commission, available by permission of the comptroller general, were separated from the general records. Day after day, dusty packs of folded, tied claims, some in the original cedar chests of the claimants, came to light. Included in many were such records as wills and testaments, letters and diaries, maps and surveyors' reports, newspapers and magazines, plantation accounts and crop inventories, parish records, and county poll lists. The tens of thousands of pages of oral testimony, covering the interviews and statements of persons ranging from the humblest members of society to key figures of government, promptly changed the problem from a paucity of material to overwhelming masses of documents. In their entirety the records are a Middletown survey of the Confederacy.

How were these records to be handled? By year, by state, or by region? A selection was suggested by the fact that the cases in excess of $10,000 had been designated for special investigation by the commissioners. These petitions contained the documents of the wealthy planter Unionists. However, the witnesses were assembled on a scale large enough to provide a cross section of Southern society during the Civil War.

The disallowed cases were not in these files, and the majority of them have not been systematically preserved. Some reverted to claimants or to their heirs. Others remained in the custody of attorneys. Cases subsequently appealed were transferred, with their accumulated records, to the Court of Claims, and can now be found in the Justice Department of the National Archives. Cases never reopened were examined in the House File Room, and have now been transferred to the Legislative Department of the National Archives. For every claim disallowed by the commissioners, however, a brief summary covering only the decision was printed in a four-volume set, of which only fifty copies were issued. Of these, only three broken sets are known to be in the hands of private persons. Complete sets are available in the House File Room and the Federal Bureau of Investigation. The summary reports for the allowed cases have never been printed.

The Southern Claims Commission records are concerned exclusively with quartermaster and commissary goods. The Court of Claims had original jurisdiction over the so-called cotton cases, under the Captured and Abandoned Property acts, and these records are stored in the Justice Department of the National Archives. They furnish another avenue for study of the Unionist minority, to be treated separately from this study at a later time. Frequently a claimant appears in the records of both agencies.

Visits to the home towns of the three commissioners—Glens Falls, New York, Burlington, Vermont, and Keokuk, Iowa—provided supplementary biographical material. I am particularly indebted to the late Lydia Howell, who allowed me the use of her father's library in Keokuk and gave me both some key items therefrom and the benefit of her recollections. A few legal firms which furnished attorneys before the commission are still active in Washington, and visits to these offices disclosed fragments of records and valuable information as to legal procedures.

Dr. Brainerd Dyer of the University of California, Los Angeles, first aroused my interest in this subject, and my great debt to him as an inspiring teacher and warm friend is not easily acknowledged. Professor Fletcher M. Green of the University of North Carolina shared his wide knowledge of the period with me, first as his student and then as his colleague. Thus, from his learning, he gave focus to my special interests. The late Professor James G. Randall included me in his always generous word and deed for younger men interested in the field over which he had such mastery.

I express my appreciation to the librarians of the National Archives, of the Library of Congress, of the University of North Carolina, and of the University of California, Los Angeles, for their continual aid. I am deeply indebted to the Carnegie Foundation for a grant-in-aid to complete this volume and to the Social Science Research Council and the Huntington Library for grants to pursue further investigations into the intellectual background of the Southern Unionist. Kathleen Harper and Glenn Gosling of the University of California Press were tireless in their assistance. There are many special obligations to those others not herein named whose help entered into the making of the volume in ways small or large.

During nearly a decade of pilgrimage and research, so many people contributed their interest, their practical aid, and their special knowledge, that it is clear such friendliness alone enables the investigator to stay the course.

FRANK W. KLINGBERG

University of North Carolina
August 27, 1954

CONTENTS

CHAPTER I

THE PERSISTENCE OF UNIONISM IN THE SOUTH

WITHIN a few dramatic months in 1861, the Southern Unionist met the first and, in some ways, the most severe test of his convictions. His efforts to arrive at a peaceful solution of the national crisis, which had found expression in the Crittenden Compromise proposals and the Virginia Peace Convention, had failed. He found himself, suddenly, no longer of the majority of his fellow citizens who had opposed secession. He was a man apart, regarded by his community, and often by his friends, with suspicion or with hostility and contempt. A sudden and violent *coup d'état* had made him an alien in his own state and in his own community. The government in Washington, to which he still gave his allegiance and for which, in many instances, he had rendered military service, was arming against him and his section. And within his state, precipitate action and force, rather than reason and compromise, were now accepted policy. In the end he necessarily became a traitor to his state and to the Confederacy.

The Reverend John T. Clark, an Episcopal minister of Halifax County, Virginia, ably described the ostracism of the Unionist. A native Virginian, who had inherited "a large fortune, & many slaves," Clark had voted for a Union candidate to the constitutional convention in Virginia in 1861 and had refused to vote for the ordinance of secession. "I was denounced at the time," he wrote, "as an Abolitionist, A southern man with Northern feelings, A dirt eater, a Submissionist; & my friends were very uneasy & thought I had ruined my character, & it was for a good while under a cloud."[1]

Faced with the actuality of secession, most Southerners who had opposed the trend of events went, of course, with their state and section. North and South, men divided into three groups. A small, vocal, and bellicose minority in each section called only for force and a show of strength. Another small minority, confirmed in its dissent against the decision of the region, organized for resisting the program of their government.[2] The majority of men on both sides of the Mason-Dixon

---

[1] Statement of the Reverend John T. Clark to Special Commissioner M. F. Pleasant, Feb. 10, 1873, in his own case [claimed $8,532, allowed $5,255 in 1873]. Commissioners of Claims Number 13330, General Accounting Office files. Hereafter cited as C. of C. No. 13330, GAO files.

[2] Two studies of the minority of protest in the North, which corresponded with the Unionist group in the South, are Wood Gray, *The Hidden Civil War, the Story of the Copperheads* (New York, 1942), and George Fort Milton, *Abraham Lincoln and the Fifth Column* (New York, 1942).

Line, who had continued to the last to hope that war could be averted, shortly found themselves in the army, wearing unfamiliar blue or unfamiliar gray.

Historically, there were many reasons for loyalty to the Republic to continue into the war years. Southern internal sectionalism did not vanish with secession. A million whites, occupying an area in the Appalachian highlands as large as a kingdom of western Europe, were almost untouched by the plantation pattern of Southern life. These hill-country men were a well-known center of opposition to the Confederate government. At the Alabama secession convention, when W. L. Yancey called all "coöperationists" traitors, Nick Davis, of Madison County, is said to have challenged him to bring a force of men to the Tennessee Valley where, he promised, "we will meet him at the foot of our mountains, and there, with his own selected weapons, hand to hand, face to face, settle the question of the sovereignty of the people."[3]

In South Carolina, contemporary accounts described the indignation of six hundred small farmers of the Greenville district who advanced on that town to force the state back into the Union.[4] As late as July 4, 1861, the New York *Tribune* called for active support for the "loyal people of the Southern States," who had gathered at the Greenville convention. These mountain men were of strategic importance, the *Tribune* suggested, and the "best guaranty for the continuance of the Federal Government" would be a military campaign to rescue the anti-secession areas of Mississippi, Alabama, Georgia, and North Carolina, in order that the loyal highlands could form a Union state of their own "in the very heart of the slave-holding country."[5]

Obviously, the South was not as unified as the dominance of its major crops would suggest. The rich alluvial bottom lands, where sugar and cotton prospered, were only oases in the sandy plains, the dense pine forests, or the impassable swamps which formed so large a part of the southern coast lands. In the piedmont areas of every state that

---

[3] H. C. Nixon, *Lower Piedmont Country* (New York, 1946), p. 26.

[4] J. W. De Forest, "Chivalrous and Semi-Chivalrous Southerners," *Harper's New Monthly Magazine*, XXXVIII (March, 1869), 339–347. De Forest added that when Governor Ben Perry went out to meet them, to explain that "the government under which you were born no longer exists" and that they owed their allegiance to the Confederacy, half of them were said to have returned to the mountains, and the other half joined the Southern army at Manassas. De Forest's papers covering his service as an officer in the Freedman's Bureau in South Carolina are revealing documents on reconstruction. See John William De Forest, *A Union Officer in Reconstruction*, edited by James H. Croushore and David M. Potter (New Haven, 1948), *passim*.

[5] "The Loyal Southerners," New York *Daily Tribune*, July 4, 1861, Vol. XXI, No. 6308, p. 4.

seceded, the struggle between plantation and family farm, which helped to split Virginia, for instance, into two states, was in process. Statistics on landholdings in the border states of the Mississippi Valley in the late 1850's show a trend toward ownership of smaller homestead acreages like the diversified farms of the agrarian West.[6] And, as Charles W. Ramsdell has maintained, improved farm machinery, transportation facilities, and increased immigration were, by 1860, setting the natural and impassable limit for the slave system.[7]

Moreover, the political monopoly of the cotton leaders of the South was being challenged by increasing production of the staple in India and Egypt. This fact helps explain the weakness of cotton as a weapon of diplomacy. The three important years following 1860 were to show further that the demand for wheat in England would rival the demand for raw cotton, especially as a cotton surplus rested in English warehouses. Wheat importations to Britain from the North increased from 2 million quarters in 1860 to 3½ million quarters in 1861. By 1862 they had risen to more than 5 million quarters.[8] On August 17, 1864, James Mason wrote hopefully from London that good harvests in Europe during the summer of 1863 promised that the North would not again be able to "supply the deficiency of Southern products by the export of Northern grain, and thus effect their exchanges without any important drain of specie."[9] However, by this date, the supplies of Northern wheat, military events in the states, emancipation, and cotton from the Middle East had already served to weaken the demand in Britain for the recognition of the Confederacy.

Scattered throughout the South were men who welcomed the internal and external challenges to the dominant interest. Sugar planters and

[6] Two studies of trends in land ownership, based on statistics, are Frank L. and Harriet C. Owsley, "The Economic Basis of Society in the Late Ante-Bellum South," *The Journal of Southern History,* VI (1940), 24–45, and, by the same authors, "The Economic Structure of Rural Tennessee, 1850–1860," *ibid.,* VIII (1943), 161–182.

[7] Charles W. Ramsdell, "The Natural Limits of Slavery Expansion," *Mississippi Valley Historical Review,* XVI (1929), 151–171.

[8] It has been estimated that England had manufactured and stored in its warehouses 300 million pounds of cotton above the demands of normal production. See Sir Arthur Arnold, *The History of the Cotton Famine* (London, 1864), pp. 54, 81, and George McHenry, *The Cotton Trade* (London, 1863), pp. 49–51. See also Louis B. Schmidt, "The Influence of Wheat and Cotton on Anglo-American Relations during the Civil War," *Iowa Journal of History and Politics,* XVI (1918), 400–439; "Indian versus American Cotton," *The London Economist* (April 13, 1861); Eli Ginzberg, "The Economics of British Neutrality During the American Civil War," *Agricultural History,* X (1936), 147–156; and Frank L. Owsley, *King Cotton Diplomacy* (Chicago, 1931), chap. xix.

[9] James M. Mason to Judah P. Benjamin, Aug. 17, 1864, in the letters of James M. Mason, Manuscript Division, Library of Congress. On June 23, 1862, Mason had written that recognition was delayed because of these large stocks.

industrialists, particularly, desired a more diversified economy. The prospect that the rising Northern industrialism would spread to the South, had been anticipated by Calhoun when he was an advocate of the protective tariff. This industrial development, a fact today, was for the moment delayed by the westward pull of the farm frontier aided by the railroads, and the eastward pull of English cotton markets. But there is considerable evidence that an alliance between Northern capital and Southern resources was likewise more than a possibility and that some influential leaders in both sections expected it. Other men, impassioned by the crisis, were calling for immediate action. In the North, the extremists applauded the abolitionists and the Union, without regard for the interests of the cotton kingdom. In the South, the planters deified their economic system in the name of state rights and the Constitution. It was a time, as Avery Craven has pointed out, when "by the strange twistings of Fate, the three great strands of development in the life span of a generation of Americans, were tangled together in such a way as to push reason aside and to give emotion full sway." Westward expansion had magnified the issue of constitutional rights and sharpened sectional differences. The growth of industrial power posed the problem of minority and majority rights. And finally, "humanitarian impulses and awakened religious feelings supplied the emotions with which sectional positions and sectional interests could be glorified."[10]

Even without such geographic and economic factors as were involved, it seems clear that the Jeffersonian individualism of a Southern agrarian society would hardly have produced an immediate and unquestioning unanimity of opinion. Further, Southern Unionism drew strength from the ties of blood, of education, of religion, of politics, and of a common history which could not be wiped out at a single blow. During the period of rapid American expansion, the people, it must be remembered, moved south as well as west.[11] In three generations, Jefferson Davis' family had lived in Pennsylvania, Georgia, western Kentucky, Louisiana, and Mississippi. Nathaniel Wright Stephenson has called attention to the fact that about half of the leading men in the plantation areas of the Southwest were born in the North. Mississippi was typical of this new order in the South, and of the six great names in the history of the state before the war, not one of these pioneers

---

[10] Avery Craven, *The Coming of the Civil War* (New York, 1942), p. 15.

[11] For discussions of migrations from the South into the Northwest, see H. C. Hubbard, " 'Pro-Southern' Influence in the Free West, 1840–1865," *Mississippi Valley Historical Review*, XX (1933), 45–62, and Wood Gray, *op. cit.*

was born there. Jacob Thompson was born in North Carolina; John A. Quitman in New York; Henry S. Foote in Virginia; Robert J. Walker in Pennsylvania; Sergeant S. Prentiss in Maine; and Jefferson Davis in Kentucky. "These men," Stephenson wrote, "used the political philosophy taught them by South Carolina. But it was a mental weapon in political debate; it was not for them an emotional fact."[12]

The strength of "the cause of the Union" in the arena of Southern politics is likewise a well-established fact. Before the war, the South had never voted solidly as a section. Southerners had divided their votes, and sometimes almost equally, between the Whig and Democratic parties.[13] The chasm of sectionalism revealed by Lincoln and Breckinridge in 1860 was more decisive in the electoral college than in the popular vote. In the Border states, truly representative of both points of view, widespread support developed for every compromise proposal. Clay's central valley voted for moderation, by supporting the Bell-Everett and Douglas tickets rather than those of Lincoln or Breckinridge.[14] And this valley, it should be added, had its tributaries in the deep South. In Mississippi and Louisiana, especially, the old-line Whigs, many of whom had known Clay personally, cast their votes reluctantly, but generally made their choice between Bell or Douglas.[15] A tragedy of the war is the fact that these areas, which had entertained the hope of peace, were to serve so largely as the battleground wherein the issue was resolved by force and destruction.

For such loyal individuals the cause of the Union was not held to be the exclusive property of the North. And frequently that conviction was firmly based in the political and economic reasoning which

[12] Nathaniel W. Stephenson, *The Day of the Confederacy* (New Haven, 1920), pp. 29–30.

[13] Totals on the popular vote in five presidential elections, compiled from Edward Stanwood, *A History of Presidential Elections* (Boston, 1888), pp. 138, 158, 176, 191, and 210. In 1840 the Whig vote in the existing states which later seceded was 253,974 for Harrison to 223,253 Democratic votes; in 1844 Clay polled 252,916 Whig votes to Polk's 279,145; in 1848, the Whig choice of Zachary Taylor brought 290,757 votes from the South, to 279,761 Democratic votes for Cass; in 1852 the Whig vote for Scott dropped to 238,303, whereas the Democrats polled 307,778 for Pierce, and in 1856 the last Whig presidential candidate, Millard Fillmore, drew 310,317, to 431,954 for Buchanan. These totals do not include South Carolina, where the legislature made the choice, and in the early period exclude Texas and Florida, which had not yet attained statehood.

[14] See Stanwood, *Presidential Elections*, p. 234, for the vote by states in the 1860 elections. Bell's total of 588,879 popular votes plus the Douglas vote of 1,376,957 more than equals the Lincoln vote totaling 1,866,452. The popular vote for Douglas in the Southern and Border states was 163,534; for Bell, 516,018, and for Breckinridge, 571,052, the Douglas strength coming largely from the Border states.

[15] For the influence on postwar attitudes of the former Whigs in this area, see David H. Donald, "The Scalawag in Mississippi Reconstruction," *Journal of Southern History*, X (1944), 447–460.

made "the Constitution and the Union" a familiar Whig slogan. During the period of the Whig ascendancy, the issue had been political rather than sectional, as Southern planters, Northern capitalists, and prosperous Western yeomen united to form the backbone of the party. From the Ohio valley, wheat, pork, and other marketable commodities moved south along the rivers, destined for the plantations, and many planters were ready to ally themselves with the urban Whigs of the North who were spinning more cotton in their mills each year. "The Cotton Whigs" of Massachusetts, for their part, not only recognized their dependence upon the South for raw materials but also believed that the plantation market was the very basis of Northern prosperity. They joined the planters in supporting internal improvements and fought with the shipowners whose interests were largely tied to the seacoasts. In 1846, Ralph Waldo Emerson noted briefly but bitterly in his *Journal*, "Cotton thread holds the Union together; unites John C. Calhoun and Abbott Lawrence. Patriotism for holidays and summer evenings with rockets but cotton thread is the union."[16]

As a "national party," the Whig opposition at the time of Jackson had used shifts in economic, social, and political power in both sections to increase its strength. During the following decades, the party furnished the great compromisers, and their driving purpose was always the preservation of the Union. Moreover, even on the slavery issue, the Whig apostles of moderation, North and South, were capable of supporting reforms for their own section before casting aspersions on the institutions of the other. Horace Greeley's early response to Calhoun's frequent attacks on conditions in Northern factories is revealed in his statement to an antislavery convention in Cincinnati in 1845. "If I am less troubled . . . by the slavery prevalent in Charleston or New Orleans," he wrote, "it is because I see so much Slavery in New York. . . . Whenever opportunity to Labor is obtained with difficulty, and is so deficient that the employment class may virtually prescribe their own terms and pay laborers only such shares as they choose of the product there is a very strong tendency to Slavery."[17]

In the same way, the Whig party of the upper South attracted some men who saw gradual emancipation as the only solution for slavery. The Emancipation Convention of Frankfort, Kentucky, on April 25, 1849, brought together 150 delegates from twenty-four counties. Present

---

[16] Edward Waldo Emerson and Waldo Emerson Forbes, eds., *Journals of Ralph Waldo Emerson with Annotations*, VII (Boston, 1912), 201. Hereafter cited as Emerson, *Journals*.

[17] New York *Tribune*, June 20, 1845, p. 1, col. 3.

were the two senators, Henry Clay and Joseph R. Underwood, as well as a number of prominent Kentucky slaveholders who were advocates of freedom for their slaves. Clay, his hopes for the presidency having dwindled, had come forward on the issue so positively that he was, according to one commentator, "looked to as the head of this [the Emancipation] party—though too old to take an active part in the campaign." In his well-known letter to Richard Pindell at this time, Clay combined a scheme for colonization with a proposal that slaves born after 1855 or 1860 should become free when they had attained the age of twenty-five.[18]

In Congress, T. L. Clingman, a North Carolina Whig, voted in 1844 for the repeal of the famous Gag Rule because he believed it added strength and fury to the cause of the abolitionists. Kenneth Rayner of the same state, who owned a hundred slaves, incurred the journalistic wrath of such Democrats as W. W. Holden when he called slavery the misfortune rather than the blessing of his section. At the same time, he warned that the abolitionists had "thrown back the cause of non-slavery in the South, at least a century."[19] Even Emerson was not always the radical abolitionist. In 1851 he suggested compensation as an answer to the problem of slavery, when he wrote in his *Journal*, "We will buy the slaves at a hundred millions. It will be cheaper than any of our wars. It will be cheap at the cost of a national debt like Engand's."[20] If the course of reform could have followed the national pattern set by England, where rival industries, such as cotton and wool, reformed each other, or where agriculture and industry, supported by humanitarians, legislated for each other, the American tradition for compromise might have solved the slavery problem.

The reluctance of the die-hard Whig planters to join with the Southern Democrats appears in the election returns of 1860.[21] These men of moderation had a disdain for the so-called "fire-eaters" of the South which almost equaled their contempt for the abolitionists of the North. They considered that both groups were sacrificing the Union for their own selfish purposes. The very stratification of Southern society, moreover, contributed to political division between Whigs and Democrats

---

[18] For further discussion of these and other proposals, see Clement Eaton, *Freedom of Thought in the Old South* (Durham, N.C., 1940), pp. 247–279, especially pp. 265–266. Clay's proposal included the suggestion that slaves should be hired out by the state for a period of three years before their emancipation, to pay their expenses to Liberia.

[19] *Ibid.*, pp. 267–268.

[20] Emerson, *Journals*, VIII (1912), 203.

[21] Stanwood, *History of Presidential Elections*, p. 234, and James G. Randall, *Lincoln the President* (New York, 1945), I, 193–200.

on this point. When in the 1850's an erratic cotton market combined with an inflation during which slave prices skyrocketed, the great planters, because of their large holdings, were cushioned against the decline in cotton profits. Furthermore, the large plantations were largely immune to the effects of the high price of slaves, since they usually produced their own. The small planter, on the other hand, lacked the capital to buy slaves if he needed them or, in some cases, to retain those he owned. Thus he and the yeoman farmer were attracted to the Democratic party, which thrived on attacks against the moderates in the South, in much the same way that the Republicans thrived on abolition. Indeed, where the plantation prevailed, the intensity of feeling against the idea of emancipation seemed often to vary inversely with the economic status of the individual. The poor whites feared the Negro as an economic competitor. Frequently, the fewer the slaves a Southerner had, the more intensely he hated an abolitionist. Such a man as James Coles Bruce of Virginia, who had inherited a fortune amounting to about two million dollars and an aristocratic tradition, could view the problem through Jefferson's eyes. A Whig, an Episcopalian, and a Harvard graduate, he preserved "sufficient detachment and wisdom to criticize slavery and to uphold the Union cause in the Virginia Secession Convention."[22]

For many men, then, secession was a difficult decision. The use of the word "secession," rather than "revolution," stressed the belief of many Southerners that violence was not involved. Alexander H. Stephens and his supporters, commonly known as "coöperationists," believed that their plan for a convention of the Southern states would result in an amended constitution which would save the Union. Even if the Washington government rejected this constitution, Stephens argued, New York, Pennsylvania, and Ohio, together with the Western states, would either join with his constitutional party or abstain from any hostile attitude, thereby isolating New England. Many coöperationists maintained that the sectional aspects of Lincoln's election were not great cause for alarm. If the President proposed to take action injurious to the institution of slavery, he would be restrained by the will of the whole people. And they further pointed out that although the Republicans had won the presidency, they had not gained control of Congress nor of the Supreme Court.

In the same way, the so-called "Reconstructionists" based their hopes for a peaceful settlement on the obvious opposition of the majority of

[22] Eaton, *Freedom of Thought in the Old South*, p. 35.

people, North and South, to violence. They hoped that all the Northern states, with the loss only of New England, would be led in time to join the new union that was forming. Some of them believed that once a state became independent it might reënter the Union, after negotiating for favorable terms. With these expectations, a vote for secession was by no means always a vote for independence, and even less often a vote for war.

A brief review of the votes on secession, in the eleven states which formed the Confederacy, will show the depth of resistance within each state in the early days of 1861, when the tide of popular sentiment for the Confederacy was at a high point. The decision to secede in South Carolina had been unanimous. But, although Georgia was the first state to consider South Carolina's course, the vote, on January 18, 1861, stood 208 to 89, with Alexander H. Stephens and Herschel V. Johnson voting "no." In Alabama, one-third of the delegates voted against secession, in a count of 61 to 39, with the minority vote coming from the counties where the free population predominated.

Mississippi, with a slave population next in numbers to that of South Carolina, passed the secession ordinance by a convention vote of 84 to 15 on January 9, 1861. One day later, on January 10, Florida joined the South, registering 62 yeas and 7 nays on secession. In Louisiana the convention vote on January 26 was 113 to 17, but the popular majority registered for secession stood at only 20,448 to 17,296. On February 1, Texas joined the solid block of states in the lower South by passing the ordinance, 166 to 8.

In the four Border states, which eventually joined the Confederacy, the issue was always in doubt, and in each case secession was rejected before it was finally accepted. In Virginia, the stanch majority for the Union maintained its strength until April 17, three days after the firing on Fort Sumter, and on that occasion secession won by a vote of 88 to 55. Two weeks earlier, on April 4, the Virginia convention had voted 88 to 45 against passage of the ordinance. The stormy sessions in Tennessee continued throughout the period, with test votes showing Union majorities until May 6, when the legislature, in secret session, called for a secession referendum in what the Louisville *Journal* described as "as bitter and insolent a mockery of popular rights as the human mind could invent." The vote of the people on June 8 stood at 104,913 to 47,238 for secession, with eastern Tennessee registering 32,923 against leaving the Union, to 14,780 favoring such a step.

Arkansas passed the ordinance on May 6, by a vote of 65 to 5, but only two months earlier, after listening to an address by Jefferson Davis, the same convention had registered itself 39 to 35 against joining the South. In the same way, the first convention in North Carolina, called in November, 1860, voted strongly for the Union and, on its adjournment on December 22, made no provision for reconsidering this decision. But on May 20, 1861, surrounded by seceded states, the governor called an extra session and the ordinance was adopted by unanimous vote.[23] Of this secession period, Richard Parham, of Benton County, Mississippi, wrote: "I believed the attempted dissolution was the work of politicians and not the people. I advocated this publicly and privately." As the Yancey forces gained strength, Parham doubled his activities in favor of the "policy of a general convention of delegates from all the States . . . to create a pause—and give opportunity to deliberate—being convinced, as I am now that the people of the Southern States and of the whole country were opposed to any precipitate action on the subject of secession."[24]

The march of events in Vicksburg was detailed, from the Unionist point of view, by L. S. Houghton, in a letter written to Lincoln on August 29, 1863. After the election of 1860, Houghton wrote, "The Union Party here were ready and willing to accept the choice and Sustain You in upholding the integrity of the Government. . . . But Sir Secession and rebellion, was a foregone conclusion in the hearts and minds of the Party who (unfortunately) had Control of Our State Government." The call for a secession convention was issued, with only twenty days' notice, giving "no time for Understanding or any Consideration by the People as to the Questions involved." The party press "set to work to Mislead and Madden the ignorant portion of Our People." Finally, since Vicksburg was known as a strong Whig center, and also because it was situated at a key point for the control of navigation on the Mississippi, a "large Military force" was sent to the city, and the Unionists were informed "that if we did not cease our Opposition We should be imprisoned, Shot or Sent out of the Country."

[23] For a discussion of the general secession movement, see James G. Randall, *The Civil War and Reconstruction* (New York, 1937), pp. 183–192, 245–257. For a contemporary and contrasting account as to dates and votes, see Horace Greeley, *The American Conflict* (Hartford, 1866), I, 347–348, 452, 485–486. A penetrating analysis of the divergent elements that combined to make secession possible in a key state of the upper South is available in J. Carlyle Sitterson, *The Secession Movement in North Carolina* (Chapel Hill, 1939).

[24] Testimony of Richard N. Parham, Benton County, Mississippi, before Special Commissioner Henry F. Dix, Jan. 9, 1873, in his own case (claimed $12,479, allowed $8,467, in 1873), C. of C. No. 360, GAO files. Parham, an old-line Whig who had voted for Bell and Everett, had written a series of articles against secession which continued after the election of Lincoln and which were published in the "Eagle & Engineer, a newspaper in Memphis."

By such tactics, Houghton asserted, opposition was silenced, and "probably about One fourth of the Union Party from fear of Consequence, and from doubts as to the ability of the United States as a Government to Sustain itself—Went Over to the Party in Power here, and soon became active participants in the rebellion." But at this time, as throughout the war, there remained a small group who "stood silent, but Stood firmly as ever by their first love, and Patiently waited the hour that should deliver them." By 1863 Houghton could add: "The Season of deliverance has Come at Last; But it has found us exhausted! And worst of all Misunderstood! Unfortunately to the Victorious army Now here, all of us appear alike, and they seem Unwilling to regard any as Union Men, and hence all must be treated quite alike."[25]

For a short time during the early period of the secession movement, a three-way division of opinion appeared in all states. William F. Martin, who subsequently served as a general in the Confederate army, described the situation in Natchez, Mississippi. "We had three parties down there," he said, "the secessionists *per se*, the cooperation party, and the Unionists *per se*. . . . I was what you might call a cooperationist." He had voted for Union delegates to the state secession convention. He had, he believed, made the last Union speech that was made in the state of Mississippi, at a time when "the current of public sentiment was so great that it was difficult for a man occupying the position I did to make such a speech without getting into personal difficulty."

Martin's explanation of his own position gives the reasoning of a "coöperationist." He had long feared that slavery would be the cause of a war, he said, and wanted to "postpone the evil day," in the hope that a better solution could be found. His concern had been to find "some means . . . to rid us of slavery, because I never had any great fondness for the institution although I had been the owner of slaves from my youth up," and as a result he had become a colonizationist. But as crisis grew and feeling became more intense, Martin began to despair of a peaceful solution. Pursuing a last hope, he "came to Washington City and spent about a month here to see whether the war was inevitable, and if there was no way of avoiding it, and if such was the case I made up my mind we had better make the best fight we could and go to work and get ready for it." When his month in Washington had convinced him "that the war *was* inevitable," he proceeded to New England and New York where, having authority,

---

[25] L. S. Houghton to Abraham Lincoln, Vicksburg, Mississippi, Aug. 29, 1863, in R. T. Lincoln MSS, Vol. 122, Nos. 25912–25914, Manuscript Division, Library of Congress.

he purchased arms and equipment for his own military company at Natchez, and for the state of Mississippi. On his return home he "went into it with all my heart and soul. . . . I took a company of cavalry from there [Natchez] and was a General at the close of the war."[26]

The difficult decision which faced Robert E. Lee, Alexander H. Stephens, and Samuel Houston, was thus shared by many other men. Governor Houston was deposed from the governorship of Texas, and retired to his farm bearing the stigma of "hoary-headed traitor," for his refusal to act with the Confederate government. He expressed the convictions of many loyal men when he wrote, "Recognizing as I do the fact that the sectional tendencies of the Black Republican party call for determined constitutional resistance at the hands of the united South, I also feel that the million and a half of the noble-hearted, conservative men who have stood by the South even to this hour, deserve some sympathy and support." He reminded the people of Texas that although Lincoln had won the election, "we have to recollect that our conservative Northern friends cast over a quarter of a million more votes against the Black Republicans than we of the entire South. I cannot declare myself ready to desert them," he continued, "until at least one firm attempt has been made to preserve our constitutional rights within the Union."[27]

The contrast between the opinions of two men in one state—Robert Toombs and Alexander Stephens, in Georgia—illustrates the widely differing points of view of those groups which finally joined together to create the Confederacy. While Toombs was wiring from Washington, on December 23, 1860, that "secession by the fourth of March next should be thundered from the ballot box by the unanimous voice of Georgia," Stephens was warning that "revolutions are much easier started than controlled, and the men who begin them . . . seldom end them. . . . The selfish, the ambitious, and the bad will generally take the lead . . . and before tearing down even a bad Government we should first see a good prospect for building up a better."[28]

In a letter to Hamilton Fish in 1870, Kenneth Rayner of North Carolina, who had served in Congress from 1839 to 1845, described the dilemma of many old Whigs. While in Congress, he had been "national

---

[26] Testimony of William F. Martin, of Natchez, Mississippi, identified as "President of a railroad, a lawyer, and a planter," before the commissioners of claims, Washington, Dec. 12, 1877, in the case of Catherine S. Minor, Natchez, Mississippi [claimed $64,155, allowed $13,072 in 1879], C. of C. No. 7960, GAO files.

[27] Sam Houston to J. M. Calhoun, Jan. 7, 1861, in Amelia W. Williams and Eugene C. Barker, eds., *The Writings of Sam Houston, 1813–1863*, VIII (Austin, 1943), 230.

[28] Ulrich Bonnell Phillips, ed., *The Correspondence of Robert Toombs, Alexander H. Stephens and Howell Cobb* (Washington, 1913), II, 504–505.

and conservative" in his course and had "fought secession & disunion for 20 years." Even after Lincoln's election he had opposed secession—he wrote, "until the moral pestilence of the spring of 1861 swept over the South, dethroning reason, & paralysing the efforts of the best Union men of the country." When the war began, "he had succumbed to the storm for a time swept along almost insensibly by a current which it seemed impossible to resist." Ten years later, he was convinced that "the hardest fate is that of those men at the South who fought against secession & disunion—and yet are . . . [its] victims."[29]

The rapid crystallization of opinion after November, 1860, when the votes for the four presidential candidates had marked the shades of opinion in the country, is seen in the positions of the candidates themselves only five months later. Abraham Lincoln, the enigma from Illinois, was sitting in the White House, having called out the militia on April 15, 1861, and declared a blockade of the ports of South Carolina, Georgia, Alabama, Florida, Mississippi, Louisiana, and Texas. John C. Breckinridge, the candidate of the deep South, was serving as a brigadier general in the Confederate army. More significant is the fact that the two candidates representing compromise had likewise declared their positions: Stephen A. Douglas for the North, and John Bell for the South.

The Southern Unionists represented the rock-and-rib segment of that large body of opinion in the South which had, in varying degrees, opposed the war. Although they were often termed "home-grown Yankees" by their neighbors, their concern was not to identify themselves with the North but was, rather, as one of them said, for the "cause of the Union and the people of the Confederacy."[30] Senator Benjamin H. Hill of Georgia gave his own description of the Unionists, while testifying before the Southern Claims Commission in 1877 on behalf of his friend Alfred Austell of Fulton County. "We had a class of native men of the South," he said, "who were always called Union men—they were opposed to secession and to the war and willing at any time to make terms with the United States and come back." They were allowed to entertain such sentiments, he added, because "everybody knew from their character that they would not be treacherous, that is, they would not subject themselves to criminal prosecution for

---

[29] Kenneth Rayner to Hamilton Fish, Nesbitt's Station, Mississippi, Jan. 31, 1870, in Papers of Fish, Manuscript Division, Library of Congress.

[30] Summary Report in the case of Georgia M. Erwin, Osceola, Arkansas [claimed $52,615, allowed $1,211.12 in 1878], C. of C. No. 294, Justice Department, National Archives.

infidelity to the Confederate government. At the same time they were, in heart, out-spoken Union men. . . ."[31]

Recent studies of the Southern home front demonstrate that real unity was seldom achieved under the Confederacy.[32] Almost from its inception the Confederate government recognized that influential Union men remained throughout the South. On August 8, 1861, the Act of Banishment set a period of forty days during which all residents of the region who still adhered to the government of the United States must "depart from the Confederate States . . . [or] be treated as alien enemies."[33] Fourteen days later, the passage of the Sequestration Act outlined the policy of confiscation of the property of "alien enemies."[34] The first conscription act, passed on April 16, 1862, was an early acknowledgment that voluntary enlistment had not sufficiently filled the ranks, in spite of the apparent enthusiasm for the Southern cause. By September of the same year, a direct call from the central government was substituted for the conscript power previously exercised by the states.

The impressment laws and "taxes-in-kind" measures, passed in an effort to facilitate the distribution of supplies, seemed generally to increase disaffection. The price-ceiling features of the impressment laws aroused bitter criticism, especially during the last year of the war when fixed prices were far below market value. Robert Toombs protested that the acts were discriminatory because "capitalists, merchants, manufacturers, speculators, and extortioners," who had profited by the war, were exempt, while the burden was borne by the "agriculturalists . . .

[31] Senator Benjamin H. Hill, testifying before the claims commissioners, Washington, Dec. 5, 1877, in the case of Alfred Austell, Fulton County, Georgia [claimed $15,222, disallowed in 1877], File Room, House of Representatives. Hill's own career is a commentary on the times. A Whig and a Bell-Everett man, he had advocated the Union until the secession ordinance was adopted. He was elected, to the Confederate senate on a moderate ticket and served there until the close of the war. On December 6, 1875, he was elected as a Democrat to the United States Congress where he served in the House until March 4, 1877, when he took the Senate seat which he retained until his death on August 16, 1882. See Haywood J. Pearce, *Benjamin H. Hill, Secession and Reconstruction* (Chicago, 1928), for his biography.

[32] See Charles W. Ramsdell, *Behind the Lines in the Southern Confederacy* (Baton Rouge, 1944), Georgia L. Tatum, *Disloyalty in the Confederacy* (Chapel Hill, 1934), Ella Lonn, *Desertion during the Civil War* (New York, 1928), and Frank L. Owsley, *States Rights in the Confederacy* (Chicago, 1925).

[33] James D. Richardson, *A Compilation of the Messages and Papers of the Confederacy, Including the Diplomatic Correspondence, 1861–1865* (Washington, 1905), I, 131.

[34] For arguments supporting and opposing these acts and outlining the reasons for their passage, see *The Sequestration Cases before the Hon. A. G. Magrath. Report of Cases under the Sequestration Act of South Carolina, in the City of Charleston, October term, 1861* (Charleston, 1861). James L. Petigru, the famous South Carolina Unionist, presented an especially able argument in opposition to the theory underlying these laws (pp. 22–25).

[who] have been the great sufferers in this war both in blood and treasure."[35]

In August, 1863, Jonathan Worth was prophesying that the war could not last long, since "the want of subsistence and returning sanity of our women will contribute much to close it."[36] Six months later, on February 3, 1864, Jefferson Davis justified his request for a second suspension of the writ of habeas corpus by referring to the serious state of public morale. He told the Confederate Congress:

In certain localities men of no mean position do not hesitate to avow their disloyalty and hostility to our cause, and their advocacy of peace on terms of submission to the abolition of slavery. In districts overrun by the enemy, or liable to their encroachment, citizens of well-known disloyalty are holding frequent communication with them, and furnishing valuable information to our injury, even to the frustration of our military movements.[37]

Such opposition was, however, more often disaffection than positive Unionism. In some cases, indeed, it grew out of an extension of the very arguments on state rights which had formed the core of secession. In others, it represented the protest of persons who, having been swept into secession by the course of popular sentiment, were now following the ebbtide of disillusionment. The genuine Unionist of the "rock-and-rib" stamp, on the other hand, had seldom wavered in his course. His conviction had been strong enough to resist the early enthusiasm for the Confederacy and durable enough to withstand four years of bitter war.

The Federal government, like the Confederate, took legislative recognition of this minority within a minority. Lincoln was well aware that opposition to secession had persisted in the South after the firing on Fort Sumter and his call for troops. His mail included letters from influential Southerners who exposed the weaknesses of the Confederacy and outlined plans for victory and reunion.[38] In his formulation of

---

[35] The Milledgeville (Georgia) *Confederate Union*, June 30, 1863.

[36] J. G. de Roulhac Hamilton, ed., *The Correspondence of Jonathan Worth* (Raleigh, 1909), p. 251. Worth added that the "last-dollar and the last man" were abusing the peace articles of W. W. Holden, "but the fact that he had the largest and most rapidly increasing circulation of any journal in the state indicates the current of public opinion."

[37] Dunbar Rowland, ed., *Jefferson Davis, Constitutionalist: His Letters, Papers, and Speeches* (Jackson, Miss., 1923), VI, 165.

[38] For letters which, in their own way, are political essays on the status of the South under the Confederacy from the Unionist point of view, see L. S. Houghton to Lincoln, Vicksburg, Mississippi, Aug. 29, 1863, in R. T. Lincoln MSS, Vol. 122, Manuscript Division, Library of Congress; Richard H. Parham to Lincoln, Marshall County, Mississippi, Dec. 16, 1862, in *ibid.*, Vol. 95; Thomas S. Bacon to Lincoln, New Orleans, Louisiana, Feb. 5, 1864, in *ibid.*, Vol., 141; and C. P. Bartrand to Lincoln, Little Rock, Arkansas, Oct. 19, 1863, in *ibid.*, Vol. 128.

policies, throughout the war, the President repeatedly made careful distinctions between loyal and disloyal men in the South. Army orders had specified that loyal persons were to be given receipts, redeemable after the war, for quartermaster and commissary goods furnished to authorized officers of the Union army as it moved south. Congress, too, had accepted this discrimination, especially in the Captured and Abandoned Property acts, which set up a special fund, from the proceeds of goods commandeered, from which the loyal owners could receive restitution by proving, before the Court of Claims, that they had "never given any comfort to the present rebellion."[39]

For men of influence and substantial property, with whom this study is chiefly concerned, such a standard was especially difficult. As they were prominent in the community, the pressures upon them were strong. Their ownership of large estates meant heavy financial and other obligations to the Confederate government. Their convictions were constantly being tested by tax measures, impressment of goods, and support of bond issues. Their holdings of cotton, sugar, rice, or tobacco were major sources of Confederate strength. Obviously, a course of active resistance or neutrality for such individuals was more difficult than it was for men of little or no property, living in remote areas.

By 1871, when the claims commissioners[40] began their investigations, the Unionists had been stateless for a decade. They had been subject to social pressure and to the stringencies of security measures. With the arrival of the Union armies, their property, in common with the property of the most ardent Confederate, had usually fallen prey to the troops, and such indemnity for the loss as had been promised them as "loyalists,"[41] by military or legislative edict, had been summarily canceled during Radical reconstruction. Their leadership in the community had been liquidated.

In a letter written at the Continental House, Washington, on November 12, 1872, the Reverend George B. Mortimer revealed the frustration of the Unionist. "I am here (I feel) to Contend against all the prejudices of the Sections, and while I am not here to shield the South I will not restrain the truth." He requested a hearing for $10,860 worth of

[39] 12 *U.S. Stat. at L.*, 820.

[40] Variously designated as the claims commissioners, the commissioners, or the Southern claims commissioners, by which name they were commonly known to the press and people of their time. The official title, as used in published reports, was "The Commissioners of Claims appointed under Act of Congress of March 3, 1871."

[41] The terms "loyal" and "loyalist" are used throughout this study, as they were in the records under review, to indicate Southern Unionism and Unionists.

quartermaster and commissary stores furnished to the army of General William Tecumseh Sherman. "I may be allowed to say that I am an American, am now, and always have been for the Union," Mortimer continued. "I have imperilled my peace, ostracised my family, lost my time, spent my means, and endangered my life again and again to . . . preserve my principles. I am not yet weary in well doing. . . . The property I ask pay for will provide me . . . means to live upon. Without it I am reduced to poverty and want."[42]

The "loyalty test" prescribed by the Southern Claims Commission, to which Mortimer was appealing, demanded a life of treason to the Confederacy. The three commissioners interpreted "aid and comfort to the enemy" in its broadest sense. Voting for secession candidates, furnishing a horse for a Confederate soldier, and even paying Confederate taxes or selling goods to the Richmond government, would normally defeat a claim. The standard set by this test, when met in its entirety, amounted to conscientious objection to the Southern cause.

In addition, the examination of each petition required the most exact facts as to the quantity and the value of each item claimed. Because Northern strategy was directed as much against Southern matériel as against Southern institutions or the Confederate army in the field, massive quantities of quartermaster and commissary supplies were confiscated. Indeed, the battle to supply the invading armies and to weaken the Southern home front became modern civilian warfare, directed against the production and transportation of goods and the livelihood of noncombatants.

The strategic importance of these commodities at first escaped the attention of Northern authorities. Their concern was centered on the staple crops of cotton, sugar, rice, and tobacco, used as exportable sources of credit. But as the war progressed, it was realized that corn, wheat, and cattle provided the real elements of survival for the South. Thus the Federal policy of authorizing supply officers to commandeer goods from the countryside served the triple purpose of supplying the army, depleting the stocks of the Confederacy, and encouraging Unionists, by the prospect of reimbursement in the currency of the United States, to stand firm. As the value of Confederate money declined with each year of the war, the appeal of Federal money became increasingly decisive.

In the light of all these facts, the 701 men and women who filed

---

[42] George B. Mortimer to Orange Ferriss, commissioner of claims, from the Continental House, Washington, D.C., in his own case, Copiah County, Mississippi [claimed $10,860, allowed $6,255 in 1873], C. of C. No. 17537, GAO files.

claims before the Southern Claims Commission for $10,000 or more
assume a role of major importance in the history of the Confederacy.
They represented the landed and propertied class, whose Unionism has
received less attention as a group than has the disaffection in the hill
country or the border areas. The total amount claimed by these 701 professed Southern Unionists was $22,582,422.83, which is, by itself, about
2 per cent of the public debt of $1,126,381,096 listed in the Report of
the Secretary of the Treasury to the Confederate Congress on October
1, 1864.[43] Approximately half this amount, or $11,923,532.21, was
claimed from the two states of Louisiana and Mississippi. Of these
large claims, here under intensive study, 164 came from Louisiana, 152
from Mississippi, 120 from Virginia, 68 from Arkansas, 65 from Tennessee, 60 from Georgia, 33 from Alabama, 12 from South Carolina,
11 from North Carolina, 7 from Florida, 6 from Texas, and 2 from
West Virginia.[44]

It must be remembered that the claims prepared in these amounts
did not represent the total wealth or resources of the individual claimants, for only quartermaster and commissary "stores and supplies"
which had been officially taken or furnished to the Federal army constituted a basis for a claim. The fact, then, that 576, or 82 per cent,
of the claimants were the owners of farms or plantations and that the
figures listed in their claims did not include their losses at the hands
of the Confederates or their assets as represented by slaves or cotton,
gives a glimpse of the real measure of loss of the propertied class which
they represented.[45]

The record of Southern Unionism found in the claims is of course
representative, rather than all-inclusive. Of the many factors which
discouraged other men and women of like circumstances and sentiments
from filing claims, two are especially important. The costs of preparing the claim, assembling the necessary evidence, and meeting attorneys' fees and other necessary expenses were often insurmountable
obstacles in the impoverished South, especially when there was little
real assurance that awards would be made. Further, at least six years
of repudiation, combined with an accumulated bitterness toward the
North which had grown up in most Southern communities by 1871,
undoubtedly discouraged many an honest Unionist. Finally, the fact
that jurisdiction was confined to quartermaster and commissary sup-

[43] J. L. M. Curry, *Civil History of the Confederate States, with some Personal
Reminiscences* (Richmond, 1901), p. 112.
[44] For a compilation of the amounts claimed and allowed in cases involving over
$10,000 prepared from the cases themselves, see chap. ix of this study.
[45] For the breakdown of occupations, compiled from the cases, see chap. ix.

plies meant that eligibility for filing a claim was limited to those areas into which the Union army penetrated.

The total of 22,298 Southerners who filed petitions in varying amounts with the Southern Claims Commission is, therefore, an impressive one, especially as a breakdown according to the area from which they were filed shows a comparatively even distribution between all the states that seceded. Equally significant is the fact that, of the 16,991 cases prosecuted to conclusion, about 41 per cent met the strict loyalty and property tests imposed by the commissioners, and were allowed.[46]

Three-quarters of a century after Appomattox, E. Merton Coulter in the new coöperative History of the South has written: "The Civil war was not worth its cost. It freed the slaves, upset a social and economic order, strengthened the powers of the national government, and riveted tighter upon the South a colonial status under which it had long suffered." In the light of all assembled evidence, and with the benefit of historical perspective, he concludes, "What good the war produced would have come with time in an orderly way; the bad would not have come at all. Its immediate effects on the South were glaring and poignant; those more fundamental were less evident and long-drawn out."[47] The prophetic position taken by the Southern Unionist in 1861 cannot, perhaps, be more succinctly summarized, though many contemporary historians challenge the assumption that the slave labor system was on the wane in 1860 and that revolutionary changes in the fabric of Southern life could have been effected without revolutionary means.

Granting that the Unionists constituted a small fraction of the Southern population, their potential value was correspondingly high. In order to avoid the tyranny of the mass, it is as important to weigh the value of individual opinions as it is to ascertain the voice of the many. In this respect the South and the North sinned equally in submerging the Unionist. The Southern people failed to heed his warning about the impossibility of peaceful secession and the dangers of a "Balkanized" United States divided into economically unstable and strategically vulnerable units. The Northern people allowed the doctrine of "constructive treason" to inundate his influence during reconstruction at the very moment when the results of the war had justified his resistance to it.

---

[46] See Frank W. Klingberg, "The Southern Claims Commission: A Postwar Agency in Operation," *Mississippi Valley Historical Review*, XXXII (1945), 195–214.

[47] E. Merton Coulter, *The South During Reconstruction, 1865–1877* (Baton Rouge, 1947), p. 1. A recent penetrating examination of the causes of the Civil War is presented in Kenneth M. Stampp, *And the War Came; the North and the Secession Crisis, 1860–1861* (Baton Rouge, 1950).

CHAPTER II

TWILIGHT CITIZENSHIP

As THE Union armies advanced into the South, they made much use of the Southern Unionists. The practice of obtaining supplies from the Southern countryside was acknowledged by an official order in 1862 that certificates of the kind and quantities of such supplies were to be issued, "payable at once if known to be the property of loyal men, [or] . . . payable after the suppression of the rebellion on proof that the owner has not given aid or comfort to the enemies of the United States after the date of receipt."[1]

In actual practice, the Federal order of 1862 was applied with considerable flexibility, at the discretion of the officer in command. Certificates were more common than cash payments. Sometimes the vouchers followed prescribed printed forms. General Nathaniel P. Banks, in the Shenandoah campaigns, prepared a special receipt reproduced here as a sample:

Department of the Shenandoah

(Culpeper,) Va., (July 28,) 1862

This certifies that there have been received from the farm of (R. L. Patterson of Culpeper County) Va., the following military supplies:

(forty tons hay $20 per Ton)

(Sixteen head cattle average net weight 450)

(Four hundred and fifty Pounds)

Said supplies will be accounted for on the property return of Captain (James I. David) Assistant Quartermaster United States Army, for the (Second Quarter) of 1863

The owner of said property will be entitled to be paid for the same after the suppression of the rebellion, upon proof that he has from this date conducted himself as a loyal citizen of the United States, and has not given aid or comfort to the rebels.

Done by authority of Major General BANKS,

Special General Order of April 2, 1862

Captain (Jas. I. David, A. Q. M.)

(Cavalry Brigade)[2]

Frequently, receipt of goods was acknowledged on scraps of paper, on which the only official marks were the signature and identification of the officer in charge. More often, no voucher was given.[3]

---

[1] In 1862 the annual report of the Quartermaster's Department noted that Union troops had been instructed "to make such use of the products of the country into which they were moving." See *Official Records*, Series III, Vol. II, p. 806.

[2] See claim of Richard L. Patterson, Culpeper, Virginia [claimed $19,900, allowed $9,075], C. of C. No. 823, GAO files. The handwritten parts of this voucher appear in parentheses.

[3] Almost invariably the cases submitted to the commissioners of claims contain a variety of passes, safeguards, and especially letters from Union soldiers and officers.

Letters from Union officers often deplored the haphazard accounting for such supplies as were taken. General Leonard F. Ross wrote sadly to Richard H. Parham of Benton County, Mississippi, that "this indiscriminate taking of property is unauthorized by our Commanding Officers ... but many of the subordinates either lack the will or the ability to enforce obedience. ... This state of things in the army has caused me much pain." Parham and Ross had become warm friends while the Union officer was stationed in Benton County. Disillusioned by the Federal policy of guilt-by-association, Ross concluded, "War brings in its train nearly every evil & every crime known to our race. The Lord grant that we may soon be enabled to see some light break through the dark clouds that now envelop the land."[4]

General Order No. 100 had specified that "the United States acknowledge and protect in hostile countries occupied by them ... strictly private property," with the reservation that "this rule does not interfere with the right of the victorious invader to tax the people, or their property, to levy forced loans, to billet soldiers, or to appropriate property, especially houses, land, boats or ships and churches, for temporary and military purposes."[5] The Revised Army Regulations of 1861, as corrected to June 25, 1863, further provided that "all property, public or private, taken from alleged enemies, must be inventoried and duly accounted for. If the property be claimed as private, receipts must be given to such claimants or their agents."[6] Such inventories had been made by order of General Andrew Jackson after the battle of New Orleans.[7] Congress, in its postwar period, chose to repudiate such claims, on the ground that they were not recognized by the international laws of war and could not be established by army regulations.[8]

In addition to the informal and temporary boards, provision was

---

[4] See claim of Richard H. Parham, Benton County, Mississippi [claimed $12,479, allowed $8,467 in 1873], C. of C. No. 360, GAO files. The letter is signed simply "Leonard F. Ross," and was written at "Headquarter's division," with no further identification. Parham owned a plantation of eleven hundred acres and had from forty to fifty "hands" on the place. On December 16, 1862, Parham wrote Lincoln regarding conditions in the South and enclosed a letter from Ross urging Parham to run for the United States Congress from Mississippi. "I would like very much to see you elected ... ," Ross wrote. "If you desire the position and I can do anything to advance your interests will you ... let me hear from you on this subject." See Richard H. Parham to Abraham Lincoln, written from Marshall County, Mississippi, Dec. 16, 1862, in R. T. Lincoln MSS, Vol. 95, Manuscript Division, Library of Congress.
[5] No. 37 in General Orders No. 100; *House Executive Document No. 100,* 43d Cong., 1st Sess.
[6] 12 *U.S. Stat. at L.,* 767, sec. 22.
[7] U.S. Congress, *American State Papers,* Vol. IX, "Claims," (Washington, 1832–1861), Claim No. 752.
[8] *House Report No. 134,* 43d Cong., 2d Sess., p. 206 n.

frequently made, in occupied areas, for permanent agencies. In Tennessee, boards were established at Nashville, Knoxville, Clarksville, McMinnville, Jasper, and Chattanooga.[9] The Driver Board at Nashville, appointed on March 13, 1863, by order of General William S. Rosecrans, was made up of three citizens and two officers of the army, and continued its operations from March 16, 1863, to November, 1864. Charged with responsibility for investigating the damages sustained from military forces of the United States by citizens of Nashville and vicinity, the board reviewed the facts and made recommendations.[10] Final authority, however, rested with Quartermaster General Montgomery C. Meigs, who admitted that he was not "skilled by profession and education in the rules of evidence" and made "intuitive" decisions. In no case did he "hesitate to reject or modify or to report favorably" upon a claim, whether his decision agreed or disagreed with that of the Driver Board and of its witnesses.[11]

The severe attitude of this board, itself, is revealed in a long letter written by its recorder, William Driver, to Senator Zachariah Chandler on June 20, 1866, from Nashville. Driver advised "passing a Law . . . while you have the Power (while these Conquered territorys are where they belong, where they placed themselves and where they should be kept if need be Forty years to come)." The letter warned that it was "a fixed 'Leagued' determination all over the South to have such Claims paid—and they won't want for *aid even from Men* in Blue." Only a law outlawing any claims from the South would "end all Log Rolling forever." As for the "loyal Citizens of those States, when they come to be states," they could obtain justice by bringing suits into their district courts against "Leading Wealthy Rebels, obtain Judgment, and sell their Lands." Driver added that of the twenty-two hundred claimants before his board, only forty-two were found loyal, in cases ranging in amounts claimed from $20.00 to $188,000. Of some $4,000,000 claimed, only $140,747.46 was recommended for allowance by the board and this "on account of Loyalty and excessive Poverty of Claimants."[12]

[9] The records of these boards were subsequently of great service to claim agents in seeking out promising cases to press against the government.

[10] Memorandum relative to Tennessee Claims, March 18, 1876, in "Miscellaneous Letters Received," 1876, Records of the Southern Claims Commission, Treasury Section, National Archives.

[11] Letter of M. C. Meigs, quartermaster general, to Asa O. Aldis, president of the Southern Claims Commission, Nov. 10, 1871, in Record Book F, "Letters Sent, Claims," 1871, War Department, National Archives.

[12] William Driver to Zachariah Chandler, Nashville, Tennessee, June 20, 1866, in the Papers of Zachariah Chandler, Vol. 4, Manuscript Division, Library of Congress.

New Orleans was likewise the scene of a permanent board throughout the four years of occupation. Established by General Benjamin F. Butler to condemn captured property and determine the allegiance of the owners, the commission was made up of three army officers and served as a fact-finding agency. General Nathaniel P. Banks continued this sequestration commission, using members of his own staff. In a few instances, cash payments were made to Unionists by General Samuel B. Holabird, custodian of the funds. "I did make some payments for sugar out of funds in my hands, on the order of the Commission, and I had some difficulty in settling these accounts [with the Quartermaster's Department], because it was all informal."[13] When General E. R. S. Canby arrived in 1864, he again limited the powers of the agency to auditing claims and recording an opinion as to the "justice and propriety of the evidence" for future reference.[14]

The complications which followed a simple transaction in the field, whereby an army supply officer gave a receipt for goods to a Southern Unionist, grew out of the fact that all three branches of the national government became involved. The constitutional guarantee that private property could not be taken for public use without just compensation, collided sharply with the war powers of Congress to provide for the common defense. In brief, a testing ground for private versus public rights in time of war constantly arose.

The Quartermaster and Commissary departments gradually classified the war claims into three different types. Claims growing out of destruction of property from military necessity were disallowed as losses sustained by the fortunes of a war for the public defense, regardless of whether they arose in the North or in the South. When claims were based on specific contracts with government departments, the department itself was empowered to pay. The third group, into which the claims of Southern Unionists for stores and supplies fell, based its demands on verbal or written agreements between officers of the government and private citizens. Both parties to the transaction had acted on the assumption that the government was thus obligated. Nevertheless, the indefinite legal status of the claim delayed any compensation during the war. Since the transactions involved goods furnished for the use of the army in an orderly and prescribed manner,

[13] Statement of General Samuel B. Holabird "regarding operations in the Dept. of the Gulf, made for the information & use of the Com'rs of Claims," Jan. 5, 1875, in the case of James Wood, Orleans Parish, Louisiana [claimed $142,805, allowed $7,643.25 in 1877], C. of C. Nos. 406, 408, 409, and 560, GAO files.
[14] *Ibid.*

the departments in Washington could not rule them out as losses incurred by damage, destruction, and the fortunes of war. However, since these claims lacked the binding power of the usual legal contract, the supply departments could, and usually did, withhold payment pending a clarification of their validity.

With delay, still another complication arose. The army orders outlining procedures for payment had been issued without the direct consent of Congress. Since the appropriation power rested with the legislature, such sanction could be required. Congress did, during the earlier war period, give that sanction indirectly, through regular appropriations to the supply departments to meet the costs of the war. But when, on July 4, 1864, the Congress acted directly to remove from the jurisdiction of the departments all claims for quartermaster and commissary stores arising in the South, it set one of the first of those sectional distinctions which were to characterize postwar legislation. As the law was worded, this voiding action was accomplished by a provision that the quartermaster general and commissary general could entertain the claims of loyal citizens "of states *not* in rebellion" for supplies taken for army use. In essence, this act merely gave Congressional sanction to a function already being performed by the departments.[15]

As a result, a man living in Kentucky could file a claim with a government department as a matter of right, whereas his neighbor living across the state line in Tennessee could not do so, regardless of his loyalty. This prohibition held even if the petitioner could show active service in the Union army or active aid to the Union cause in Tennessee, to prove his loyalty. This restriction applied even if the property from which the supplies had been taken was in the South but belonged to a resident of the North whose loyalty was not in question. By this act, therefore, Congress returned to itself full power over all claims of this description arising in the rebellious states. The constitutional right to file the claim in the form of a private bill in Congress, which dated from the Revolution, was not disturbed. But since no representatives from the South sat in Congress at that time, and since the same majority was required to pass a private claim as had been required to pass the so-called limiting act of July 4, 1864, it is clear why only a few isolated claims from the seceded states received any consideration in Congress for the rest of the decade.

During the debates on this bill, the injustice of such a sectional dis-

---

[15] *Cong. Globe*, 38th Cong., 1st Sess. (July 2, 1864), p. 3499.

tinction was vigorously protested, particularly by men from the Border states. Questioned by James H. Lane, of Kansas, as to why loyal men in disloyal states should thus be excluded, Senator Lyman Trumbull of Illinois explained, "We discriminate against them because of the difficulty of arriving at the facts. ... " The Southern Unionists were entitled to payment, he said, but the hour had not yet arrived. "Where the country has been in a state of insurrection to open the door for men to prove their loyalty, would be, I fear, dangerous at this time."[16]

Although the members of Congress from the Border states favored a more liberal policy toward the claims of loyal men in the "late insurrectionary regions," they were finally influenced by the interests of their own constituency to support the bill. Its passage confirmed a right which had existed largely in prospect, and hastened payment which might otherwise be subject to an interminable delay. Senator Reverdy Johnson supported the bill by describing the losses to his constituency during the Antietam and Gettysburg campaigns when "the armies were fed almost entirely by the citizens of Maryland." The bill, he argued, would provide that "a Maryland citizen who upon that occasion fed with stores or supplied the Army in another with commissarit stores shall be paid, unless it shall turn out that he was disloyal."[17]

In the final arguments before passage of the measure, Lazarus W. Powell, of Kentucky, added his regret that the bill had not included "something better for those states which have been subject to invasion." He considered the bill inadequate and discriminatory. Nevertheless, the Border State men had "been trying for two years to get some legislation on this subject," and the proposed bill would "do some good to some meritorious persons who have been made utterly penniless by taking everything they had to feed our armies, and I know at this late state of the session we can get nothing else. ... "[18]

As it was concerned with commissary supplies, the law had only a limited operation. No claims were paid by that office unless they were accompanied by official receipts for the property, or unless the property was found to have been entered on the returns of commissary officers. Since such evidence was not often at hand, the prospect of reimbursement was slight. But in the case of quartermaster stores, more active relief was granted. The quartermaster general appointed agents to investigate the claims in the area in which they had arisen.

---

[16] *Ibid.*
[17] *Ibid.*
[18] *Ibid.*, p. 3500.

These officers visited the claimant and took sworn statements of witnesses both for and against the claims. The largely ex parte procedure of this examination is indicated by the fact that not until June 15, 1880, was the petitioner protected to the extent that he received notice of such investigation and the privilege of cross-examining witnesses.[19]

The case of Richard L. Patterson demonstrates with what rigidity the territorial restrictions were applied. The loyalty of the claimant—a Northerner by birth and by conviction, but a resident of Virginia—was early established. He held the prescribed vouchers and documents. Since he lived in Culpeper, not far from Washington, and had retained enough funds to finance the prosecution of his claim, he marshaled every resource at his command to recover his losses.

Quartermaster General M. C. Meigs, on January 5, 1869, followed the policy of the department in rejecting such claims on the basis of the act of July 4, 1864. With Patterson's unpaid claim before him, Meigs wrote to John M. Schofield, secretary of war: "This then appears to be a case not without difficulty. On one side is the faith of the Government pledged through its proper and authorized Officers that the owner of the property will be entitled to be paid for it after the suppression of the rebellion on certain conditions." The evidence before the department showed, he said, that Patterson had satisfied a most careful examination into his loyalty and had proved ownership of the property concerned. The government had "given its word." But, Meigs concluded, the act of Congress left no alternative but to refuse payment "in view of the policy and apparent intent" of that body.[20]

The sectional limitations written into this act brought the courts into the picture, as they had added their own complications through a series of opinions respecting the status of the South and of Southerners. To the average Southern loyalist, the involved reasoning of the Supreme Court, in the Prize cases, served to confuse rather than to clarify his status. In its decision that citizens in seceded states owed "supreme allegiance" to the national government and that " in organizing this rebellion they have acted as States," the Court labeled the Southerner a rebellious citizen and an alien enemy and set the boundaries of the insurrectionary regions. The Court held that *"all persons residing within this territory whose property may be used to increase the revenues of the hostile power are, in this contest, liable to be*

---

[19] 21 *U.S. Stat. at L.*, 586.

[20] M. C. Meigs, quartermaster general, to John M. Schofield, secretary of war, in the claim of Richard L. Patterson, Culpeper, Virginia [claimed $18,900, allowed $9,705 in 1871], C. of C. No. 632, GAO files.

treated as enemies though not foreigners."[21] By this reasoning, in a civil war the power of the nation over its own rebellious citizens became greater than it could have been over alien enemies, as it added, to the belligerent rights of war over alien enemies, the sovereign right to confiscate and punish for treason.

This reasoning, it is true, was in one sense a legal rationalization of the peculiar and contradictory position of the Washington government itself during the first years of the war. Even with the blockade in full effect, Seward had maintained a "no war" policy, and Lincoln held to the theory that the true governments of the Southern states had merely been temporarily deposed. The Federal government conceded the *de facto* status of the Confederate government, but it could not admit it in principle. At the same time, a state of war existed, and laws of war applied. The so-called "double-status" theory developed from this unprecedented situation. Justice Robert G. Grier described this phenomenon of expediency, in the majority opinion, as follows:

The law of nations ... contains no such anomalous doctrine as that which this Court [is] now for the first time desired to pronounce, to wit: That insurgents who have risen in rebellion against their sovereign, expelled her Courts, established a revolutionary government, organized armies, and commenced hostilities, are not *enemies* because they are *traitors;* and a war levied on the Government by traitors in order to dismember and destroy it, is not a *war* but it is an "insurrection."[22]

The decision in the Prize cases made the legal relations between the sections subject to both international and national law. However severe this principle could be, it had the advantage of permitting a flexibility of policy. A distinction could be drawn, as it was in the amnesty proclamations and usually in the various confiscation acts, between "loyal citizens" within a state and "traitors," without prospect of immediate challenge.

The sectional distinctions which grew out of the confused status of the Southern states, however, increased the problems of the Southern Unionist before the law. From time to time, flagrant war had existed, not only in states proclaimed as in rebellion, but in Missouri, Kentucky, Maryland, West Virginia, and temporarily in parts of Indiana, Ohio, and Pennsylvania. According to the reasoning of the Court in *Ex parte Milligan,* the war in Missouri, Kentucky, Maryland, and West Virginia, as it involved resident insurrectionists engaged in guer-

---

[21] 2 Black 673–674.
[22] 2 Black 670.

rilla warfare, took on, for given periods, the characteristics of a civil war. A state of insurrection was held to have existed in these sections for a limited time, but the states themselves were never declared to be in insurrection. Since the states could be deemed "loyal," their citizens retained all the rights of "loyal" citizens. The presumption of loyalty remained, and only those citizens or groups of citizens who were shown to be in fact disloyal were subject to the sovereign and belligerent powers of the government. Moreover, the belligerent rights applied only to those periods which were held to have contained the characteristics of "civil war."

In Indiana, Ohio, and Pennsylvania—where organized resident insurrectionists offered no real threat, as they had on occasion in the loyal Border states—the army action fell under the classification of "invasion." Thus it was held that at no time or in no limited area within these three states had "insurrection" or "civil war" existed, and no belligerent rights of the government were, therefore, held to apply to any of their citizens at any time except, of course, those sovereign rights of the government which applied to any individual in any loyal state with respect to treason.[23]

As the precise relationship of residents of the South to the Federal government became clouded by the dual status theory, inevitably problems developed over property titles in commonwealths engaged in rebellion. The Unionist was vitally concerned with the confiscation acts, which furnished the weapons for economic strangulation. The Confederacy acted first, with provisions, on May 21 and August 30, 1861, for the sequestration of all Northern debts and property within the Southern states. By August 6, 1861, however, the Northern Congress had inaugurated a series of confiscation acts which, in theory, first appropriated all Southern property and then, in various forms, promised its return under circumscribed provisions. Both sections, it may be noted, could find the precedent for expropriation in the writings of a hero of their common past. Thomas Paine, in *Common Sense*, had proposed in 1776 that the American Revolution be financed by confiscating the property of loyalists and Englishmen, and the Continental Congress had acted on his suggestion on January 24, 1776.

The most extreme statement of Federal policy appears in Lincoln's

---

[23] *Ex parte Milligan*, 4 Wallace 140. The Prize cases had held that the war in Missouri, Kentucky, Maryland, and West Virginia, because these states included resident insurrectionists organized or engaged in rebellion, was civil war even though these states were not proclaimed as in rebellion. See Prize cases, 2 Black 636. See also William Whiting, *War Powers under the Constitution of the United States* (Boston, 1871), pp. 238–241, 460.

proclamation of July 17, 1862, which provided that all estates and all property of persons who did not cease to aid, countenance, and abet the "rebellion" would be liable to seizure and confiscation.[24] Further, he specified that it was the duty of the President of the United States to cause this property to be seized and applied, either directly or through its proceeds, to the support of the Federal army.[25] General Henry W. Halleck had previously enunciated the military policy which extended belligerent rights to property on the ground that war gave to "one belligerent the right to deprive the other of everything which might add to his strength and enable him to carry on hostilities."[26] William Whiting had made a similar pronouncement regarding the effect of martial law on contraband. Those civil and municipal restraints which protected private property could not, he argued, be applied to a state of war since, by such reasoning, "no defensive war can be carried on; no rebellion can be suppressed; no invasion can be repelled.... Not a gun can be fired *constitutionally*, because it might deprive a rebel foe of his life without *due process of law*—firing guns not being deemed 'due process of law.' " War powers, while they lasted, must therefore be held to be "as lawful, as constitutional, as sacred, as the administration of justice by judicial courts in time of peace. They may be dangerous; war itself is dangerous; but danger does not make them unconstitutional."[27]

In practice, however, this theory was more a threat than a weapon, and Northern policy during the war normally protected titles to private property within the Confederacy.[28] In this respect, the central question was invariably concerned with how far such property (especially cotton), or the holding of property within the Confederate States, constituted "aid and comfort to the enemy." In 1864, in the case of Mrs. Elizabeth Alexander's cotton, Chief Justice Salmon P. Chase had clearly related the possession of private property within the

---

[24] 13 Wallace 130.
[25] 12 *U.S. Stat. at L.*, 590.
[26] Henry W. Halleck, *International Law in Peace and War* (New York, 1861), p. 446. Precedents for this ruling were cited in Henry W. Wheaton's *Elements of International Law*, Pt. 4, chap. 2, secs. 5–11.
[27] Whiting, *op. cit.*, pp. 49, 52.
[28] J. G. Randall has commented on the contradiction of policy (in the light of Lincoln's assurances to the people of the South) which this power over Southern property suggests. "The existence side by side of two opposing legal principles is understandable," Randall writes, "if we remember that the insurrectionary theory was not in fact applied as against Southern leaders and their adherents. They were not held personally liable as insurrectionists as were the leaders of the Whiskey Insurrection; but the Confederacy was in practice treated as a government with belligerent powers." See J. G. Randall, *Constitutional Problems under Lincoln* (New York, 1926), p. 517.

Confederacy to assistance to the Southern cause. "It is said that, though remaining in rebel territory, Mrs. Alexander has no personal sympathy with the rebel cause," he wrote, "and that her property therefore cannot be regarded as enemy property." But, he continued, since the court could not, in the first place, "inquire into the personal character and dispositions of individual inhabitants of enemy territory . . . all the people of each State or district in insurrection against the United States must be regarded as enemies until, by the action of the legislature and the executive, or otherwise, that relation is thoroughly and permanently changed."[29]

Chase reasoned that as a resident of the South, Mrs. Alexander— regardless of her political convictions or her wishes in the matter—was, by holding cotton, furnishing aid and comfort to the secession government. In the same way that destruction of the enemy's commerce and navigation was held to be a legitimate act of war, so the "sinews" of military power on land became subject to capture or destruction by an invading army. The Confederate government itself had acknowledged that cotton was "one of their main sinews of war," the Chief Justice pointed out. It represented the "chief reliance" of that government for the purchase of arms in Europe. Furthermore, it was "a matter of history, that rather than permit it to come into the possession of the national troops, the rebel government has everywhere devoted it, however owned, to destruction." For example, Chase noted, the value of cotton destroyed at New Orleans, just before its capture, had been estimated at "eighty millions of dollars."[30] This concept was clearly phrased by James S. Framer, one of the commissioners on the British-American Claims Commission. "The capture or destruction of property on land belonging to individual enemies," he wrote, "is justified by the modern law of nations, if there be military reasons for it; in the absence of good military reasons such captures are generally without the support of public law."[31]

By 1869, however, the Supreme Court held, in *United States* v. *Padelford,* that "the rights of possession in private property are not disturbed by the capture of a district or county or a city or town until the captor signifies by some declaration or act, *and generally by actual seizure,* his determination to regard a particular description of property as not entitled to the immunity usually conceded in conformity with the

[29] 2 Wallace 419.
[30] *Ibid.*, p. 420.
[31] Hale's Report to the Secretary of State, Nov. 30, 1873, reproduced in *House Report No. 134*, 43d Cong., 2d Sess., p. 239.

humane maxims of the public laws." The right to remedy, by this
decision, was dependent upon proof of loyalty, but there could be proof
of ownership without proof of loyalty, and the effect of the act of
March 3, 1863, therefore, did not constitute immediate confiscation
since the "property of the original owner, is, in no case, absolutely
divested."[32]

For purposes of clarification, this decision distinguished between
four classes of property in the South during the war: that which
"belonged to the hostile organizations, or was employed in actual hostilities on land," and therefore became, wherever taken, the property
of the United States; property which "at sea became lawful subject
of capture and prize," where title was changed not by capture alone
but by regular judicial proceeding and sentence; property "which
became the subject of confiscation," including most of the property
in the South (but such property usually remained unaffected in the
possession of its proprietors until special consideration proceedings
were provided); and finally, "A peculiar description known only in
the recent war, called captured and abandoned property," with which
type the Padelford case was concerned. For this last class of property, the government became the trustee, the Court explained, with
the power to determine, itself, whether or not the proceeds should be
restored to the owner. By the Padelford decision, it was held that
restoration of the proceeds became "the absolute rights of the persons
pardoned," if they had applied within the prescribed two years from
the close of the war.[33] However, as this time limit was almost never
observed, the statute of limitations intervened to bar recovery, and
the right was largely an academic one.

In view of the foregoing circumstances, it may be wondered why
any Southern Unionist had, by 1871—when the Southern Claims Commission was established—managed to retain any hope that he would
ever receive the payment promised by army officers. If he had closely
followed the various events in Washington, here briefly sketched,
which affected his status, he must often have despaired. But he could
continue to *assume* his right to a claim, on the basis of the assurance
given him by army officers at the time of the transaction in the field.
And he could find further hope in the attitude of the executive branch
of the government in Washington.

Lincoln's view of the war, from its beginning, offered early assur-

---

[32] 9 Wallace 540. Review for precedent of the Padelford decision in *United States
v. Klein*, 13 Wallace 138–139.
[33] *Ibid.*, p. 136.

ance that the rights of "loyal" Southerners would be preserved. This theory, as it was described by William Whiting, held that the "war waged by this government was . . . a personal war against rebels; a war prosecuted in the hope and belief that the body of the people [of the South] were well disposed toward the Union, and would soon right themselves by the aid of the army." For this reason, Whiting continued, "Congress declared and the President proclaimed, that it was not their purpose to interfere with the private rights of domestic institutions."[34] The policy of pardon and amnesty in Lincoln's proclamation of December 8, 1863, applied also, with certain exceptions, in the case of each subsequent proclamation. It provided "full pardon . . . with restoration of all rights of property, except as to slaves, and in property cases where rights of third parties shall have intervened," to all Southerners willing to subscribe to the oath that they would "henceforth faithfully support, protect, and defend the Constitution of the United States."[35]

The question arises: Was the average Southerner within Confederate lines aware of the special privileges promised by executive proclamations, and even by act of Congress? The Unionists of substantial property, here under review, were usually aware of these assurances and governed their actions accordingly, even under the Confederacy. Dr. John Rhodes, of St. Mary's parish, Louisiana, told the claims commissioners, for example, that he had kept his sugar on his plantation, instead of marketing it or surrendering it to Confederate authorities, "relying fully on President Lincoln's proclamation that all those who didn't commit themselves in any shape in aiding or assisting the confederates should be compensated for the loss of their property. I kept my obligations most religiously."[36] Johnson's general amnesty proclamation of December 25, 1868, which removed all reservations (as will appear in a later chapter), was the logical extension of those assurances given by Lincoln, upon which the Southern Unionists had relied.

During the war, Congress had likewise drawn distinctions favoring "loyal" Southerners, in enacting such legislation as the acts of July 2, 1862, on abandoned lands, and of March 3, 1863, regarding captured and abandoned property. The latter measure was especially important to the Southern Unionist, since it not only guaranteed in-

---

[34] Whiting, *War Powers*, p. 235.

[35] 13 *U.S. Stat. at L.*, 737.

[36] Testimony of Dr. John Rhodes before the commissioners, Washington, April 3, 1874, in his own case [claimed $59,650, allowed $21,971 in 1874], C. of C. No. 21324, GAO files.

demnity for the cotton, rice, sugar, or tobacco with which this act was chiefly concerned but named the Court of Claims as the adjudicating body and set aside all proceeds from the sale of the commodities to apply toward the promised indemnity. In this act in particular, therefore, Congress, by a friendly gesture toward reinstatement of loyal Southerners, renounced part of the full belligerent rights it had assumed. Failure to prove loyalty, however, voided the trusteeship obligation, and the property held in trust, or its equivalent value, reverted to the status of confiscated property.[37]

In addition to his dealings with the supply officers of the army seeking his hogs, corn, horses, or cattle, the Southern Unionist often had dealings with the Treasury agents appointed to carry out the provisions of the Captured and Abandoned Property Act. In theory, these agents were appointed to comb the territory under occupation by the army, making the necessary distinctions respecting the loyalty of individual Southerners and furnishing the proper receipts through which reimbursement could be obtained, by friends of the Union, from this fund especially set aside in the Treasury for this purpose. By January, 1864, an executive order signed by Lincoln and the secretary of the Treasury offered any person in the Confederacy who would bring his products to the Federal lines and take an oath of loyalty, 25 per cent of its value in "notes of the United States or Treasury notes." For the remainder, a receipt was issued, the duplicate of which was to be deposited in the Federal Treasury. If, at the end of the war, the owner could prove his consistent and continued loyalty, he was assured of receiving the balance due him in the currency of the United States.[38]

In practice, however, these regulations were perverted and distorted in the field, either through laxity on the part of the agents or by the extensive and inflationary trade operations which were carried on largely by private parties.[39] At times, as General E. R. S. Canby pointed out, whole campaigns were obstructed by dishonest traders and speculators who profited equally at the expense of the South and of the invading army. One Union officer wrote, "My hard-earned reputation as a soldier is being frittered away hourly by

[37] 12 *U.S. Stat. at L.*, 591. In the case of Mrs. Alexander's cotton, the Supreme Court had held that Congress could use the "belligerent right of confiscating," which with regard to the Captured and Abandoned Property acts meant that Congress could require the forfeiture of the property of all persons in the Confederacy, loyal and disloyal, on the ground that all inhabitants of enemy territory were enemies. See 2 Wallace 404.

[38] *Cong. Globe*, 38th Cong., 2d Sess. (Jan. 16, 1865), pp. 271–272.

[39] *House Report No. 24*, 38th Cong., 2d Sess. (March 1, 1865), pp. 1–4.

Southern Traitors and Northern thieves. Cotton is the corrupting element."[40] In an investigation of these activities conducted by a special committee of the House of Representatives, Grant, Sherman, and Canby were especially critical of these illicit operations. Canby, in particular, deplored the activities of these "unprincipled men, actuated only by the instincts of gain ... who follow in the track of the army, traffic in its blood, and barter the cause for which it is fighting, with all the baseness of Judas Iscariot, but without his remorse.[41]

The concern shown by Congress at that time in regard to these operations was not, as E. Merton Coulter has shown, shared by all departments of government. "The treasury, influenced by powerful private industries," Coulter writes, "clung to the idea that a continuance of this trade was worth more as an economic advantage to the north than its stoppage would amount to as a military weapon against the south." Whatever legal or moral questions were involved, the total effect of all these measures was to drain the resources of the South and of Southerners.[42]

The important role played by the Court of Claims, especially as it had been assigned responsibility for cases under these Captured and Abandoned Property acts, calls for a brief review of its functions. This court, founded on February 24, 1855,[43] was open at the beginning of the war for suits filed by any citizen whose property had been taken for public use. But of the three judges sitting in 1862, two had been appointed by Democratic presidents. John J. Gilchrist of New Hampshire was a Pierce appointee, and Edward O. Loring of Massachusetts had been nominated by Buchanan. The third member, Joseph Casey, was a Lincoln man appointed to his position in May, 1861.[44] The Republican Congress, therefore, reorganized the court at the same time that it placed the cotton cases under its jurisdiction. The act of March 3, 1863, provided that claimants must show loyalty to the United States and, at the same time, increased the number of judges to five, to make way for two Lincoln appointees, Ebenezer Peck, of Illinois, and David Wilmot, author of the Wilmot Proviso. No limitation was placed on the jurisdiction of the court, however, by this re-

[40] *Official Records*, Series I, Vol. 41, Pt. II, p. 238.
[41] *House Report No. 24*, 38th Cong., 2d Sess. (March 1, 1865), pp. 1–4.
[42] For a careful study of the effects of these trading operations, see E. Merton Coulter, "Commercial Intercourse with the Confederacy in the Mississippi Valley, 1861–1865," *Mississippi Valley Historical Review*, V (March, 1919), 377–395.
[43] 10 *U.S. Stat. at L.*, 612.
[44] Casey was appointed to succeed George P. Scarborough of Virginia, another Pierce appointee, who resigned from the court when his state seceded from the Union.

organization act. If loyalty could be proved, any citizen might file suit to recover compensation for property taken.[45]

In the October term, 1863, the court's opinion in the case of *Grant* v. *United States* set its first precedent for claims arising from the Civil War. The claimant, William S. Grant, an army contractor for commissary and quartermaster supplies in Arizona, filed suit for compensation for various military supplies and a flour mill burned by Union troops in order the prevent the property from falling into the hands of Confederate sympathizers. Justice Wilmot delivered the opinion of the court, holding that destruction of the property under the given circumstances constituted in law a "taking" for public use, and awarded the claimant a judgment of $41,530 as the value of his property.[46]

The cotton, sugar, rice, and tobacco cases arising out of the Captured and Abandoned Property acts were protected from such summary cancelation, as the act of July 4, 1864, had applied only to quartermaster and commissary claims. The favorable position of the so-called "cotton cases" arose from certain conditions: the organic act had not only specified the tribunal before which these cases could be heard but had established a trust fund, which meant that no appropriation would be required by Congress in their settlement. Another distinction was that Congress itself had acted in authorizing these cases, whereas army claims arose from operational procedures and lacked specific Congressional sanction.

The "cotton cases" before the Court of Claims, therefore, became an exception to the policy of repudiation during that period in the 1860's when restrictive legislation against the South served Congress in its struggle for dominance. At the same time, these cases served the courts as a chief tour de force in the decisions on loyalty. As Congressional reconstruction became more severe, the Court of Claims became more lenient as to what constituted loyalty. Meanwhile those few "Southern loyalist" claims which had been reported out of committee and reached the floor of Congress, played a strategic part in presenting the case of the Southern Unionist.

In most cases, it is true, the benefit of a hearing was the chief source of satisfaction, since few claims were allowed. The Court of Claims, as stated above, provided a slow and expensive means of adjudication

---

[45] 12 *U.S. Stat. at L.*, 765.
[46] 1 Court of Claims 41. Hereafter cited as Ct. Clms.

and was limited to the "cotton cases."[47] Less than two dozen claims reached the floor of Congress in the form of private bills. When a hearing was obtained, however, the claimants could argue that their right originated in a policy approved and implemented by all branches of the Federal government during the war, and could produce specific evidence to show a loyalty to the Union which often reached heroic proportions. Since claims also involved two points of major importance—the status of Southern property and the effect of amnesty—court rulings on these points also became important spearheads in the drive for recognition of the rights of the South.

The "cotton cases," in particular, set the stage for those Supreme Court decisions which, in the late 'sixties and early 'seventies, were to mark an improvement of the status of citizens of the South, at least in the eyes of the law. Indeed, during the dark period of Congressional reconstruction, the slow but reasonably certain operation of the Court of Claims was one source of hope for the Southern Unionist, especially as its decisions were approved or expanded on appeal to the Supreme Court. For, with the exception of a joint resolution of July 28, 1866, which extended the jurisdiction of the Quartermaster and Commissary departments to include claims of loyalty citizens from Tennessee with Northern claims,[48] the acts of Congress during this period became more, rather than less, restrictive as they applied to the claims of the Southerners.

Claims from Unionists in the South thus stood side by side with political restoration and enfranchisement as a major point of argument in the growing attack on Radical policy. These claims had the advantage of presenting specific cases which often refuted the convenient argument that all Southerners had united to overthrow the Federal government and that punishment could therefore be meted out to the entire section. The two avenues open for pleading these cases, during the late 'sixties, served as forums in which the doctrine of constructive treason could be challenged.[49]

---

[47] By 1888, the Court of Claims had allowed only an estimated $9,864,330.75 for cases which had appeared before it growing out of the Captured and Abandoned Property Act. See James G. Randall, *The Confiscation of Property during the Civil War* (Indianapolis, 1913), p. 50.

[48] 14 *U.S. Stat. at L.*, 370. The counties of Berkeley and Jefferson, in West Virginia, previously excluded, were also admitted to the court's jurisdiction by a similar joint resolution of June 18, 1866. *Ibid.*, p. 360.

[49] Professor Jonathan T. Dorris has thrown valuable new light on the legal status of Southerners before the law during the war and reconstruction years in his *Pardon and Amnesty under Lincoln and Johnson* (Chapel Hill, 1953). A similar service for the North is available in the work of Harold M. Hyman, *Era of the Oath* (Philadelphia, 1954).

In summary: with the arrival of peace the Southern Unionists found that the payment they had been led to expect on the cessation of hostilities was restricted, by Radical policy, to the point of repudiation. For the claimant, of course, his loss was as great whether it resulted from looting, from depredation, from military action, from seizure of his cotton, for which he might have received some reimbursement through the Court of Claims, or from the orderly process, implying a definite obligation, by which he had furnished livestock and grain to an authorized officer of the Supply Department. From the standpoint of the government, and of international law, it was equally obvious that some distinctions would have to be drawn. The ruling that held that those losses from destruction were not allowable which were caused by the fortunes of war, was consistent with the laws of war, and applied to Northerners as well as to Southerners. In quartermaster and commissary claims, inequity was sharpened by the fact that both the Southern Unionist who voluntarily offered his supplies and the army officer who received them had acted with the assurance that ready compensation could be expected.

CHAPTER III

CONGRESS RECONSIDERS THE CASE OF THE SOUTHERN UNIONIST

CONGRESS has never been so concerned with the status of the South as it was during the bitter years between 1861 and 1871, when that section of the country was largely without representation in Washington. From the point of view of Congress, the decade of the 'sixties may, for emphasis, be said to have been divided into two periods: the first, roughly until 1864, a period of enforced unionism; the second, marked by Congressional reconstruction, one of forced secession. During the war, Washington legislators, with a tenacious perversity, had continued to pass legislation for the seceded states, on the theory that the loyal state governments had been only temporarily "subverted."[1] Conversely, the doctrine of constructive treason, with its tenet that any resident of the late insurrectionary region was, *ipso facto,* an enemy who must be held guilty of treason until he could prove his innocence, operated to disfranchise and territorialize an entire section. Thus Congress succeeded "at last" in establishing the South as a separate "nationality," as Senator Daniel W. Voorhees of Indiana pointed out in an attack on Radical measures. Having "sought in vain in all the four quarters of the earth for recognition," he continued, "the Southerners had been able to find it . . . at the hands of those who speak for the administration on this floor."[2]

Because the debates in Congress over the formation of the Southern Claims Commission serve to set forth most of the arguments advanced by representatives of both sections, they may here be reviewed in some detail. Indeed, the Forty-first Congress itself (March 4, 1869, to March 3, 1871), which passed the legislation, marks something of a turning point. It is significant because of what it accomplished, but also because it contained advocates of that new point of view toward the South which was beginning to foreshadow a happier future. This Congress was the first since the war to include representatives of all of the lately seceded states, and a substantial number of its members were able, therefore, to challenge the vociferous and confirmed vindictives. It marked the growing strength of the Liberal Republican movement and saw the split between Sumner and the Grant admin-

---

[1] Preamble of the Proclamation of Pardon by the President of the United States, Dec. 8, 1863, 13 *U.S. Stat. at L.,* 737.

[2] Charles S. Voorhees, comp., *Speeches of Daniel W. Voorhees of Indiana* (Cincinnati, 1875), p. 234.

istration on the Santo Domingo question. It passed the Texas-Pacific railroad bill and, by Lyman Trumbull's amendment of the appropriation bill in its final session, made a beginning toward reform of the Civil Service. The partial repeal of the Test Oath marked a step toward general amnesty. And, according to the New York *Daily Tribune,* its establishment of the Southern Claims Commission was an "important measure to the late rebellious States."[3]

The make-up of the Senate itself reveals an interesting cast of characters who were to enact legislation creating the commission. Of the seventy-six senators, twenty-nine had served, in some official capacity, a party other than the one which had elected them to Congress.[4] The roll of the Senate showed fifty-four Republicans, eight Union Republicans, twelve Democrats, and one each from the Conservative and Union Conservative parties. The New England and Middle Atlantic states were represented by sixteen Republicans, one Union Republican, and one Democrat; the Northwest, West, and Far West by sixteen Republicans, five Union Republicans, one Union Conservative, and three Democrats.

Most significant was the role of the Border states; in these states, sectional issues and the drive for more moderate measures reached the greatest momentum. The one region with a Democratic majority (seven Democrats and four Republicans), its senators took a leading part in the enactment of legislation designed to assist Southern loyalists. From the seceded states, only recently readmitted, came eighteen Republicans (of whom nine had served as officers in the Union army), two Union Republicans, one Conservative, and a lone Democrat, Dr. Homer Miller of Georgia, who was also the only veteran of the Confederate army in the Senate. In passing, it may be noted that the average period of what the Philadelphia *Public Ledger* called "unrepentance" for the Southern states, not counting Tennessee, had been "eight years and two months."[5]

---

[3] New York *Daily Tribune,* March 7, 1871, Vol. XXX, No. 9334, p. 1.

[4] Senators who had served the Whigs in some official capacity were Davis (Ky.), Vickers (Md.), Hill (Ga.), Miller (Ga.), Pool (N.C.), Brownlow (Tenn.), Fessenden (Me.), Sumner (Mass.), Wilson (Mass.), Sprague (R.I.), Howell (Iowa), Chandler (Mich.), Howard (Mich.), Ramsey (Minn.), Sherman (Ohio); Democrats turned Republican were Willey (W.Va.), Fowler (Tenn.), Buckingham (Conn.), Hamlin (Me.), Cameron (Pa.), Trumbull (Ill.), Ross (Kan.), William (Ore.), Carpenter (Wis.); former Free-Soilers were Blair (Mo.), Sumner (Mass.), Wilson (Mass.); and from the Antislavery party were Hamlin (Me.) and Nye (Nev.). These affiliations with other parties are listed from information recorded in *The Biographical Directory of the American Congress, 1774–1927* (Washington, D.C., 1928).

[5] The Philadelphia *Public Ledger,* Feb. 23, 1871, Vol. LXX, No. 129, p. 2.

The discussion in the Senate on the issue of claims from the South centered around the responsibility and ability of the government to pay, the proper agency for judging the claims, the problem of evaluating them, and chiefly the controversial question of what constituted loyalty. The advocates of remedial legislation for Southern Unionists attacked the concept of guilt-through-association, and corruption of blood, and eulogized the services and sacrifices of the loyal men of the South. The antagonists concentrated on various constitutional theories which would treat the occupied regions as conquered provinces, guilty of having committed state suicide and having forfeited their rights; Southern Unionists thereby would be placed beyond the pale of national responsibility. As in debate on other contested reconstruction measures, the climate of opinion was supercharged, and logic often succumbed to passion.

In the initial discussion of Senate Bill 249, around which measure debate on the right of compensation for loyal Southerners was to center for two years, Daniel D. Pratt of Indiana contended, "Sir, the records of patriotism during the world's history do not show sublimer examples of fortitude than were furnished by southern loyalists during this devastating war." Not only their liberty and property had been threatened or destroyed, but also the bonds of kinship, and social, domestic, and religious ties, and "every monument of title by which man holds rights of the State perished like flax in the flames."[6]

These men, said Frederick A. Sawyer of South Carolina, had "stood up in the dark hours of the rebellion for the old flag and the integrity of the Union just as fully and on exactly the same principles as ... the man who lived in Boston or New York."[7] They had, according to Francis P. Blair of Missouri, been "exposed to every possible peril ... the loss of their property and the hazard of their lives; while the loyal men of the North slept quietly and profoundly in their beds, many of them."[8] Garrett Davis, of Kentucky, charged that Radical policy, not wishing to make "*any* concession," had objected on technicalities "for about six long years," during which Congress had been trying to provide for loyal Southerners in spite of the vindictives. He therefore suggested that the Committee on Claims "bring in a bill offering a reward for the discovery of an invention" which would provide a proper way of determining loyalty.[9]

---

[6] *Cong. Globe*, 41st Cong., 2d Sess. (April 27, 1870), p. 3019.
[7] *Ibid.*, 41st Cong., 3d Sess. (Feb. 28, 1871), p. 1790.
[8] *Ibid.*, p. 1791.
[9] *Ibid.* (March 3, 1871), p. 1971.

For the extreme opposition, George F. Edmunds of Vermont challenged a provision of S 249 which established loyalty by either speech or conduct, charging that "if a man has fought all day against the United States and talked loyalty all night ... he can come under the Bill." Under such a definition, any Southerner who had a claim or "expected to have one ... or thought the rebellion was going to slunk," could make an "excellent speech" to his "uncle, to his aunt, to his cousin, that after all he thought the rebellion was a mistake; that he would have been much better satisfied to have been on the other side; as, I believe, General Lee did." Lee, he felt sure, could "come under this bill without the least doubt."[10]

The true status of the South, Edmunds maintained, had been outlined by the Supreme Court, which had "decided unanimously ... in the Prize cases, upon the distinct and exact point that every person, without regard to his personal wishes, sentiments, feelings, without regard to his personal conduct, who resided within the territorial limits held by the forces in armed hostility," subject to the "*de facto* and temporary governments there existing, was ... [just as much] an enemy in the public sense ... as if he had been the commander of the confederate forces."[11]

But the advocates of relief, seizing on the tenet that secession governments had, indeed, been only "temporary governments," and citing those executive decrees and acts of Congress which had distinguished between the rights of loyal and disloyal individuals within the states, took the stand that loyal men of the region were, and had always been, within the Union. This distinction between the individual and the seceded state had, they said, been "preserved throughout the war,"[12] and no "single official act of the government during the late war ... treats the South as a foreign country or as an alien country."[13]

Carrying forward this argument, Sawyer pointed to the substantial aid rendered the Union cause in the South by those groups who were either openly loyal to the Union or opposed to Confederate measures. What would have been the effect on the South, he said, if this "doctrine of Senate lawyers," that all Southerners were "alien enemies," had

[10] *Ibid.*, 41st Cong., 2d Sess. (June 6, 1870), p. 4149.

[11] *Ibid.*, 41st Cong., 3d Sess. (Feb. 28, 1871), p. 1792. This was one interpretation of the Prize cases which had defined the conflict as both a war and a rebellion, and the Southerners as "rebels" and belligerents.

[12] *Ibid.*, 41st Cong., 2d Sess. (April 27, 1870), p. 3017.

[13] Francis P. Blair of Missouri, in *ibid.*, 41st Cong., 3d Sess. (Feb. 28, 1871), p. 1791. Challenged by Sherman (Ohio) on this statement, Blair replied that "those who took up arms simply, not the loyal men" were involved.

been proclaimed in 1862 and 1863? Obviously, he concluded, "every man, woman, and child in the entire South would have been a rebel from the necessity of the case," and would have conducted himself as such.[14] Recognition of loyal Southerners had been denied by Congress, these men insisted, whereas disloyal Northerners were absolved from guilt by virtue of their residence. Deploring the sectional discriminations of Radical policy, Samuel C. Pomeroy of Kansas demanded, "Did we not have as bad a fire in the rear as we had in the front?"[15] And Willard Warner, of Alabama, protested the injustice of a policy which, while abrogating honest obligations to loyal Southerners, "would pay the last farthing to Mr. Vallandigham or to the Knights of the Golden Circle who were doing what they could to destroy the government others fought to save."[16]

On the question of money for the South, opponents of the measure protested that the late Confederacy was, by repudiation of its war debts, in a better financial position than the North. Southerners, they insisted, must realize that the war was devastating to both sides, and that the government could not afford to pay on any large scale. Not only had a tremendous national debt been incurred; the real costs must also be assessed on local and state levels, where much of the expense of equipping and furnishing troops and supplies had been borne. An already overburdened government could not, therefore, permit a new "raid upon the Treasury" without facing bankruptcy.[17]

But obviously the South was "not out of debt," Francis P. Blair replied. "Since the carpet-bag governments have been established there they have been run into debt deeper than the northern states."[18] William Sprague, of Rhode Island, went further by maintaining that "the main national income is now from the South."[19] And Joseph Flower challenged national honor, with the charge that it was "the act of a highwayman to take property from friends and refuse to pay a dollar."[20] On the question of the obligation of the government to pay, and any danger of overpayment, Willard Warner of Alabama expressed his confidence that "the discrimination would be against the people of the South rather than in their favor," since it would be exercised "to ex-

---

[14] *Ibid.*, 41st Cong., 3d Sess. (Feb. 28, 1871), p. 1791.
[15] *Ibid.*, 41st Cong., 2d Sess. (March 4, 1870), p. 1686.
[16] *Ibid.* (June 13, 1870), p. 4409.
[17] See the remarks of William M. Stewart of Nevada in *ibid.*, 41st Cong., 3d Sess. (Feb. 28, 1871), p. 1791 and of Jacob M. Howard of Michigan in *ibid.*, 41st Cong., 2d Sess. (June 6, 1870), p. 4147.
[18] *Ibid.*, 41st Cong., 3d Sess. (Feb. 28, 1871), p. 1790.
[19] *Ibid.*, 41st Cong., 2d Sess. (June 13, 1870), p. 4409.
[20] *Ibid.* (June 6, 1870), p. 4148.

clude loyal men from fear of paying rebels, rather than paying rebels through the belief that they are Union men."[21]

The service of Southerners in the Union army was repeatedly used as an example of the loyalism which could not be questioned. Daniel Pratt, of Indiana, read into the *Globe* the statement of the adjutant general showing the number of Southerners who had served in the Union army.[22] (See table 1.)

TABLE 1

States in which recruited	Approximate number of white enlistments	Number of colored enlistments	Total
Virginia	880	5,723	6,603
North Carolina	3,200	5,035	8,235
South Carolina	......	5,462	5,462
Georgia	160	3,486	3,646
Florida	2,050	1,044	3,094
Alabama	2,296	4,469	7,265
Mississippi	984	17,869	18,853
Louisiana	5,488	24,052	29,540
Texas	2,132	47	2,179
Arkansas	5,942	5,526	11,468
Tennessee	24,940	20,133	45,073
	48,072	93,346	141,418

Specific test cases of loyalty were also cited as typical of the unjust discrimination resulting from the limiting act of July 4, 1864. Joshua Hill, of Georgia, described the case of a woman of his acquaintance, a citizen of Tennessee who owned a plantation in Mississippi. Although Grant himself had been a witness to her loyalty and to the validity of the claim for 8,000 bushels of corn taken by his army, her claim had nevertheless been rejected on the basis of her residence. "Had she lived further north than the State of Tennessee," he said, "had she lived in Missouri or Kentucky, she would have recovered her claim."[23] And John Scott of Pennsylvania, a member of the Committee on Claims, cited the instance of an Alabaman who held certificates from a commanding general and had presented "unquestioned" evidence of loyalty, but who was refused payment on the sole issue of his residence. Is

[21] *Ibid.* (June 13, 1870), p. 4410.
[22] *Ibid.* (April 27, 1870), p. 3018.
[23] *Ibid.*, 41st Cong., 3d Sess. (Feb. 28, 1871), p. 1790.

such a man a citizen of this country, Scott demanded, and, if so, is he not entitled to payment?[24]

But Jacob Howard, of Michigan, called on international law in order to establish his doctrine that continued residence in an insurrectionary state voided any established rights of citizenship, as it inevitably implied aid and comfort to the enemy. He cited William Pitt's refusal to compensate and indemnify the loyalists of the American Revolution on the ground that they were inhabitants of a country at war with England, and maintained that Southern loyalists, likewise, had no standing in the Constitution. Immediately challenged on this point with the argument that the Revolutionary loyalists had, in fact, received compensation, Howard insisted that such payments as were finally made were allowed only on the ground of the generosity of Parliament, rather than as a matter of established policy.[25]

Occasionally the political potentialities of Bill 249 were suggested. Thomas C. McCreery, a Democrat from Kentucky, charged in the heat of debate that the word "loyalty," whatever its first significance may have been, "now means an unflattering devotion to the fortunes of the Radical party, and has no connection whatever with efforts made to preserve or destroy this nation." For example, he said, General Thomas J. Morgan, a Union hero in the Cumberland Gap retreat, but still a Democrat, was "not loyal enough to hold a seat in the last Congress although a large majority of the qualified electors of his district had voted for him." On the other hand, the former Confederate, General James Longstreet, who "may be a Radical," was "loyal enough to hold the surveyorship of the port of New Orleans."[26] Apparently McCreery's suspicion remained with him throughout the debate, in spite of the clearly defined Radical opposition, for he was the only senator from the Border states, and the only Democrat, who voted against the bill in its final form.[27]

There was, perhaps, some logic in McCreery's fear that, regardless of their opposition, the Republicans might use claims as a means of building up their party in the South. Willard Warner of Alabama had recognized this possibility, in arguing that Southern Unionists should be put "on the same basis" with Union men of the North. How, he asked, could the "great Union party" tell those "two or three thousand Union soldiers who came from the mountains of Alabama into

---

[24] *Ibid.*, 41st Cong., 2d Sess. (June 13, 1870), p. 4408.
[25] *Ibid.* (June 13, 1870), p. 4411.
[26] *Ibid.* (April 27, 1870), p. 3020.
[27] For McCreery's votes on six related measures, see the table which appears later in this chapter.

our Army, 'You have no standing in the courts of your country; you have no claims for property arising during the war which your country feels itself bound to respect'?" No one, he declared, could maintain that position, " and yet build up in those States a great party true and loyal to the Government and to the principles and purposes of the great Republican party of the country."[28]

But if this particular measure sought deliberately to subsidize Republicanism in the South, it fell far short of its mark, as will appear later. The sustained opposition of the Radicals suggests that it was never a "party measure." Further, as claims presumed possession of property, few former slaves would be involved. If money were to build the party there were, as had been demonstrated, simpler ways than the elaborate claims procedure for distributing it. In any case, both the split support for the bill and the subsequent action of the commission appointed by Grant offer small grounds for the assumption that this was a Republican measure to sustain the Republican party in the South.

Although by far the largest part of the debate revolved around the question of determining what constituted loyalty, some attention was directed to the problem of deciding the value of property claimed. "What value, for example, could be set on crops," said James W. Nye, of Nevada. "Fields of green rice were out. . . . It was fed to the horses. Who is going to value that? Would the rice have ripened and been full, if not cut when green?" All loyal men would say "yes," he thought, nor would the chances of its being subject to the usual blight be considered.[29] But for the most part, such arguments were dismissed as another manifestation of the strategy of delay over technicalities. Government departments had already, in any case, established policy, in these respects, which were designed to take care of abuses.

The following chart, prepared to list the members of the Senate during the Forty-first Congress, with a glimpse at their native states and their army identification,[30] shows that the issue was drawn more largely on sectional than on party lines. The fight for the claims of Southern Unionists found its chief support from the men in the Southern and Border states, regardless of their political affiliation. The strongest opposition came from the New England and Middle Atlantic

---

[28] *Cong. Globe*, 41st Cong., 2d Sess. (June 13, 1870), p. 4409.
[29] *Ibid.* (June 6, 1870), p. 4151.
[30] Biographical information, as to birthplace and identification with the Union or Confederate armies, and attendance at the Republican National Convention of 1860 are recorded as they appear in the *Biographical Directory of the American Congress 1774–1927* (Washington, 1928).

states; the West and Far West were almost evenly divided as to votes. Six roll calls on measures or motions affecting this legislation are here recorded. They cover a period from June 6, 1870, to March 3, 1871, on which day Congress, in a rider to the Army Appropriation Bill, passed the bill establishing the Southern Claims Commission.

In order to emphasize the sectional features of these votes, they have been tabulated in six groups representing the Border states, the South, New England, the Middle Atlantic region, the Northwestern and Western states, and the Far West. In the column giving voting record, number 1 shows the vote on a motion to pass over S 249, which attempt, on June 6, 1870, was defeated by a vote of 32 to 14.[31] On the same day, an amendment absolving the government of all responsibility to pay was also lost by a vote of 29 to 14 (number 2).[32] A week later, on June 13, a vote on adjournment to avoid consideration of the bill was defeated by a tie vote, 18 to 18 (number 3).[33] Lacking final action on this bill, the McDonald amendment to the Army Appropriation Bill was introduced during the closing days of the session. This amendment provided that loyal men of the South be placed "on equal footing" with loyal men of the North, by repealing the act of July 4, 1864, in order to allow citizens of all states to present their claims to the Quartermaster and Commissary departments. On February 28, 1871, a vote to table this amendment was killed, 31 to 13 (number 4),[34] and shortly afterward, the amendment passed the Senate with some revision, 33 to 22 (number 5).[35] The substitute amendment as reported out of the conference committee, which created the commission as a compromise between the House and Senate bills, passed the Senate on March 3, 1871, by a vote of 25 to 21 (number 6)[36] and established the Southern Claims Commission.

A straight vote favoring aid to loyal Southerners is indicated by italics. In table 2, the votes are broken down into: A, absent; Y, yea; and N, nay.

---

[31] The motion was made by Zachariah Chandler of Michigan. See *Cong. Globe*, 41st Cong., 2d Sess. (June 6, 1870), p. 4147.

[32] Vote on George H. Williams' (Oregon) amendment to S 249 providing that the bill involved no obligation on the part of the government to pay claims allowed. See *Cong. Globe*, 41st Cong., 2d Sess., p. 4148.

[33] Vote on adjournment to avoid consideration of S 249. A second vote to adjourn was defeated Yeas 16, Nays 17, with no changes in votes but with more members absent. See *ibid.* (June 13, 1870), pp. 4412, 4413.

[34] Vote on the Cornelius Cole (Calif.) motion to table the McDonald amendment to HR 2816. See *Cong. Globe*, 41st Cong., 3d Sess. (Feb. 28, 1871), p. 1788.

[35] Vote on McDonald's revised amendment to HR 2816. See *ibid.* (March 1, 1871), p. 1821.

[36] Vote on the substitute for McDonald's amendment which created the commissioners of claims, in *ibid.* (March 3, 1871), p. 1973.

TABLE 2

State and senator	Party	Born	Army	Voting record					
				1	2	3	4	5	6
BORDER STATES									
DELAWARE:									
Bayard, Thos. F............	Dem.	Del.	......	A	A	Y	N	Y	Y
Saulsbury, Willard.........	Dem.	Del.	......	N	N	A	A	A	A
KENTUCKY:									
Davis, Garrett..............	Dem.	Ky.	......	N	N	N	N	Y	Y
McCreery, Thos. C.........	Dem.	Ky.	......	N	N	Y	N	A	N
MARYLAND:									
Hamilton, Wm. T...........	Dem.	Md.	......	N	N	A	N	A	A
Vickers, George.............	Dem.	Md.	......	N	N	A	N	Y	Y
MISSOURI:									
Blair, Francis P.............	Dem.	Ky.	Union	..	..	..	N	Y	Y
Drake, Charles D...........	Rep.	Ohio	......	N	A	Y	..	..	..
*Schurz, Carl...............	Rep.	Germany	Union	N	N	A	A	Y	Y
WEST VIRGINIA:									
Boreman, Arthur I..........	Rep.	Pa.	......	N	N	Y	N	Y	A
Willey, Waitman T..........	Rep.	W. Va.	......	N	N	A	N	Y	A
SOUTH									
ALABAMA:									
Spencer, George E...........	Rep.	N. Y.	Union	N	N	N	N	Y	Y
*Warner, Willard............	Rep.	Ohio	Union	N	N	N	N	Y	Y
ARKANSAS:									
McDonald, Alexander.......	Rep.	Pa.	Union	N	N	N	N	Y	A
Rice, Benjamin F............	Rep.	N. Y.	Union	N	N	N	N	Y	Y
FLORIDA:									
Gilbert, Abijah.............	Rep.	N. Y.	......	N	N	A	A	A	N
Osborn, Thomas W.........	Rep.	N. J.	Union	N	N	Y	Y	N	Y
GEORGIA:									
Hill, Joshua................	Union Rep.	S. C.	......	A	A	A	N	Y	Y
Miller, Homer..............	Dem.	S. C.	Confed.	A	A	A	A	Y	Y
LOUISIANA:									
Harris, John S..............	Rep.	N. Y.	......	N	N	N	N	Y	A
Kellogg, Wm. P.............	Rep.	Vt.	Union	N	N	A	N	Y	A
MISSISSIPPI:									
Ames, Adelbert............	Rep.	Me.	Union	A	A	A	N	N	A
Revels, Hiram R............	Rep.	N. C.	Union	A	A	A	N	Y	A
NORTH CAROLINA:									
Abbott, Joseph C............	Rep.	N. H.	Union	A	A	N	A	Y	A
Pool, John.................	Rep.	N. C.	......	A	A	N	A	A	A

* Delegate to the Republican National Convention, 1860.

TABLE 2—*Continued*

State and senator	Party	Born	Army	Voting record 1	2	3	4	5	6
SOUTH—CONTINUED									
SOUTH CAROLINA:									
Robertson, Thos. J	Rep.	S. C.	......	N	N	N	N	Y	Y
Sawyer, Frederick A	Rep.	Mass.	......	A	A	A	A	Y	A
TENNESSEE:									
Brownlow, Wm. G	Rep.	Va.	......	A	A	A	A	Y	N
Fowler, Joseph S	Union Rep.	Ohio	......	N	N	N	N	Y	A
TEXAS:									
Flanagan, J. W	Rep.	Va.	......	A	A	A	N	Y	Y
Hamilton, Morgan C	Rep.	Ala.	......	Y	Y	A	Y	N	A
VIRGINIA:									
Johnston, John W	Cons.	Va.	......	A	A	A	N	Y	Y
Lewis, John F	Rep.	Va.	......	A	A	N	A	Y	A
NORTHWESTERN AND WESTERN STATES									
ILLINOIS:									
Trumbull, Lyman	Rep.	Conn.	......	Y	Y	A	Y	N	N
Yates, Richard	Union Rep.	Ky.	......	A	A	Y	A	N	Y
INDIANA:									
*Pratt, Daniel D	Rep.	Me.	......	N	N	N	N	Y	Y
Morton, O. H. P	Union Rep.	Ind.	......	A	A	Y	N	Y	N
IOWA:									
Harlan, James	Rep.	Ill.	......	Y	Y	Y	A	A	N
Howell, James B	Rep.	N. J.	......	Y	Y	A	A	N	A
KANSAS:									
*Pomeroy, Samuel C	Rep.	Mass.	......	N	A	N	N	N	N
Ross, Edmund G	Rep.	Ohio	Union	N	N	N	A	Y	A
MICHIGAN:									
Chandler, Zachariah	Rep.	N. H.	......	Y	Y	A	A	N	N
Howard, Jacob M	Rep.	Vt.	......	Y	Y	Y	Y	N	A
MINNESOTA:									
Norton, Daniel S	Union Cons.	Ohio	......	A	A	A	..	..	..
Ramsey, Alexander	Rep.	Pa.	......	N	A	N	N	A	N
Stearns, Ozora P	Rep.	N. Y.	Union	..	..	..	A	N	N
NEBRASKA:									
Thayer, John M	Rep.	Mass.	Union	A	A	N	N	A	Y
Tipton, Thomas W	Dem.	Ohio	Union	N	N	A	N	Y	Y
OHIO:									
Sherman, John	Rep.	Ohio	......	Y	Y	A	Y	N	Y
Thurman, Allen G	Dem.	Va.	......	N	N	A	N	A	A
WISCONSIN:									
Carpenter, Matthew	Rep.	Vt.	......	N	Y	Y	A	A	A
Howe, Timothy	Union	Me.	......	N	N	N	A	Y	Y

* Delegate to the Republican National Convention, 1860.

TABLE 2—*Concluded*

State and senator	Party	Born	Army	Voting record 1	2	3	4	5	6
FAR WEST									
CALIFORNIA:									
Casserly, Eugene	Dem.	Ireland	......	N	N	A	N	A	A
Cole, Cornelius	Rep.	N. Y.	Union	Y	Y	A	Y	N	Y
NEVADA:									
Nye, James W	Rep.	N. Y.	......	Y	A	Y	A	N	Y
Stewart, Wm. M	Rep.	N. Y.	......	A	A	Y	Y	N	Y
OREGON:									
Corbett, Henry W	Union Rep.	Mass.	......	A	A	Y	Y	Y	N
Williams, George	Union Rep.	N. Y.	......	Y	Y	Y	A	A	N
MIDDLE ATLANTIC STATES									
NEW JERSEY:									
Cattell, Alexander	Rep.	N. J.	....	A	A	A	A	A	A
Stockton, John P	Dem.	N. J.	......	N	N	Y	A	Y	A
NEW YORK:									
Conkling, Roscoe	Rep.	N. Y.	......	A	A	A	A	N	N
Fenton, Reuben Z	Rep.	N. Y.	......	A	A	A	N	Y	A
PENNSYLVANIA:									
*Cameron, Simon	Rep.	Pa.	......	A	A	A	A	A	N
Scott, John	Rep.	Pa.	......	N	N	Y	N	Y	N
NEW ENGLAND STATES									
CONNECTICUT:									
Buckingham, Wm. A	Rep.	Conn.	......	A	A	A	Y	N	N
Ferry, Orris S	Rep.	Conn.	Union	Y	Y	A	A	A	A
MAINE:									
Hamlin, Hannibal	Rep.	Me.	......	N	N	A	Y	N	N
Morrill, Lot M	Rep.	Me.	......	A	A	A	A	A	A
MASSACHUSETTS:									
Sumner, Charles	Rep.	Mass.	......	Y	Y	Y	A	A	A
Wilson, Henry	Rep.	N. H.	Union	A	A	N	Y	N	Y
NEW HAMPSHIRE:									
*Cragin, Aaron N	Rep.	Vt.	......	A	A	A	A	N	N
Patterson, James W	Rep.	N. H.	......	Y	A	A	A	A	A
RHODE ISLAND:									
Anthony, Henry B	Rep.	R. I.	......	N	Y	A	Y	N	N
Sprague, William	Rep.	R. I.	......	A	A	N	A	A	Y
VERMONT:									
Edmunds, George F	Rep.	Vt.	......	Y	Y	A	A	N	N
Morrill, Justin S	Union Rep.	Vt.	......	A	A	A	Y	N	N

* Delegate to the Republican National Convention, 1860.

In quick review, a history of various bills which were debated on the floor of the Senate during this session shows the strategy by which the relief measure was finally passed. On March 30, 1869, Benjamin F. Rice of Arkansas forced the issue by presenting S 224, "to provide for the auditing and adjudicating and payment of certain claims" of loyal citizens of the South, and requested that it be referred to a specially created committee of five, bypassing the regularly constituted committees. Rice reminded his colleagues that bills of this kind had repeatedly been introduced and referred either to the Committee on Claims or the Committee on the Judiciary but had never been satisfactorily reported.[37] Timothy Howe of Wisconsin, chairman of the Claims Committee, rose to defend his committee which, he said, was "pretty well agreed as to what sort of a report should be made," but had not had the time, in the press of business demanding attention, to prepare a bill.[38]

This threat, however, caused Howe two days later, on April 1, to introduce S 249 providing for "the settlement of claims for quartermaster and commissionary stores furnished to or taken by the United States within the States in Rebellion," by specifying that the claims were to be filed in the House during a two-year period, and be referred to the quartermaster or commissary general who would "examine and award on proof of loyalty."[39] The bill was ordered printed but was not reported until a year later, on March 4, 1870.[40] The Radical press, which had maintained steady hostility to such measures, viewed the appearance of the bill on the floor of the Senate with some alarm. A representative comment appeared in the Washington column of the Warren County *Times* of Glens Falls, New York, the home of Orange Ferriss, who was to serve as one of the three commissioners. "A great question has to-day been brought up in the Senate," wrote the correspondent, one which promised to affect the finances of the country more materially "than any that has been agitated since the close of the war. . . . Let this door once be opened and it will take more money to foot the bills than it would to pay the government debt. Every person in the South will be able to prove his loyalty." An attempt to estimate "the amount of greenbacks that it would require to cover up the tracks made by Sheridan in the Valley of the Shenandoah and Sherman

---

[37] *Ibid.*, 41st Cong., 1st Sess. (March 30, 1869), p. 346.
[38] *Ibid.*
[39] *Ibid.* (April 1, 1869), p. 439.
[40] *Ibid.*, 41st Cong., 2d Sess. (March 4, 1870), p. 1681.

in his march to the sea," alone were enough to suggest that "there would
be no end to the claims."[41]

On the floor of the Senate, Howe's bill was immediately attacked
by Cornelius Cole of California, who prophesied that provision for such
claims would probably involve "50 thousand millions" of dollars. Howe
replied, and, drawing on his experience on the Claims Committee,
quoted $5,000,000 as the figure which would probably cover the entire
amount.[42] It is interesting to note that ten years later, after investigating 22,298 claims, the Southern Claims Commission had allowed
exactly $4,636,920.69, which is remarkably close to Howe's figure. Wil-
son, of Massachusetts, backed Howe in the belief that "some settlement
was desirable," but warned against the fraud and false swearing which,
in his experience, were the rule in such cases. He pointed out, however,
that of the claims for $17,000,000 already presented to the Quarter-
master and Commissary departments, probably not more than $2,500,-
000 had been allowed. According to Wilson's figures, the Quartermaster
Department had received seventeen thousand claims, amounting to
$14,000,000, and had paid "less than a half million." During the same
period the Commissary Department had "studied" some five thousand
claims, amounting to nearly $3,000,000, on which the payment allowed
had been less than a quarter of a million dollars.[43]

During the ensuing year the bill was frequently discussed, but almost
as frequently discussion was prevented by objections from opponents
of the bill. Typical was the protest of Senators Sumner and Conkling,
on December 12, 1870, to a motion for the consideration of this "much
debated bill," and it was allowed to lie over.[44] Meanwhile, as the history
of the times shows, the power of the Radicals was being challenged
with more effect as each day passed. By August, 1870, with the fall
elections in prospect, Schuyler Colfax wrote to Henry B. Anthony,
president pro tempore of the Senate, of his concern over the dwindling
fortunes of the Republican party. The "ceaseless Dem. misrepresenta-
tion," he wrote, "the natural tendency of a people like ours to try to
change, & the unjust & sharp attacks of our own leading papers—
together with the removal of the strong cohesive power of the Reconstruction issues—have all tended to weaken us somewhat. . . ."[45]

[41] Warren County *Times*, Glens Falls, New York, Vol. I, No. 20, March 11, 1870,
p. 2, col. 3, under the "Washington Letter" dated March 4, 1870.
[42] *Cong. Globe*, 41st Cong., 2d Sess. (March 4, 1870), p. 1682.
[43] *Ibid.* (March 4, 1870), p. 1684.
[44] *Ibid.*, 41st Cong., 3d Sess. (Dec. 12, 1870), p. 55.
[45] Schuyler Colfax to Henry B. Anthony, Washington, Aug. 7, 1870, in "Letters of
Schuyler Colfax," Manuscript Division, Library of Congress.

The Congressional elections in November, 1870, furnished a fresh challenge to Radical supremacy, by increasing the Democratic representation in the House to a total of 100, of whom 17 had been officers in the Confederate army. The Republican count of members was reduced to a total of 143. From this moral victory, the South took on new courage. The "succession of Democratic victories in the Southern States is producing a great deal of . . . uneasiness in Radical quarters here," wrote the Washington correspondent of the Norfolk *Virginian* on December 30, 1870. Editorially, the *Virginian*, in commenting on this dispatch, sounded a word of warning against too much enthusiasm too soon. "We repeat," wrote the editor, "our people must be cautious in their movements and should scrupulously avoid furnishing the enemy with ammunition when we see his cartridge box empty on his hip. Just now a blunder would be a crime against constitutional liberty and our hopes of the future."[46]

Meanwhile, from Washington came another dispatch, which commented with some satisfaction on the hints of growing disaffection within the Republican party. A "prominent Western Democrat," wrote the correspondent, had made the statement that the Democrats and the Revenue Republicans were "likely to unite to secure the organization of the House in the Forty-second Congress." Further, there seemed to be good prospects of success for this pooling of forces, since "objections which have heretofore been urged against this coalition have, to a great extent, been met and obviated."[47]

The effect of the elections on the attitude of the members of this lameduck Congress who had opposed all or part of Radical policy, began to show itself in a renewed vigor in their speeches. And the Southern press, which had for the most part followed a policy of sniping at Grant, Butler, and other Radical leaders, took on a more positive tone. This change of tone appeared most vividly in Georgia, where the controversy over the seating of the states' delegates to Congress had produced the bitterest attacks against the administration. Encouraged by the mandate of the election, however, the Atlanta correspondent to the Cincinnati *Commercial* had written, "The innocent reader who is aware of the fact that seven Senators have already been elected for this state since the war and not one has yet got in, would naturally inquire what we want with any more. We love to have them around. If we can't have two in, like other States, we will get the best of them

---

[46] The Norfolk *Virginian*, Dec. 31, 1870, Vol. XI, No. 33, p. 1, and the editorial page.
[47] *Ibid.*, Dec. 26, 1870, Vol. XI, No. 29, p. 1.

by having half a dozen or more out."[48] By early February of 1871, the Savannah *Daily Republican* was "encouraged by the very decided vote in the House to seat Corker, the Representative-elect from the Fifth District of Georgia," and by the "unexpected majority in the Senate against the admission of certain pretenders to seats from Georgia." These hopeful signs, together with the prospect of the repeal of the test oath "now regarded as certain," were "circumstances of great and gratifying significance," the *Republican* concluded. "Neither could have happened a year ago with the same bodies, and the change augurs well for the country."[49]

On the issue of claims from the South, the increased moderate Democratic strength in the House—where private claims originated—no doubt suggested to the Radicals that if they were to control claims legislation, the time was growing shorter in which effective action could be taken. In any case, the issue was suddenly forced in the closing days of this Congress when, on February 28, 1871, Alexander McDonald of Arkansas introduced a surprise amendment to the Army Appropriation Bill which not only revised the limiting act of July 4, 1864, to admit claims from the South, but included an appropriation of $500,000 to pay for such claims from the South as were allowed by the department. Under the provisions of this bill, claimants from the South would have been entitled to immediate payment once they had received the sanction of the department, without review by Congress. The second section of the amendment, as submitted, went even further in providing the repeal of "all laws or parts of laws making a discrimination against loyal claimants because of residence."[50] This section was immediately attacked, notably by John Sherman, of Ohio, who charged that it "repeals international law, it repeals the law of war, it repeals all law."[51] For obvious reasons, the remaining strength of the Republicans was promptly mustered, and this particular provision was voted out of the amendment.

During two days of heated debate which followed, the best efforts of the Radicals, however, could not succeed in tabling the McDonald amendment, although they did succeed in eliminating those features which seemed, from their point of view, most dangerous. Commenting on the surprising strength of the measure, the Philadelphia *Public Ledger* noted that "the Democrats, and Southern [Republican] Sena-

---

[48] *Ibid.*, Dec. 14, 1870, Vol. XI, No. 19, editorial page.
[49] The Savannah *Daily Republican*, Feb. 1, 1871, Vol. LXX, No. 26, editorial page.
[50] *Cong. Globe*, 41st Cong., 3d Sess. (Feb. 28, 1871), p. 1788.
[51] *Ibid.*, p. 1789.

tors, except Hamilton of Texas, voted solidly together."[52] To the New York *Tribune* it was "evident that the Southern Senators had made up their minds to force the amendment through," in spite of the fact that Sherman called it a "monstrous proposition," and Conkling predicted that it would "beggar any nation on earth" to pay the claims. The Southern senators held, however, that "a loyal man in the South was as good as a loyal man in the North," and it was clear that "a majority of the Senate favored the amendment."[53]

In the form in which it passed the Senate on March 1, the amendment did extend the act of July 4, 1864, to include loyal citizens of the South, and repealed "such parts of said act as make a discrimination between loyal claimants because of residence." It also provided that service in the United States Army during the war be held as prima-facie evidence of loyalty "unless some act of disloyalty shall be proven to have been committed after such service."[54]

Alarmed by the increasing strength of the Democrats, the New York *Times*, commenting on the 25 to 21 vote which had passed the amendment, expressed the hope that the bill would "not be concurred in by the House unless it obtain a more intelligible idea of what is intended, and what may be accomplished, than can be derived from the proceedings of yesterday." If its purpose was "to embrace only claims for stores supplied to the Union army, and for which regular vouchers were given," said the *Times*, "justice would seem to be on its side." But the phrase "loyal claims" could cover reconstruction claims and claims for damages "and nobody knows what besides. The whole thing," the paper concluded, "has at this moment an ugly aspect."[55]

Meanwhile the *Tribune* likewise viewed the proceedings with suspicion, but took some comfort from the fact that, although the House also seemed to favor the payment of these claims, its Committee on War Claims had "carefully examined the subject," and preferred that they be "thoroughly investigated by a commission appointed for the purpose, in order that the loyalty of the claimants may be proved beyond a doubt," before they were passed on to the accounting officers of the Treasury Department. The Senate debates, said the *Tribune* writer, estimated $1,000,000 as the total amount involved. Whether this figure was correct, he noted, would "depend entirely upon the strictness of the test of loyalty prescribed, and there is danger that it will exceed $10,000,000.00."[56]

---

[52] Philadelphia *Public Ledger*, March 1, 1871, Vol. LXX, No. 134, p. 1.
[53] New York *Daily Tribune*, March 1, 1871, Vol. XXX, No. 9329, p. 1.
[54] *Cong. Globe*, 41st Cong., 3d Sess. (March 1, 1871), p. 1821.
[55] New York *Times*, March 2, 1871, Vol. XX, No. 6067, p. 4.
[56] New York *Daily Tribune*, March 2, 1871, Vol. XXX, No. 9330, p. 1.

On March 1, the House, which to that time had not debated any Southern claims bill, relying upon the "careful consideration of the Committee of Claims during the present Congress," received a bill from Representative William B. Washburn of Massachusetts, the chairman of the House Committee on War Claims. This bill was substantially the one which finally passed both houses, providing as it did for three commissioners, appointed by the President, who would receive and examine claims from the South and report on them to Congress for approval and appropriation. Washburn reported that his bill had the unanimous approval of his committee which, having submitted it to the different departments of government, was convinced that it was "now as unobjectionable as it can be made."[57]

The House bill reached the Senate on March 2 and, on motion of Senator Cole of California—who had hitherto consistently opposed all such measures—the Senate agreed to a conference.[58] Cole himself served on the conference committee in which the House bill, with slight modifications, was substituted for the McDonald amendment. With little comment in the House, but with a final flash of oratory in the Senate— where Conkling and George F. Edmunds, of Vermont, made a last vigorous attack—the bill passed both branches, and was signed by the President on March 3, 1871.

Such men as Wilson and Cole, yielding to political expediency, had switched their support to the compromise measure. In reporting the substitute, Senator Cole reminded his colleagues that both branches had now voted in such a way "as to distinctly recognize the propriety of a payment of the claims of the loyal citizens in States once in Rebellion." In view of this fact, he believed it to be wiser to allot the responsibility to "a commission of responsible and intelligent gentlemen, men of character and capacity . . . of ability and learning, rather than to some 'irresponsible clerk' in the quartermaster or commissary departments."[59] At the same time the stanch supporters of the McDonald amendment, still holding that loyalists North and South should be treated on the same basis and by the same agency, voted for the substitute bill.

President Grant acted quickly in naming the three commissioners who, as will appear in the following chapter, were all Republicans of Radical persuasion. On March 8, five days after the act had passed, he

---

[57] *Cong. Globe*, 41st Cong., 3d Sess. (March 1, 1871), p. 1849.
[58] *Ibid.* (March 2, 1871), p. 1880. The joint committee consisted of Cole (Calif.), Thayer (Neb.), and Blair (Mo.) from the Senate, and Dickey (Pa.), Beck (Ky.), and Logan (Ill.) from the House. See *ibid.* (March 3, 1871), p. 1915.
[59] *Ibid.* (March 3, 1871), p. 1971.

announced his selection of Asa Owen Aldis of Vermont, Orange Ferriss of New York, and James B. Howell of Iowa, and on March 10 these three men were approved by the Senate. Within a week, the three appointees gathered in Washington to make their preliminary plans.

On April 10, the same day that the House passed the bill to remove disabilities from all Southerners except members of the Confederate Congress, Confederate army and navy officers, and members of state conventions voting for the ordinance of secession, the offices of the Southern Claims Commission were opened for business in the Hood Building. During its first day of business, claims to the amount of approximately $300,000 were filed, and the long-awaited tribunal for the adjudication of quartermaster and commissary claims from the South was at last an established fact.

The Radicals had been forced to yield on the issue of the right of Southern Unionists to a hearing on their claims. But they had been able, for the moment at least, to divert from an unpredictable House the full responsibility for initiating private claims. The power of investigation had been placed in the hands of three Grant appointees who could assemble and digest proper, rather than partisan, evidence respecting loyalty. Further, by the terms of the act, these three men had been given wide discretion in the matter of determining what should constitute loyalty, and, from their past records, it seemed likely that their rulings in this regard would be well grounded in the Radical doctrine.

At the same time, the Southern Unionists, too, could take some comfort from the fact that they had achieved at least a measure of success in an area which had consistently been barred to them since July 4, 1864. Exactly ten years and one day after Lincoln's first inaugural, Congress had finally provided the means by which loyal men of the South could file their claims with some real hope of success.

CHAPTER IV

THE SOUTHERN CLAIMS COMMISSION IN OPERATION

FROM TIME TO TIME during the controversies over proper procedures on claims growing out of the war, the advantages of creating a commission for their settlement had been suggested. In 1865 Hugh McCulloch, secretary of the Treasury, had proposed this method to the attorney general, James Speed. Speed, however, had replied that he was "of opinion . . . that jurisdiction cannot be conferred upon a commission, appointed either by the President or the Secretary of the Treasury."[1] In January, 1869, during a debate in Congress over the Sue Murphy case, Senator Charles Sumner made the same suggestion in a summary speech reviewing the status of war claims under international law. Sumner held that residents of an insurrectionary region had no legal right to compensation on the basis of bounty or generosity. But in view of the supercharged atmosphere surrounding the issue, he suggested that a commission for "classifying these claims, specifying their respective amounts, circumstances, and evidence of loyalty," would make it possible for Congress to know "precisely the extent and character of these claims before legislating thereon."[2]

The commission-type of procedure embodied in the act of March 3, 1871, was to some extent controlled by all three branches of government. Asa Owen Aldis, whose philosophy guided the organization and rules of the body, commented in 1872 that "this commission allows the same latitude of inquiry in its oral hearings that the committees of the Senate and House allow, and admits any evidence they think will reasonably aid their inquiries."[3] At the same time, the rules set up by the commission drew heavily upon the practices and precedents established by the Court of Claims.[4] The emphasis upon cross-examination of claimants and witnesses, the requirements for admissible evidence, testimony under oath, and the concerted effort to test the claimant's case against counterevidence assembled for the government were in line with judicial procedure. Rulings regarding loyalty and the status

---

[1] James Speed to Hugh McCulloch, Attorney General's Office, July 5, 1865, *Senate Exec. Doc.*, 40th Cong., 2d Sess., No. 22, pp. 16–19.
[2] Charles Sumner, *His Complete Works* (Boston, 1900), XVII, 10–31.
[3] 2d Gen. Rept. of C. of C., *House Misc. Docs.*, 42d Cong., 3d Sess., No. 12, p. 4.
[4] 10 *U.S. Stat. at L.*, 612. The court was established to "hear and determine all claims founded upon any law of Congress, or upon any regulation of an executive department, or upon any contract, express or implied, with the government of the United States . . . and also all claims which may be referred to said court by either house of Congress."

of property in the South likewise were based on Court of Claims and Supreme Court decisions growing out of the Captured and Abandoned Property acts. Finally, both the recommendations drawn from evidence as to the loyalty of each claimant and the validity of his claim with respect to property were completely subject to the approval of Congress, which, year after year, received not only these recommendations but all of the accumulated evidence in each case as well.[5]

In view of the wide discretionary powers of the commissioners, skeptics of the period might well regard with some suspicion the men whom Grant would select from a "large number of retiring members of Congress who [were] candidates for these positions."[6] On the day following his appointment of Asa Owen Aldis, Orange Ferriss, and James B. Howell, the Washington *Daily Morning Chronicle* commented editorially: "The Southern men very generally express dissatisfaction at the Commissioners appointed to examine Southern Claims. They do not know Judge Alder [*sic*]; they prefer someone else to Mr. Ferriss, and they think that while Mr. Howell is an honest man, he is not a just or unprejudiced man."[7]

The choice of Judge Aldis, of Vermont, for president of the commission was fortunate, since he brought to the important position a mind trained in judicial procedure and a knowledge of the international law involved in the whole theory of the status of the South. His father, Asa Aldis (1770–1847), a graduate of Brown University in 1796, had served as a judge of the Supreme Court of Vermont and was one of the leading lawyers in the state.[8] Of special interest is the fact that the elder Aldis, who had been orphaned at the age of five, had himself filed one of the loyalist claims growing out of the American Revolution. The orphaned boy brought suit in a Massachusetts court

---

[5] 2d Gen. Rept. of C. of C., in *House Misc. Docs.*, 42d Cong., 3d Sess., No. 12, p. 39.

[6] Philadelphia *Public Ledger*, March 7, 1871, p. 1. According to the *Ledger*, former Senator Jacob M. Howard of Michigan declined the chairmanship of the commission because "it would necessitate a large amount of the hardest kind of labor, and oblige him to remain away from home most of the time for two years." See *ibid.*, March 13, 1871, p. 1. The Michigan delegation, however, proposed Richard Strickland for the position. His application, bearing the signatures of Senator Howard and Zachariah Chandler, together with the names of some twenty-three other prominent men, went to Grant on March 4, 1871. See R. Strickland to Hon. A. T. Ackerman, attorney general, in Appointment Papers, Record Group 60, Justice Department, National Archives.

[7] The Washington *Daily Morning Chronicle*, March 9, 1871, Vol. IX, No. 109, editorial page.

[8] The memorial sketch on Judge A. O. Aldis, delivered before the Vermont Bar Association on October 4, 1903, presents his background. His father, Asa Aldis, is described as "for more than thirty years the most sagacious, influential and distinguished man and jurist in the vicinity, if not in the state." See Hon. Edward A. Sowles, *Memorial Sketch of Asa Owen Aldis* (Montpelier, Vt., 1904). Hereafter cited as *Memorial Sketch*.

for land belonging to his father which had supposedly been confiscated because of "the suspicion of toryism" surrounding the family. The court restored the property.[9]

As the *Chronicle* account indicates, Asa Owen Aldis was not a familiar figure in the Grant machine. His record, however, showed a career of public service which was substantial rather than spectacular. He was graduated from the University of Vermont in 1829, and afterward attended the Harvard Law School,[10] where Charles Sumner was a classmate.[11] Following his graduation from Harvard, he entered his father's law firm, in 1832. In 1857 he was elected to the Supreme Court of Vermont. According to a contemporary account, he retired from this bench in 1865, "largely in consequence of deep affliction from the loss of three lovely daughters and of the delicate health of others of his family, and accepted an appointment as United States consul at Nice, which office he held with high credit for five years."[12]

While at Nice, according to one of his eulogists, he was especially charged to keep close watch in this "great European resort of Southern chivalry," and during the reconstruction period, "his advice was frequently sought by Congressmen, Senators, and the President, as to their future course in the light of the sentiment of foreign countries."[13] He returned from Nice in 1869,[14] again because of the poor health of his children; in 1870 he was recommended—by Luke Poland, who had served with him as an associate justice in Vermont—for the post of chief justice of the Court of Claims, to take the place of Judge Joseph Casey, who was about to retire.

Poland, who had himself been offered the position on the court, gave Aldis an unqualified endorsement. "I know of no man in the whole

---

[9] See the sketch of Asa Aldis, Sr., in *The Vermont Historical Gazetteer: A magazine embracing a History of Each Town, Civil, Ecclesiastical, Biographical and Military* (Burlington, Vt., 1871), II, 322–323.

[10] *Memorial Sketch.* According to another account, he began a course of law at St. Albans, entered Harvard Law School in April, 1831, remaining there during that year and, in January, 1832, entered Yale Law School in New Haven, where he remained until June. See Lewis Cass Aldrich, *History of Franklin and Grand Isle Counties, Vermont* (Syracuse, N.Y., 1891), pp. 226–227.

[11] In a letter recommending Aldis for the post at Nice, Charles Sumner wrote to Seward from Boston, on August 18, 1865, "The Judge and myself were fellow students in the Law School at Cambridge & I have followed his career ever since. He was not only an eminent lawyer, but he was a strong Anti-Slavery man from the beginning." See Appointment Papers, State Department, National Archives.

[12] See Aldis' obituary in the Burlington *Free Press*, June 26, 1901, XLVII, No. 152.

[13] *Memorial Sketch.*

[14] Aldis' passport, issued on September 26, 1865, as he was leaving for Nice, describes him as fifty-four years of age, 5 feet 7 inches tall, "forehead, High & full; Eyes, light blue; Nose, short; Mouth, medium size; Chin, short; Hair, brown; Complexion, Fair; Face, Round," and a native-born citizen. See Appointment Papers, State Department, National Archives.

country who would fill the place better than he," he wrote the attorney general. "He had every advantage that education could give," in addition to a fine record on the Vermont Supreme Court. Poland added that although the salary for the Court of Claims position was "too small . . . that is not a matter of importance to Judge Aldis as he is a man of ample fortune."[15] No exact evidence is available, but it seems likely that Poland's strong recommendation may have had something to do with Aldis' appointment as president of the Southern Claims Commission.

In contrast to Judge Aldis, who could not be described as a practicing politician, both Orange Ferriss and James B. Howell had served as elected members of Congress: Ferriss in the House from 1865 to 1869, and Howell in the Senate, where he filled the vacancy caused by the resignation of James W. Grimes, from January 18, 1870, to March 3, 1871. Ferriss was fifty-seven years old when he received his appointment as commissioner of claims, and had just completed his two terms in the House. Perhaps his best-known speech while in Congress came during the impeachment proceedings against President Andrew Johnson. Ferriss had voted against impeachment in December, 1867, but during the Stanton controversy, he finally, on March 2, 1868, made a strong charge against the President. He described Johnson as "an apostate Executive, who had used the power of his high office to thwart the will of the people; whose perfidy had well-nigh rendered of no avail all the fruits of a terrible but successful civil war." Now Johnson, with the summary removal of Stanton, had "completed the full measure of his infamy by the deliberate violation of a criminal statute in a last abortive attempt to absorb in himself all the powers of the Government."[16]

Of Puritan-Quaker lineage, Ferriss was born at Glens Falls, New York, on November 26, 1814, and, except for periods of public service, he lived all his life in that community. Through his mother he was a descendant of John Alden, "a fact of which he was very proud," according to one of his biographers.[17] He studied law in Glens Falls in

---

[15] Luke P. Poland to Amos T. Ackerman, attorney general, Washington, July 1, 1870, in Appointment Papers, Court of Claims, Record Group 123, Justice Department, National Archives. Attached is a letter from R. W. Clark, recommending Aldis as "a gentleman of culture, a ripe scholar and an able Jurist."

[16] *Cong. Globe*, 40th Cong., 2d Sess. (March 2, 1868), Appendix, pp. 232–235.

[17] J. A. Holden, *"In Memoriam," Orange Ferriss, 1814–1894* (Glens Falls, 1894), Glens Falls Public Library. Hereafter cited as *In Memoriam*. This thirty-six-page brochure, published on Ferriss' death, contains tributes from many local and national personages. The final pages, which contain the Resolution of the Glens Falls Bar on the occasion of his death, reproduce numerous letters received by his family at that time, including notes of sympathy from Hon. W. Strong, former justice of the United States Supreme Court, the Hamlins, the Morrills, and Miss Lizzie Sherman, the daughter of John Sherman.

the office of Hon. William Hay, and later was graduated from the University of Vermont. Admitted to the bar in 1840, he was, in the next year, appointed surrogate of the county by Governor William H. Seward. An "ardent Whig" in politics at this time, he subsequently became "as partisan a Republican."[18] Another admirer made the observation that "in striking contrast with the conduct of so many public officials of the post-bellum days ... the subject of this sketch, upheld by his Quaker-Puritan honesty, lived an incorruptible life, and came out no richer than he went into politics, perhaps poorer pecuniarily."[19] Ferriss returned to Glens Falls in 1880 when the Southern Claims Commission expired, but moved again to Washington in 1888 to serve as second auditor of the Treasury. He remained in this position until 1891, when he was retired because of the election of Cleveland.[20]

According to a prominent Iowa Republican, James B. Howell was "the first Editor in that State to espouse the cause of General Grant for the Presidency."[21] Born near Morristown, New Jersey, on July 4, 1816, he grew up on a farm in Licking County, Ohio. In 1833 he entered Miami University, from which he was graduated in 1837. Subsequently, he studied law in the office of Judge Hocking H. Hunter, of Lancaster, Ohio, and in 1839 was admitted to the bar. In 1840 he was the Whig candidate for prosecuting attorney in Licking County. Although he failed of election, he reduced the "usual Jackson majority of one thousand or thereabouts ... to one to two hundred."[22]

In the spring of 1841, bad health determined him to "find a home or a grave in the 'great West'," and he made his way on horseback to Chicago and then to the Iowa territory. Here he settled at Keosauqua and began the practice of law. Always interested in politics, he purchased the Des Moines *Valley Whig* in 1845, more for the purpose of giving "his party a live and efficient organ," than with any idea of deserting the legal profession. Gradually, however, in an area and a period when "almost every lawyer was a politician," he became more involved in party issues and politics.[23] In 1849 he moved his paper to

---

[18] *Ibid.;* see also A. W. Holden and Joel Munsell, eds., *A History of the Town of Queensbury in the State of New York* (Albany, N.Y., 1874), pp. 107–109; and a typewritten biography in the Crandall Free Library, Glens Falls, New York.

[19] *In Memoriam.*

[20] *Biographical Directory* (1913), pp. 640–641.

[21] Letter from William W. Belknap, March 16, 1869, Keokuk, Iowa, for the Republicans of Iowa recommending Howell for the position of minister resident to Guatemala, in Appointment Papers, State Department, National Archives.

[22] William H. Barnes, *The History of the Congress of the United States* (New York, 1871), pp. 1–6, Keokuk, Iowa, Public Library.

[23] *Ibid.,* p. 3.

Keokuk, where he established the *Daily Gate City,* the paper with which he was identified until his death.[24]

As Whig influence declined in the state, he associated himself with the young Republican party, and was one of the signers of the call for the convention which organized the party in Iowa. In 1856 he was a delegate to the National Convention which nominated John C. Frémont. He continued his party activities, largely through the editorial columns of his paper, and in January, 1870, was chosen to fill the seat in the United States Senate made vacant by the resignation of Senator James W. Grimes.[25] While in the Upper House, his longest speech was on the subject of land grants to railroads; in this he advocated a limitation on the period in which the railroad companies could hold their land, and a maximum price at which they could sell it.

A clue to the reasons for his appointment to the Southern Claims Commission appears in connection with his application for the position of minister resident to Guatemala in March, 1869. The strong Iowa delegation in Congress had united in recommending him for the post. When, however, Silas A. Hudson, "a cousin of Grants," was appointed instead, Grant was informed, by a petition, that "great & serious dissatisfaction has grown out of Mr. Howell's defeat. . . . It is not right . . . [that] so serious an injury be done to the administration."[26]

Although they represented a wide area of interests and an equally wide variety in background, the three commissioners had a number of things in common. All had been Whigs and had subsequently become Republicans on the slavery issue. All had studied law, although President Aldis' experience in this field was the most extensive. All were, moreover, in their fifties and as a result had not seen service in the Union army. Aldis was the senior member of the commission, being fifty-nine when he received his appointment. Ferriss was fifty-seven, and Howell fifty-five.

At their first meeting, the newly appointed commissioners set about

[24] See Edgar Rubey Harlan, *A Narrative History of the People of Iowa* (Chicago, 1931), V, 88–89; Caleb F. Davis, comp., *Keokuk Biographical and Historical Sketches* (n.d.), VI 401–405; the Keokuk *Weekly Constitution,* June 23, 1880, Vol. XVII, No. 44, p. 7.

[25] The Keokuk *Daily Gate City,* March 8, 1871, Vol. XXV, p. 2. The paper describes Howell as "a man of great practical sense, with all his resources constantly at his command. One who cannot be bribed or coaxed or scared or driven."

[26] The petition was signed by such men as J. W. Grimes, James Harlan, William B. Allison, and Charles Pomeroy. In a separate letter, James F. Wilson, to whom Grant had offered the position of secretary of state, also urged the appointment, as did Samuel F. Miller, a justice of the Supreme Court. A letter from George W. McCrary, a member of Congress, to Hon. R. W. Clarke, who was a personal friend of both Howell and Grant, carried the warning of the Iowa Delegation which may have prompted Grant to appoint Howell to the post of commissioner of claims.

the task of inaugurating procedures, outlining rules and forms, completing the organization, and analyzing their jurisdiction as defined by Congress.[27] A set of twenty-two Rules and Regulations shortly appeared, which indicated the evidence to be included in each claim and called for the most exact information, under oath, regarding the claimant himself, the value of each item listed, and the circumstances surrounding the purchase or seizure of the goods.

Questions arose immediately as to the division of jurisdiction between the commissioners and the Quartermaster and Commissary departments. Claims from Tennessee and West Virginia, which had come under these departments in 1866, presented one such problem. On April 9, 1871, A. T. Ackerman, a former Confederate soldier who was ruling on these claims as attorney general, had written his opinion that "the act of March 3, 1871, repeals the act of July 4, 1864, and the joint resolutions of June 18 and June 28, 1866," so far as Tennessee and West Virginia were concerned.[28] Since the commission had been organized so promptly, and since, in any case, the act creating it went into effect immediately, Ackerman held that "all such claims have been improperly submitted to the Departments since the 3d day of March, 1871."[29]

A letter confirming this division of authority appears in the letter books of the Quartermaster General's Office on May 10, 1871. It notes the withdrawal of a series of cases under the act of July 4, 1864, all of which would be presented to the Southern Claims Commission. Ackerman's opinion is confirmed by the notation that "the jurisdiction over all claims originating in the State of Tennessee presented prior to March 3, 1871, still continues with the Quartermaster General. Claims presented since that date will be adjusted by the Commission."[30]

But by November 28 of the same year, General Meigs was writing to President Aldis that, in his view, "a claimant has a right to choose whether he will prosecute a claim before the Quarter-Master General

[27] Grant's appointments were announced on March 8, 1871, and approved by the Senate on March 10, without debate. Their salary of $5,000 a year was set in the act creating the commission, which provided as well for one clerk and one shorthand reporter, each to receive $2,500 a year. 16 *U.S. Stat. at L.*, 525.

[28] A. T. Ackerman, attorney general, to George S. Boutwell, secretary of the Treasury, April 9, 1871, reproduced in the Washington *Daily Morning Chronicle*, April 10, 1871, Vol. IX, No. 136, p. 1. Joint resolutions on June 18 and June 28, 1866, had extended the jurisdiction of the Quartermaster and Commissary departments, operating under the act of July 4, 1864, to Tennessee and West Virginia respectively.

[29] *Ibid.*

[30] Quartermaster General's Office, "Letters Sent, Claims, 1871," Record Book B., May 10, 1871, p. 313. War Department, National Archives.

or before the Commission, if originating in the State of Tennessee." Meigs added that it would obviously be improper for a claimant to appear before the two tribunals at the same time. He did not, therefore, "propose to pursue the investigation of any claim after learning that it had been brought before the Commissioners." He did not include his obvious hope that the commission would follow a similar method, but he repeated that he would "gladly send to the Commission all information in this office relating to any case before them."[31]

On their part, the commissioners ruled that they would not consider, without new evidence, claims from Tennessee previously ruled upon by the Quartermaster Department. Their reasons for this ruling are described in the report on the claim of J. George Harris, a paymaster of the United States Navy, from Davidson County, Tennessee. Harris had asked for a fresh hearing on his case before the commissioners, on the ground that the award of the quartermaster general, confirmed on March 10, 1870, of "only $1 per cord for standing wood or timber, was harsh, arbitrary, and unjust." On March 11, 1870, the secretary of war had ruled that the decision of the quartermaster general on the merits of claims presented under the act of July 4, 1864, was final. In view of these facts, the commissioners wrote: "We do not deem it our duty to consider it further. . . . Were we to open this case after it has been so fully examined and finally decided by a tribunal having full jurisdiction, we might well be called upon to re-examine all the cases which have been examined by the Quartermaster and Commissary Generals adversely to the claimants."[32]

The review before the commission differed in some important respects from the corresponding examinations in the Committees on Claims in Congress, or in the government departments. Stress was placed on the presentation of the case for the government, whereas in Congress claims examined by the proper committees had been made up almost entirely of ex parte evidence which presented only the side of the claimant. Even when the committee was aware that, in the material submitted to it, the government's side of the case was not adequately presented, the members of the committee did not have time nor facilities to prepare a better case.

---

[31] M. C. Meigs, quartermaster general, to A. O. Aldis, regarding the claim of Mary E. Lacey, forwarded by the Quartermaster Department to the commission on November 28, 1871, *ibid.*, Record Book D., War Department, National Archives.

[32] Summary Report of the commissioners in the case of J. George Harris, Davidson County, Tennessee [claimed $24,822.29, disallowed in 1871], C. of C. No. 55, Justice Department, National Archives.

In general the commissioners followed the procedures of the Court of Claims as set forth in its Annual Reports.[33] Since the court's decisions were often tested by appeal to the Supreme Court, this practice brought the rulings of the commission into line with established legal practice.[34] An additional, but at the time unsuspected, advantage of adopting Court of Claims methods wherever possible, appeared in the 1880's when, under the Bowman and Tucker acts, many of the cases heard by the commission were reopened in the Court of Claims. In nearly every instance, the evidence assembled by the commissioners and usually their conclusions in each case were sustained by the court.

The act creating the commission allowed considerable latitude in the interpretation of the all-important terms "loyalty" and "stores and supplies," and these subjects are reserved for separate chapters. Two members of the board could constitute a quorum, and agreement of two members could decide all questions in controversy. The act required that a journal of the proceedings be kept, to be signed by the president of the board; that a register of claims be prepared, showing the date of presentation of each claim, its number, the name and residence of the claimant, and the subject matter and amount of the claim together with the amount allowed, if any. These records were always to be open to the inspection of the President and the attorney general of the United States, or to "such officer as the President may designate." The commissioners were required, by a provision which was inserted after some debate in the Senate, to hold all their sessions in Washington, presumably so that they would be under the close surveillance of Congress.[35]

A view of the commission in operation during its first weeks can be gained through the daily entries in the *Journal.* On April 12, 1871, according to this record, the State Department sent certified oaths of office for the three commissioners, and a certified copy of the Senate resolution approving Aldis as the president of the commission.[36] Five days later, on April 17, the quartermaster general forwarded "speci-

---

[33] James B. Howell to A. O. Aldis, Keokuk, Iowa, July 24, 1871, in Southern Claims Commission, "Miscellaneous Letters Received," Record Group 56, Treasury Department, National Archives.

[34] See Charles C. Nott and Samuel H. Huntington, *Cases Decided in the Court of Claims of the United States at the December Term for 1868* (Washington, 1868), II, iv. The office of solicitor was abolished by act of Congress on July 1, 1868, and specifications for transfer to the Attorney General's Department were made in the same act. For the rules and practices of the Court of Claims in 1870, see *ibid.*, VI, v–xix.

[35] 16 *U.S. Stat. at L.*, 525.

[36] *Journal of the Commissioners of Claims*, Vol. I, Record Group 56, Treasury Department, National Archives.

men blanks, forms and vouchers used in the examination and settlement" of claims in his office. On the same day, a letter arrived from a citizen of Cornersville, Tennessee, suggesting that some provision should also be made for reimbursing Unionists for property taken by the Confederate army: a function obviously beyond the jurisdiction of the commission.[37] On the following day, a letter from the secretary of the Treasury informed Aldis that the so-called "rebel archives" captured by the Union army or purchased by agents from the North, were available for their use.[38] Three days later, on April 21, the names of the first 150 claimants were forwarded to the Treasury Department to be checked against these records.[39]

Meanwhile, in its "Washington Notes," the New York *Tribune* reported that the commission had "found no lack of work . . . and this before the law . . . had been read in distant parts of the country." The newly created board might, the writer warned, quite easily be "a great piece of good fortune for the Washington claim agents, who were fast finding their occupation gone with the settlement of nearly all the war claims which could be paid under previous laws." This danger was very real, especially since the law establishing the tribunal "is quite vague and almost everything is left to the discretion of the Commissioners." But the columnist concluded hopefully, "It is fortunate for the interests of the Treasury and the tax payers that the Commissioners are men of high character and knowledge of public affairs, who will scrutinize all claims with great care, and prescribe stringent tests of loyalty that cannot be evaded." Any loophole which would allow claims merely upon strong testimony of loyalty would, the writer believed, result in a raid upon the Treasury in amount "so enormous that the Congress would have to reject them all or bankrupt the Treasury, and increase the public debt by hundreds of millions."[40]

By May 17, 1871, the commissioners were ready to announce that public hearings on the claims already on file would begin, to be held on each Tuesday, Wednesday, Thursday, and Friday. Mondays and Saturdays were reserved for consultation and review.[41] By the end of April, 566 claims had already been filed. During the summer months, when the commissioners themselves had adjourned, the office remained

[37] *Ibid.*, p. 8, 9.
[38] *Ibid.*, p. 9.
[39] *Ibid.*, p. 11.
[40] The New York *Daily Tribune*, April 15, 1871, Vol. XXXI, No. 9368, p. 7.
[41] *Journal of the Commissioners of Claims*, Vol. I, p. 23, Record Group 56, Treasury Department, National Archives.

open and claims poured in for totals of 1,222 in May, 1,562 in June, 1,539 in July, 1,261 in August, and 1,757 in September.[42]

In the fall months, the claims continued to pour in: 1,218 in October, 981 in November, and 686 in December; but in spite of the press of routine office business, the first Annual Report to Congress, on December 16, 1871, transmitted 580 cases which had been examined and on which recommendations were being made. Of this number, 256 were disallowed, some 26 for lack of jurisdiction and the remainder for lack of satisfactory proof of loyalty. Most of the allowed cases came from the counties in Virginia near Washington. Many of the claimants listed in this report were originally from the North. Most of them had lived within Union lines and could prove, through Federal officers or loyal Washingtonians, overt acts of loyalty. The extensive investigations which were characteristic of the later reports were not, therefore, considered necessary. About forty of these cases had been so thoroughly examined by governmental departments that the loyalty of the individual was held to have been reasonably established. Such cases had, of course, been prepared according to the specifications of the act of July 4, 1864, and were all ready for review, in anticipation of the time when the restrictions of that act respecting the South should be removed.[43]

The commissioners felt constrained, however, to take oral testimony on their own account, if possible, in these early cases. They also reviewed and digested the evidence accumulated by the government departments and prepared their own Summary Report for each one. It should be noted also that in this first Annual Report to Congress, the proportion of cases allowed, about 52 per cent, represented an all-time high. The report itself explained that in the cases which had been under surveillance "which come from regions more decidedly hostile to the Government . . . the proportion of claims in which loyalty is not satisfactorily proved . . . [is] considerably larger."[44]

At the same time, cases from the mountain regions of Tennessee, Georgia, and Alabama which, in this report, were recommended for allowance had impressed the commissioners with their evidence "of

---

[42] These figures are computed from the Register of Claims, in which each case was listed on a separate page, giving the date it was filed, the name and address of the claimant, the amount claimed together with a brief description of the type of articles listed, the commission number of the case, and the name of the attorney on record. Under this identifying information brief notations record the progress of the case, giving dates of hearings, rulings, and its final disposition.

[43] 1st Gen. Rept. of C. of C., in *House Misc. Docs.*, 42d Cong., 2d Sess., No. 16, p. 8.

[44] *Ibid.*

peril, hardship, sacrifice, and suffering, of steadfast courage and patriotic devotion to the Union, which do them honor and entitle them to the grateful considerations of the Government."[45] Regarding this first report, the New York *Times* noted that the "work of the Commission has been so thoroughly done, and the policy of excluding doubtful and uncertain claims so rigidly enforced, that it is most likely the Committee on Claims will be constrained to recommend the payments allowed by the Commission without reduction."[46]

During the second year of its operation, claims continued to be filed with regularity, if in somewhat smaller total numbers. In January of 1872, 665 claims were filed; in February, 507; in March, 743; in April, 856; in May, 742; in June, 536; in July, 540; in August, 694; in September, 649; in October, 563; in November, 413; and in December, 658. The organic act had set March 3, 1873, as the last date for filing claims, and, as this deadline approached, the volume of claims again began to rise. During January, 1873, 804 petitions were filed; in February, 1,620 cases were registered. On Saturday, March 1, in a single day 233 cases came in, and on the last day they could be filed, 1,282 cases poured into the office.[47]

At the close of business on March 3, 1873, the commissioners could report, therefore, that 22,298 claims, for a gross amount of $60,258,-150.44, had been filed, of which only 580 had been reported to Congress. Congress, thereupon, extended the life of the commission for four years, but reaffirmed its previous position that no claim could be filed after March 3, 1873, and that "all claims not so presented shall be deemed to be barred forever thereafter." This abrupt and decisive action on the part of Congress, without special warning and within a single day, became one of the issues in the subsequent controversies regarding Southern claims.

On the subject of their unfinished business, the commissioners commented that the 14,637 cases awaiting adjudication had almost all had a preliminary examination and, because they were "difficult and doubtful" and frequently involved large sums, would consume much time. Twelve of the larger cases with which they were immediately concerned, for example, involved amounts totaling $3,035,000. In most of the cases, the oral examination of witnesses which, the commissioners noted, had taken up a "large portion of our time," was nearing completion. It seemed likely, therefore, that more time could be spent in detailed

---

[45] *Ibid.*
[46] The New York *Times*, Dec. 11, 1871, Vol. XXI, No. 6310, p. 1.
[47] Prepared from the Register of Claims.

investigation of the evidence at hand. To this end and for the purpose of testing the claims adequately at the point of their origin, the commissioners urgently requested that the number of special agents allowed them, limited by law to three, be increased.[48]

On the fourth anniversary of the act which created the commission, President Aldis' recommendation that additional clerks be engaged to "speed the work and shorten the duration" of the commission, gave another view of the busy office. Aldis pointed out that, with seventeen thousand claims still on the register, the addition of expert clerical assistance would be of immeasurable benefit. These clerks could read the papers sent in from the field, list the witnesses, and examine the items and amounts claimed, in relation to the evidence. They could, moreover, mark the most material evidence for the benefit of the examining commissioner and check each name against the records in other government departments, thus adding to the evidence and avoiding duplication of effort. In addition to these routine duties, they could relieve the commissioners themselves of the heavy task of writing letters of inquiry, especially to those army officers mentioned for their part in taking the goods; and finally, they could assist by copying the items specified in the petition onto the Summary Report which bore the final judgment of the examining commissioner.[49]

With no new claims being filed, the commission could now give full time to the consideration of business already at hand. During the first two years of work, the cases in which evidence of loyalty or disloyalty were reasonably obvious had been reported to Congress. As each year passed, however, the decisions became more difficult and the technique of examination involved more details. In the first report, as has been noted, 580 cases were disposed of.[50] A year later, on December 6, 1872,

---

[48] 4th Gen. Rept. of C. of C., *House Misc. Docs.*, 43d Cong., 2d Sess., No. 18, p. 2.

[49] Asa Owen Aldis to William Lawrence, chairman of the House Committee on War Claims, included as an appendix in *House Report No. 91*, 43d Cong., 1st Sess. (to accompany HR 1565). The expenses of the commission for the fiscal year 1875 were shown in the annual report of the Treasury as follows:
Salaries and expenses, Southern Claims Commission

A. O. Aldis	5,000.00
J. L. Andum	2,305.60
C. F. Benjamin	2,500.00
S. S. Everett	1,200.00
O. Ferrins	5,000.00
T. J. Hobbs	27,000.00
J. B. Howell	5,000.00
D. R. Keller	1,200.00
T. W. Phipps	1,395.40
G. W. Seaver	1,200.00

See *An Account of the Receipts and Expenditures of the United States for the Fiscal Year Ending June 30, 1875* (Washington, 1882), p. 43.

[50] 1st Gen. Rept. of C. of C., *House Misc. Docs.*, 42d Cong., 2d Sess., No. 16, p. 7.

the second Annual Report transmitted to Congress 2,209 cases, of which 1,061 were recommended for allowance and 1,148 for rejection.[51] The third report, submitted on December 8, 1873, was concerned with 2,465 cases, with 1,092 found loyal and 1,373 disallowed by the commissioners.[52] The fourth report, in 1874, listed 2,407 completed claims and recommended that 1,163 of them be allowed and 1,244 disallowed.[53]

The fifth General Report of the commission, issued on December 20, 1875, rounded out the first five years by reporting a total of 1,561 cases, of which 775 were allowed and 786 "wholly disallowed." The total number of cases reported to Congress was, in this year, brought to 9,222, and 13,076 cases were still awaiting full examination. Of the claims already reported, 205 were from Alabama, 187 from Arkansas, 8 from Florida, 209 from Georgia, 57 from Louisiana, 151 from Mississippi, 128 from North Carolina, 44 from South Carolina, 242 from Tennessee, 318 from Virginia, and 12 from that part of West Virginia which had been included under the jurisdiction of the commission. The total amount allowed up to this time was $492,602.17; the amount disallowed was almost eight times this figure, or $3,303,742.56.[54] The sixth report, in 1876, included 1,866 cases, of which 976 were recommended as deserving of award and the rest rejected.[55]

By early 1877, when the four-year extension granted to the life of the commission on March 3, 1873, was about to expire, there remained 11,212 cases as yet unconcluded. Meanwhile, the broadside attack on the whole question of Southern war claims was reaching its peak. In the North, editorial opinion thundered against the "vast brood of claim agents" which had descended on Washington "like a perennial cloud of locusts."[56] The New York *Tribune*, which had led in the assault on "rebel claims," continued to agitate against "Confederate Rapacity," and prophesied that such claims "promised soon to make the National debt seem a trifling matter."[57] With increasing Democratic majorities, however, men from the South had begun to argue not only for the right to file claims but for representation on the boards of review.

On March 9, 1877, Lewis P. Olds of Raleigh, North Carolina, wrote

[51] 2d Gen. Rept. of C. of C., *ibid.*, 42d Cong., 3d Sess., No. 12, p. 2.
[52] 3d Gen. Rept. of C. of C., *ibid.*, 43d Cong., 1st Sess., No. 23, p. 2.
[53] 4th Gen. Rept. of C. of C., *ibid.*, 43d Cong., 2d Sess., No. 18, Pt. 2, p. 3.
[54] 5th Gen. Rept. of C. of C., *ibid.*, 44th Cong., 1st Sess., No. 30, p. 5.
[55] 6th Gen. Rept. of C. of C., *ibid.*, 44th Cong., 1st Sess., No. 4, pp. 1-2.
[56] The New York *Times*, Feb. 15, 1875, p. 4.
[57] The New York *Tribune*, Sept. 16, 1880, pp. 1-2. The *Tribune* estimated that the grand aggregate asked for by the "Solid South" for internal improvements, private relief bills, and war claims based on a refunding of the cotton tax, amounted to $1,390,970,313 in 1880.

President Rutherford B. Hayes asking to be appointed "one of the three 'Commissioners of Southern Claims' under the recent Act extending the time." He asked special consideration as "a Southern Man, and humbly conceiving that one of this board might very properly come from that section where the business lies." Accompanying this letter was an endorsement, dated November 30, 1874, from former Governor W. W. Holden, who argued that the South should have at least one of the commissioners. Olds was, Holden believed, entitled to the job as an honest man and one "supremely attached to the national government having maintained his status as a loyal man throughout the rebellion." Holden did not question the integrity of the commission as it stood, but argued that Olds would be a valuable addition "from his knowledge of the Southern people among whom he was born and reared."[58]

Alarmed by the possibility of "a new Commission of the men desired by some scheming Southern Members and Claim Agents," Commissioner Howell wrote his friend William Dennison, acting attorney general, early in March, urging that the President reappoint the present commissioners at once. Calling on "college memories of each other," Howell warned Dennison such appointments of newcomers "would cost the Government a good deal in many ways as all they want is more claims and larger amounts allowed than they can get at our hands." Besides, he added, Congress seemed entirely satisfied with the present board. "We don't want any disturbing element planted into the Commission," he added, "but desire to go on in the grooves we have made and understand."[59]

On March 6, Dennison forwarded the letter to the President,[60] and on the following day George G. Wright, chairman of the Committee on Claims in the Senate, wrote Hayes urging that the incumbent commissioners "can finish the work better than any new men—much better, and the public service demands their retention in the places they have so well filled."[61]

The three commissioners were reappointed by Hayes, and continued their work until March 12, 1880, when completed reports on all of the 22,298 cases had been filed. The seventh report, issued to Congress in

---

[58] Lewis P. Olds to Rutherford B. Hayes, Washington, March 9, 1877, and W. W. Holden to "His Excellency, the President," Raleigh, North Carolina, Nov. 30, 1874, Record Group 60, Appointment Papers, Justice Department, National Archives.
[59] J. B. Howell to W. Dennison [n.d.], *ibid.*
[60] S. Dennison to the President, Washington, March 6, 1877, *ibid.*
[61] George C. Wright to the President, Senate Chamber, March 7, 1877, *ibid.*

1877, listed 1,659 cases, of which 945 were disallowed and 714 allowed.[62]

The eighth report, in 1878, included 1,559 cases, with 657 allowed and 902 disallowed.[63] On December 16, 1879, 2,290 cases were reported, of which only 553 were allowed and 1,737 disallowed. Of the 5,702 cases not yet reported, 250 were still under investigation, but Aldis believed that all could be "decided and reported to Congress by the time the term of this commission ends, on the 10th of next March." The rest of the 5,702 cases were claims on which no evidence had been filed by March 10, 1879, and were, therefore, "barred forever thereafter" by the act of June 15, 1878.[64]

In their final report, on March 9, 1880, the commissioners summarized their ten years' work with a brief table:[65]

Number of claims disposed of in former reports	16,608
Number disposed of in this report	383
Cases "forever barred" under the act of June 15, 1878 and herewith reported	5,250
Cases previously withdrawn	57
Total	22,298
Whole amount of the 22,298 claims is	$60,258,150.44
Whole amount allowed	4,636,920.69
Whole amount disallowed	$55,621,229.75

[62] 7th Gen. Rept. of C. of C., in *House Misc. Docs.*, 45th Cong., 2d Sess., No. 4, p. 3.
[63] 8th Gen. Rept. of C. of C., *ibid.*, 45th Cong., 3d Sess., No. 6, pp. 1–2.
[64] 9th Gen. Rept. of C. of C., *ibid.*, 46th Cong., 2d Sess., No. 10, p. 4.
[65] 10th Gen. Rept. of C. of C., *ibid.*, 46th Cong., 2d Sess., No. 30, p. 2.

CHAPTER V

THE TECHNIQUES OF TESTING

THE commissioners of claims had been limited to Washington for their own deliberations.[1] It soon became clear, however, that their testing procedures could not be confined to an examination of the papers submitted by the claimant or his attorneys. Accordingly, they came to rely on two chief techniques: oral examination of the petitioner and his witnesses, and verification of the evidence by a study of his home community. In an annual report to Congress, they well described the nature of their local investigation:

> To know ... the condition of the affairs at a given place at any period of the war, the state of public opinion, the leading adherents of the Union and confederate causes, the kinds and degrees of duress and insecurity under which the adherents of the National Government rested, the opportunities for showing loyalty by word or act, the time and extent of the restoration of the authority of the Government, the disposition and activity of both the Federal and confederate commanders and other authorities, the actual military situation that controlled or justified the Federal forces in appropriating the private property of citizens to their own use ...[2]

The oral examination provided the opportunity of observing the claimant's "appearance on the stand, of judging his intelligence, fairness, and honesty, and by cross-examination of ascertaining his means of knowledge and testing his credibility."[3] In cases under $10,000, special provisions were made for holding these oral hearings at convenient spots throughout the South, using special commissioners and special agents. But men and women of substantial property, whose claims exceeded $10,000, were required to appear in person in Washington with their witnesses.

The Southern Unionist was expected to assemble all possible evidence showing his loyalty and his right to payment for property lost. In the subsequent oral examination, this evidence was thoroughly examined and checked against other records. If, for example, the petitioner had received a voucher for the goods he furnished to the Union army, and if he had managed to retain it, the receipt was considered to be good evidence. At the same time, the commissioners were unwilling to accept without question the tattered slips bearing the signature

[1] Report of John A. Logan for the Conference Committee in *Cong. Globe*, 41st Cong., 3d Sess. (March 3, 1871), p. 1915.
[2] 5th Gen. Rept. of C. of C., *House Misc. Docs.*, 44th Cong., 1st Sess., No. 30, p. 10.
[3] 1st Gen. Rept. of C. of C., *ibid.*, 42d Cong., 2d Sess., No. 16, p. 5.

of a Union officer. They knew that in many areas of the South these slips had been sold by 'their discouraged owners to unprincipled opportunists.[4]

In preparation for each hearing, the Washington office classified all the materials submitted—often using the methods of parallel columns to show the conflicting evidence—so that at the hearing the commissioners were prepared with specific questions and the claimant had an opportunity to refute any damaging evidence which had been uncovered. This oral examination was recorded in shorthand and carried great weight in the final decision.

The records of the departments of government, especially the quartermaster and commissary branches of the War Department, were regularly examined for the information they might contain.[5] The so-called "rebel archives," which had come into the hands of the Treasury officials, furnished "written contemporary evidence of the position of thousands of persons in the service of, or having dealings with the confederacy."[6] Public lists of claimants throughout the South were posted as an invitation to informants. Local records, especially the files of newspapers covering the period, were consulted for the names and local news they contained.

The commissioners encouraged their agents and representatives to collect such Southern records whenever the opportunity presented itself. Enos Richmond, a special agent assigned to Virginia, wrote frequently of having acquired Virginia poll books as he traveled from county to county. These poll books contained the names of men who had voted for or against secession at the election of May 23, 1861, when Virginia submitted the question to a popular vote. On April 15, 1872, Richmond wrote from Berryville that "Col. Isaac Mix of the 3ᵈ New York Cav. took possession of all poll books but returned to the court house all except the books containing the Names of the soldiers voting at Harper's Ferry." In the meantime he had obtained five of the six

---

[4] On May 8, 1874, S. E. Chamberlain, a special agent of the commission, wrote from Harrisburg, Virginia, that "parties were all through this country some time since, buying vouchers against the Government for quartermaster and commissary stores. . . . They bought indiscriminately (paying some 25 cents on the dollar) of any one who held them, but it seems that loyal men were not so eager to sell as those disloyal."

[5] From time to time officers of the Quartermaster or Commissary departments, or agents of the Secret Service Division of the Justice Department, made special investigations of their own. A typical letter, written in a terse, factual style, is that of A. B. Newcomb, Detective Service, Department of Justice, Washington, March 25, 1876, to Edwards Pierpont, attorney general, reporting on his investigation of a claimant before the commission. See Record Group 60, Box 94, Justice Department, National Archives.

[6] 2d Gen. Rept. of C. of C., *House Misc. Docs.*, 42d Cong., 3d Sess., No. 12, p. 7.

books recording the vote in the sixth precinct. The missing book, for the White Post precinct, was not available since it had been "stolen from the Clerk's office in the last three months."[7]

President Aldis' active interest in collecting local records appears in his correspondence with A. R. Spofford, librarian of Congress, regarding the purchase of a complete file of the *Daily Savannah Republican.* The file covered the period from 1800 to 1873, and had been priced at $1,500. However, on August 18, 1873, Spofford wrote that the purchase had finally been made at Aldis' price of $1,000. "Now," Spofford continued, "if I can procure from you a similar certificate to that you are accustomed to draw on the Fund for Captured & abandoned Property! or whatever the last appropriation is called, the Treasury will pay the amount."[8]

Perhaps one of the most extreme and, as it developed, least effective methods for testing claims was the practice of posting public lists of claimants throughout the South, giving the name of each claimant, the state and county in which he lived, and the number and amount of his claim. On April 27, 1871, a little over a month after the commission had opened for business, the Washington *Chronicle* announced that such lists had already been posted. "The Commissioners welcome information from all quarters," the *Chronicle* noted, "on this difficult problem of Southern loyalty during the war. They are anxious . . . to secure to the true loyalists . . . the sure recognition of their just demands, and nothing will conduce more to that end than the exposure of all mere pretenders by the aid of a wide publication of their names throughout the South."[9]

---

[7] Enos Richmond to the commission, Berryville, Virginia, April 15, 1872, in Southern Claims Commission, "Letters from and about Special Agents," Record Group 56, Treasury Section, National Archives. In explaining the soldier vote at Harper's Ferry, Richmond wrote that "about three hundred voters belonging in Clarke Co. had joined the rebel army and was at harpers ferry Va on . . . the election day and each company opened a poll book representing the precinct in which they voted at home."

[8] A. R. Spofford, librarian of Congress, to A. O. Aldis, Washington, Aug. 18, 1873, in Southern Claims Commission, "Miscellaneous Letters Received," Record Group 56, Treasury Section, National Archives. For a report on the efforts to collect those records of the Confederacy which were scattered throughout the South, see Dallas D. Irvine, "The Fate of Confederate Archives," *American Historical Review,* XLIV (July, 1939), 823–841, and Philip M. Hamer, "The Records of Southern History," *Journal of Southern History,* V (Feb., 1939), 3–17.

[9] The Washington *Daily Morning Chronicle,* April 27, 1871, Vol. IX, No. 151, p. 1. On August 1, 1872, Charles F. Benjamin, clerk of the commission, wrote to Aldis that he had "hurried up the preparation of the lists for each State, embracing all the claims filed up to 1,500." See Charles F. Benjamin to A. O. Aldis, Aug. 1, 1872, in Southern Claims Commission, "Miscellaneous Letters Received, 1872," Record Group 56, Treasury Department, National Archives.

From the field, the special agents wrote frequently that the lists prepared for every post office in the South were quickly torn down.[10] Just how far these lists served their secondary purposes of "deterring many from pressing disloyal and unjust claims," it is impossible to determine.[11] With the Ku Klux riding, and in view of the ingrown bitterness against Northern interference, it seems likely that many an honest Unionist hesitated to expose himself to such a rigid test before his own community. Judging from the records, these lists produced a surprisingly small number of letters. The attitude of J. C. McFerran, chief quartermaster of the Military Division of the South, was apparently shared by many other men. On June 30, 1871, McFerran wrote the quartermaster general regarding a "letter addressed to the Southern Claims Commission and referred to me by your endorsement of June 27, 1871." He made the required investigation, but concluded his report with the indignant comment, "Were it not for the endorsement thereon by the Commission and by your office I should treat it with the silent contempt such dastardly cowardice deserves."[12] The commissioners consigned such anonymous letters, signed merely "Friend," or "A Partisan," to the miscellaneous file instead of attaching them to the individual record.

The network of special commissioners and special agents established to canvass the South had precedents in the Court of Claims, which maintained a group of special commissioners for the convenience of claimants in remote areas and to obtain such local information as might support or invalidate the evidence at hand.

On June 18, 1871, a little over two months after the office of the Claims Commission had been opened, President Aldis announced that six deputy commissioners had been named and were at work in North Carolina, Tennessee, and Louisiana, and that more would be appointed for other regions in the South as quickly as qualified men could be found. By March of 1877, when the field investigations had been largely completed, the staff had grown to include 106 special commissioners distributed as follows: thirteen in Alabama, thirteen in Arkan-

---

[10] On April 15, 1872, Enos Richmond wrote from Berryville, Virginia, before starting out on a trip, "I have no list of the claims filed. The published list that was posted at the post office was torn down last Jan." See Southern Claims Commission, "Letters from and about Special Agents," Record Group 56, Treasury Department, National Archives.

[11] 1st Gen. Rept. of C. of C., *House Misc. Docs.*, 42d Cong., 2d Sess., No. 16, p. 8.

[12] J. C. McFerran, Department of Quartermaster General, United States, and Chief Quartermaster Military Division of the South to the quartermaster general, June 30, 1871, in Records of the Quartermaster General's Office, "Letters Sent, Claims, 1871," Record Book A, War Department, National Archives.

sas, six in Georgia, ten in Louisiana, fifteen in Mississippi, eighteen in North Carolina, three in South Carolina, fourteen in Tennessee, thirteen in Virginia, and one in West Virginia.[13]

Although the special commissioners assembled vital data for practically every case, large or small, President Aldis recognized the limitations to this type of field examination. In his first Annual Report to Congress he observed that, after reading the depositions submitted by the special commissioners, "one cannot but feel that the results would have been far more satisfactory if some competent person on behalf of the Government had investigated the claims and been present to examine the witnesses." The need for such expert examination was especially obvious, he believed, in the larger cases, since "high ability, ingenuity, and skill in procuring and presenting evidence to sustain them might be expected." A just decision could only be reached in such cases if they were thoroughly examined for the government "on the spot where they arose."[14]

Accordingly, on May 11, 1872, Congress made provision for traveling special agents, not to exceed three in number, who could operate throughout the South. These men were especially assigned to supervise and assist with the hearings before the local commissioners in cases involving between $5,000 and $10,000 and to make such special inquiry or searches as the larger cases required.[15]

The exact function of these three field representatives thus was governed largely by the size of the claim. The special commissioners, residing at strategic points throughout the South, were chiefly concerned with receiving and hearing claims for amounts up to $5,000.[16] Using the eighty detailed questions prepared by the commissioners, they took sworn depositions from the claimants and their witnesses and, when the claimant had paid his fees, forwarded the case to Washington, where it was usually referred to one member of the three-man

---

[13] The first six commissioners were stationed in Alexandria, Louisiana; Nashville, Tennessee; and in Fayetteville, Plymouth, and Hookerton, North Carolina. See *Journal of the Commission*, Records of the Southern Claims Commission, Record Group 56, Treasury Department, National Archives. The utility and the rapid development of the use of these special commissioners is most quickly revealed by subsequent lists of such officers. By December, 1871, twenty-nine such deputies were functioning, covering all of the Southern states. See 1st Gen. Rept. of C. of C., *House Misc. Docs.*, 42d Cong., 2d Sess., No. 16, pp. 23–24.

[14] 1st Gen. Rept. of C. of C., *House Misc. Docs.*, 42d Cong., 2d Sess., No. 16, pp. 5–6.

[15] 17 *U.S. Stat. at L.*, 97.

[16] The first commissioners were limited to claims under $3,000, but after the appointment of the special agents, their functions were extended to all claims above $5,000. See 2d Gen. Rept. of C. of C., *House Misc. Docs.*, 42d Cong., 3d Sess., No. 12, p. 4.

board for intensive review. If, after examination, he felt that further investigation was needed, the local commissioner was instructed to reopen the hearings along specific lines, and fresh depositions were prepared covering doubtful points.

The problem of finding suitable men for the field posts was difficult. They must be able to take testimony under oath, which meant that they were usually justices of the peace, United States commissioners, or men serving the public in some more or less official capacity. Their selection, in contrast to many other appointments made during the Grant administration, was very slightly influenced by political considerations. Indeed, in spite of frequent letters from congressmen or party men recommending this or that constituent as a good candidate for such a job, the appointments were almost never made as a result of such recommendations, to judge from a comparison of the letters with the full list of special commissioners in the index of the *Journal*. A report on a prospective special commissioner, for example, led to the conclusion that he would be a good man because "he has been a County & Probate Judge since 1868, and is still poor which speaks well for an Arkansas official."[17] Commenting on this problem of recruiting, George Tucker, a special agent, wrote from Jackson, Mississippi, in 1874, "There is a great pulling and hauling here and what one leading man recommends another one will not. I think we will have to pick out our men pretty much ourselves."[18]

Usually the work performed for the Southern Claims Commission was in the nature of a side line for the special commissioners, who were residents of the community in which they functioned. When Theodore W. Parmele, of Columbia, South Carolina, was offered a full-time job as a special agent on the strength of his past performance as a special commissioner, he replied, "My position as 'Special Commissioner' affords a less certain and probably less lucrative income, per se, than the one you offer, but in it I may do other business without interference with my duty... [and] I have a family to provide for from my earnings."[19]

The special agents, on the other hand, were roving representatives who usually covered several states in their operations. In addition to their direct responsibility for obtaining evidence, they were given

---

[17] John D. Edwards to the commission, Little Rock, Arkansas, April 14, 1875, in Southern Claims Commission, "Letters from and about Special Agents," Record Group 56, Treasury Department, National Archives.

[18] George H. Tucker to Charles F. Benjamin, Jackson, Mississippi, Jan. 30, 1874, in *ibid.*

[19] George H. Tucker to A. O. Aldis, Columbia, South Carolina, Jan. 24, 1873, in *ibid.*

supervisory functions. They were directed to correspond with the special commissioners and to advise them as to questions which should be put on behalf of the government. In theory, they were to be present at hearings before the local commissioners, especially in cases involving amounts of between $5,000 and $10,000, to cross-examine claimants and witnesses whenever they thought it necessary. The practice, however, was somewhat different. As Charles F. Benjamin, the clerk of the commission, put it in 1873:

> If the experience of our special commissioners in getting witnesses together in small cases within their jurisdiction, and the experience of the Commissioners themselves in cases heard orally at Washington, go for anything, it would require an almost miraculous conjunction of fortuitous circumstances to get together, at the same time and place, and in any considerable number of cases, a special agent, a special commissioner, a claimant and all his witnesses, neither the agent nor the commissioner being armed with compulsory process to secure the attendance of witnesses, and everybody concerned having his or her special business to look after.[20]

The functions of the special commissioners, as differentiated from the special agents, are sometimes difficult to define because both types of officers operated within somewhat elastic functional boundaries. On occasion a special commissioner might act as a special agent and, less frequently, special agents as special commissioners. From the standpoint of office organization, however, there were at least two differentiations in their status. The special commissioners were men authorized and entitled to take testimony under oath, whereas the special agents could not, since their jobs were considered to be largely investigative. In the second place, the special commissioners were paid entirely by the claimants, in the form of fees in amounts set by the Washington office,[21] but special agents were paid entirely by the government, and could receive no fees of any kind from claimants.

The special agents, in their capacity as investigators, followed the practices of similar agents of government departments, namely, "to inquire in the vicinity of the claimants, of respectable and credible

---

[20] Memorandum by Charles F. Benjamin, Dec. 15, 1873, in Southern Claims Commission, "Miscellaneous Letters Received, 1873," Record Group 56, Treasury Department, National Archives.

[21] The fees exacted by the special commissioners for attendance and for taking, certifying, and forwarding depositions, were limited by law. In cases where the claim did not exceed $1,000, they were limited to a charge of ten cents per folio. For persons claiming over $1,000, the fees were $3.00 for each day of actual attendance, divided pro rata among all claimants served in one day, with no more than one day's attendance fee to be collected in any one case. Twenty cents per folio was the ceiling price for taking, certifying, and forwarding the depositions. See 1st Gen. Rept. of C. of C., *House Misc. Docs.*, 42d Cong., 2d Sess., No. 16, p. 26.

witnesses, and ascertain the truth." Under these instructions, they were not required to take depositions or to confine themselves to strictly legal evidence. The philosophy underlying this function is perhaps best described in an annual report to Congress which read, "As this commission allows the same latitude of inquiry in its oral hearings that the committee of the Senate and House allow, and admits any evidence that they think will reasonably aid their inquiries, we require these agents to do the same."[22] In all cases, claimants or their attorneys were allowed to see the agent's report if they wished, in order to refute the evidence it contained.[23]

Little imagination is required to picture some of the difficulties encountered by these special agents. The physical hardships of moving from town to town—traveling by train at night and often by buggy or horseback by day, in pursuit of claimants or witnesses—were formidable in themselves. In addition, these men found themselves in a hostile environment because they were agents of the government and because they sought to disprove, or at least verify, the story told by the claimant. John D. Edwards, special agent for Mississippi at the time, wrote on September 7, 1875, "I am alone, against a crowd. In many cases claimants, attornies, and witnesses are banded by a common interest to deceive me, and prevent me from obtaining the truth; it is no exaggeration to say that there is a semi-hostility to me, in the whole community." When he went into a little town, he continued, "it is whispered about in half an hour, 'he's a government detective,' and my companion, if I have one, is the only man I can talk to with confidence." When he went out to talk with citizens, they were "on their guard . . . some of them 'forget' how so and so 'Stood,' they 'think' he was a Union man like most of the other citizens in the vicinity." Sometimes they volunteered the information that "claimant is a dangerous man, and they do not like to testify against him." In other cases they acknowledged that the petitioner had probably been a "rebel, but [they] do not like to give evidence to defeat his claim because its payment will 'bring money into the county.'" Again, Edwards continued, under the promise of secrecy "respectable men . . . tell me of circumstances which would defeat unjust claims, if I could expose them," but these informants refused to make the necessary sworn statements.[24]

[22] 2d Gen. Rept. of C. of C., *ibid.*, 42d Cong., 3d Sess., No. 12, p. 4.
[23] *Ibid.*
[24] John D. Edwards to the commission, Water Valley, Mississippi, Sept. 7, 1875, in Papers of the House of Representatives, File on Commissioners of Claims, 44th Cong., 1st and 2d Sess., Box 1, Manuscript Division, Library of Congress.

In a similar vein, Theodore W. Parmele wrote from Beaufort, South Carolina, that "most of the persons were openly hostile to the object of my visit & spoke of [the] Claims Commission as a 'Yankee Swindle,' saying no one would ever realize on their claims."[25] S. E. Chamberlain, operating in Virginia, described his difficulties in a somewhat milder manner. "I find that it required earnest efforts to obtain facts," he wrote, "and fully satisfy myself as to the loyalty or disloyalty of Claimants, so long a time having elapsed since the War and the disposition of men to establish a name of loyalty in order to make a dollar."[26] And John B. Brownlow, the son of Senator "Parson" William B. Brownlow, who served as a special agent in Tennessee, showed his own attitude in the comment that "it would seem that almost every claimant feels that Uncle Sam had more money than he can conveniently take care of and he is doing a kindness to him to relieve him of the burden."[27]

During the ten years of the commission, some thirteen men served as special agents. Of this group two, Enos Richmond, of Berryville, Virginia, appointed on May 14, 1872,[28] and George A. Tucker, of Washington, D.C., appointed on June 10, 1872,[29] served practically throughout the life of the board. Of the eleven remaining, one died within a few months after his appointment, three terminated their connection with the commission to go into business for themselves; three served actively for about a year and then, owing to the press of their own business which limited traveling time, served intermittently. Two were discharged, more for neglect of duty than for malfeasance of practice.

A commentary on the qualifications described by President Aldis in seeking suggestions for candidates appears in a letter from James O. Pierce, of Memphis, Tennessee. Pierce wrote to Aldis:

I take it for granted you would prefer a man who has lived here—and such would be my judgment. You must know, too, the sad truth that the supporters of the Government in this section are not the same high & honorable class as compose the bulk of good Society at the North. . . . From my acquaintance, which is con-

[25] Theodore W. Parmele to the commission, [n.d.] Beaufort, South Carolina, in *ibid.*

[26] S. E. Chamberlain to the commission, Harrisonburg, Virginia, April 24, 1874, in Southern Claims Commission, "Letters from and about Special Agents," Record Group 56, Treasury Department, National Archives.

[27] John B. Brownlow to A. O. Aldis, Decherd, Franklin County, Tennessee, Aug. 5, 1873, in *ibid.*

[28] *Journal of the Southern Claims Commission*, May 14, 1872, p. 93, in Record Group 56, Treasury Department, National Archives.

[29] For the oath of office as special agent taken by Tucker on June 10, 1872, see Southern Claims Commission, "Letters from and about Special Agents," Record Group 56, Treasury Department, National Archives.

siderable, and I think reaches every one who would be likely to suit, I can think of but one person whom I can recommend . . . one who has had considerable experience with the tricks of claimants & claim agents here. . . . And from personal observation of and acquaintance with him for many years, I am satisfied he cannot be bought. I regard him as thoroughly honest—he is poor because he is honest.[30]

At the same time, the men who were hired as special agents represented no set type. John D. Edwards, of Little Rock, Arkansas, took on the job of special agent while trying to establish himself there as an architect and an engineer, a profession, he commented, in which "there is not much doing at present."[31] S. E. Chamberlain had served as a colonel in the Federal cavalry and was thus "acquainted with the circumstances and to some extent with the people of the Southern States."[32] Liberty Bartlett, who served briefly in Arkansas and was one of the most outspoken and colorful men employed by the commission, had been a circuit judge in his district. Bartlett was an irrepressible letter-writer, with strong convictions regarding who should and who should not be paid and how the affairs of the commission should be conducted, and his reports were usually more concerned with his own opinions or his revolt against the mechanics prescribed for his reports than with obtaining the type of evidence required by the commissioners, and he remained in their service for only about a year.[33]

Senator William G. Brownlow, whom the commissioners had consulted in seeking qualified Tennesseans to serve both as special commissioners and as special agents,[34] nominated L. C. Houk, a lawyer of

---

[30] James O. Pierce, of the firm of Pierce and Dix, lawyers, Memphis, Tennessee, to A. O. Aldis, April 6, 1872, in *ibid.*

[31] John D. Edwards to the commission, Little Rock, Arkansas, July 13, 1874, in *ibid.*

[32] See note from Justin S. Morrill to the commission, Jan. 4, 1874, Waterford, Loudon County, Virginia, in *ibid.*

[33] After his discharge from the office of special agent, Bartlett made a strong attack on the commission which was published in the New York *Tribune.* Under the title "The Southern Claims Commission—Is It Worth What it Costs?" Bartlett pointed out that the board's machinery alone cost the government "$50,000 a year, more or less," with little benefit to the "Southern producing Unionists" who were the alleged beneficiaries of its deliberations. In his view, the commission seemed to have adopted an arbitrary rule of allowing about half the claims submitted and cutting the amounts allowed so drastically that little remained for the men of the South who had "continued loyal throughout the war." See the New York *Tribune,* Feb. 19, 1876, p. 3.

[34] On June 7, 1872, John B. Brownlow wrote the commissioners, at the request of his father, who wished President Aldis to know that "he would not have you remove Thorburgh [a special commissioner] to make place for McKinney. They are both his friends and he would not see one removed to make place for the other. My father thinks you could get a better man for Middle Tennessee than Frazer. . . . My father regards Frazer as an honest man but altogether too easy and *timid* for the place. Not a man of sufficient courage and firmness." See John B. Brownlow, Danville, Kentucky, June 7, 1872, in Southern Claims Commission, "Letters from and about Special Agents," Record Group 56, Treasury Department, National Archives.

Knoxville, who, after serving the commission off and on for some three years, went into politics and subsequently served in the House of Representatives from 1879 to 1891.[35] On the whole, however, the commissioners found that the most effective agents were not involved in politics or, for that matter, were not usually attorneys. The three men upon whom they placed the most reliance were Enos Richmond and George Tucker, who proved their ability and reliability through eight years of steady and careful work, and Richard B. Avery, a former Union officer who had married a Southern girl and opened a newspaper in Bay St. Louis, Mississippi.[36]

Instructions from Washington constantly warned the agents to pursue investigations fully. Commissioner Aldis wrote John Brownlow in 1875, "Where the proof is strong & satisfactory that the clm^t was disloyal, and probably can not be rebutted, it would seem useless to spend time in taking proof [but] where you have clear & readily accessible proof that the claim in whole or in part is fraudulent, you had better take the proof even if the claimant be proved disloyal."[37]

In their report to the home office, the agents described the variety of duties they were called upon to perform in order to fulfill their function. The files of newspapers and county court records often yielded information which would have eluded them in interviews or at hearings, and consequently they consulted all available local records.[38] A

[35] See letter of W. G. Brownlow to A. O. Aldis, Knoxville, Tennessee, June 22, 1872, in *ibid.* Brownlow wrote that he was much gratified over this appointment, since Houk "has the reputation of being a good lawyer. He is an industrious, thorough going man and a steady in habits, as well as reliable in his character. I have full confidence in his honesty: while his ability to discharge the duties imposed by the appointment is undoubted." Houk had enlisted as a private in the Union army, and was mustered out as a colonel of the third Tennessee infantry. He had served as a presidential elector on the Lincoln and Johnson ticket in 1864 and as a member of the state constitutional convention in 1865. Before going to Washington as a congressman, he had also served in the state's House of Representatives for two years.

[36] Avery applied for the job on March 21, 1877, and was accompanied by a letter of recommendation signed by Captain M. Shaughnessy, collector of internal revenue for the Southern district of Mississippi. Shaughnessy described him as "a newspaper man ... thoroughly conversant with Mississippi politics; ... a Republican, energetic and true, and ... a man sober and reliable." Another letter from C. E. Harris, attorney general of Mississippi, was filed with the application, together with several other strong endorsements including one from Henry R. Smith, postmaster of Canton, Mississippi, who, on February 1, 1877, wrote that "Capt. Avery enjoys the full confidence of the people of his state, has been the able late Editor of the Seacoast Republican, a reference to the files of which will Verify his ability as an editor and proprietor." See Southern Claims Commission, "Letters from and about Special Agents," Record Group 56, Treasury Department, National Archives.

[37] A. O. Aldis to John B. Brownlow, Washington, June 1, 1875, in *ibid.*

[38] Sometimes these court records, when they were consulted by the agents, revealed more than property information. John D. Edwards forwarded the transcript of an order he found arising out of a called session of the Quarterly Court

brief description of his activities for Friday, May 31, 1878, recounts that Richard B. Avery "went to Bryan place, and measured yard in which Scipio Gordon claims to have kept corn, fodder, hay, cow, horse and wagon in 1864. Got statement of Mayor John F. Wheaton in claim of Christian Ubele. Took testimony of Flora F. Lowe, and at night, that of A. N. Wilson in regard to their knowledge of . . . Hillyer's interest in claims proved before him, and which are still pending before the Hon. Com'r's of Claims."[39] Similarly, Enos Richmond reported from Claiborne County, Mississippi, of his investigations into the loyalty and property claimed by Mrs. Anna de N. Evans, that he had measured the wharfage charged in the amount of $3,000 which was "not a levee, it was composed of square posts 18 inches Square and fifteen feet long. These posts were placed upright and were faced with 2 or 2½ inch plank ten feet in front."[40]

The problem of getting reliable information from witnesses for the government presented the greatest difficulty the agents encountered. Those men who came forward too eagerly with information were immediately suspect as to their motives. If the information was in support of the claim, there was always the suspicion of collusion.[41] If it was against the claim, there was always the possibility that it rose out of spite or personal animosity. From time to time the agents wrote that their best information came from casual conversations as they rode about the country, from the talk in hotel lobbies at night, and local gossip picked up in livery stables and country stores. As they left one community for another, they often took pains to obtain in advance information on the community to which they were proceeding.

---

of Fayette County, Tennessee, which showed that certain Fayette County claimants had been appointed "minute men," charged with contributing toward and looking out for the welfare of indigent families of Confederate volunteers and with arming and equipping the Home Guard.

[39] Report of Special Agent R. B. Avery for the week ending Saturday, June 1, 1878, in Southern Claims Commission, "Letters from and about Special Agents," Record Group 56, Treasury Department, National Archives.

[40] Account of the testimony of Mrs. Evans taken by Special Agent Enos Richmond, November, 1875, at the Bruinsburg Plantation in Claiborne County, Mississippi. See case of Anna de N. Evans [claimed $37,395, allowed $6,770 in 1875], C. of C. No. 3036, GAO files.

[41] One especially involved investigation reported by John D. Edwards, which involved collusion, described his uncovering of "an intimate understanding between Kline and Harriss . . . from what my friend Mr. King tells me. King rooms with Kline at Clarksville . . . and Kline he tells me has received a letter from Harriss in which he taxes Kline with telling King something, which he has told Edwards which he told Harrington which he told the Commissioners—quite a house that Jack built—but if Harris' work is all square what possible objection could he have to every detail of it being known." See John D. Edwards to the commissioners, Little Rock, Arkansas, July 13, 1874, in Southern Claims Commission, "Letters from and about Special Agents," Record Group 56, Treasury Department, National Archives.

Thus John Brownlow wrote from Chattanooga in 1875, "From old merchants and others living here I can get the names of Union & reliable men in North Alabama and you had better send to me now all the Alabama cases you have before I go into Alabama which I will do in a few days."[42]

The dilemma in which many witnesses found themselves was well expressed by a citizen of Arkansas who, in response to a request for assistance in uncovering evidence for a case, wrote the commissioners, "I begin to think I am getting myself involved in a ticklish business. To tell the truth here one must have made up his mind to be a martyr. I had a terrible rough time of it for the past 14 years editing a republican newspaper and if it gets out that I am throwing light on some 'loyal' claims, I'll have the union as well as the rebel element 'down' on me."[43]

John D. Edwards wrote that some of his best information came from the Negro members of the community, especially from former slaves. "I go to negroes," he wrote, "because I find I can really get *detailed* information out of them. They always know if a man was *really* loyal, they know if the cribs were full or not, often remember the names of the mules, the oxen, in fact are generally better posted than the rich white neighbors of the claimants." The white neighbors, he concluded, were too inclined to "assert with a careless generality that 'so and so had between 50 and 100 head of whatnots, and the Federal took 'm all sir; they took everything in the county, they robbed me, and broke me up . . . so and so lost ten times what he has charged the government.' " Edwards added that the mobility of the population in his region, characteristic of the unsettled conditions of the time, added to his difficulties. He wrote: "It's impossible to get on very fast, especially when you reflect that many of these witnesses working as they do on shares as rent—change their locality nearly every year—and the roads are such that 4 miles an hour is good average speed over them on horseback."[44]

Edward's opinion of Negroes as witnesses was not shared by John Brownlow, who wrote to Washington, "I do not always find the negro reliable though he was almost invariably so during the war. I find in some sections that colored men will testify to the loyalty of a Rebel who has dealt honestly or liberally by him since the War." He added,

[42] John B. Brownlow to the commissioners, Chattanooga, Tennessee, Jan. 25, 1873, in *ibid.*
[43] Confidential letter of V. Dell, Fort Smith, Arkansas, Jan. 17, 1877, in *ibid.*
[44] Weekly report of John D. Edwards, Little Rock, Arkansas, June 27, 1874, in *ibid.*

"Where an original Secessionist has promptly paid his employees for their labor or dealt charitably by them when in distress he has no trouble in proving his loyalty." The difficulties he encountered, he continued, depended upon the area of the state in which he was operating. Franklin County, Tennessee, was, for example, "one of the most disloyal in the State. Scarcely any white Union men in the County except newcomers from the North who have settled here. . . . In East Tennessee where the large majority of the people are loyal, it is different."[45]

The expense accounts required each month contained documented receipts for money advanced for a variety of items, ranging from "Hotel bill & horse feed," to the $2.00 allowed as payment for government witnesses. Charges for subpoenas in amount from 50 cents to $3.50 were included with such miscellaneous expenses as those for French interpreters. Although no month can be listed as typical, the accounts of August, 1875, reflect a maximum load. J. D. Edwards received $272.75; Enos Richmond, $474.54; J. C. Parker, $286.50; George Tucker, $206.85; S. E. Chamberlain, $300.05; H. E. Nelson, $341.88; and J. B. Brownlow, $269.55—a total of $2,152.12.[46]

In their reports to the home office, the agents referred frequently to the so-called "claimant's rings," which were formed, they said, usually at the instigation of an attorney representing a group of petitioners. By testifying for each other, such bands of men and women could quickly produce a substantial body of testimony for their own and other cases and, by pooling their resources, could cut down on the expenses involved. The special agents were, however, very suspicious of the reliability of evidence assembled in this manner. Their attempts to break up such rings often involved them in difficulties with the attorneys, who brought a variety of charges against them before the commissioners in Washington and exerted pressure on members of Congress. In one instance, the protests of New Orleans attorneys against the operations of Enos Richmond brought about his trial before the Washington board. The burden of the charge brought against Richmond was that he considered it his duty to disprove all claims by choosing witnesses, however obtained, who would invariably testify that any petitioner was disloyal. Richmond countered by charging that his accusers were attempting to form a "claimant's ring" by offering assurance that their political influence would assist in obtaining payment

---

[45] John B. Brownlow, Decherd, Tennessee, Aug. 11, 1873, in *ibid.*

[46] For each item so allowed, careful receipts were required. These receipts are still attached to the accounts as they are preserved in the files of the General Accounting Office. In addition to the amounts listed above, Enos Richmond received $244.45 and George Tucker $145.65, due them on previous accounts.

for the claim. In their annual report for the following year, the commissioners referred to this trial with the comment that it had lasted "ten business days, in which testimony covering 660 legal-cap pages was taken . . . which resulted in a complete vindication of the agent, whose accusers were present to confront him during the entire proceeding."[47]

Both Avery and Tucker were likewise called upon from time to time to reply to charges brought against them by attorneys. Avery accounted for this harassment on the ground that he had been careful to make it plain that "the Commission was not run in the interest of the Attorneys, or claim agents who were not attorneys."[48] These small wars between the attorneys and the various special agents and special commissioners continued throughout the life of the commission. On the whole they were viewed as a healthy sign that there was no collusion between the field representatives and the attorneys who represented the claimants. Indeed, the local commissioner against whom no complaints were made was sometimes considered worthy of close inspection as to his activities, and a trusted special agent was called upon to visit him in order to determine his motives.[49]

The attorneys were, of course, most interested in obtaining allowances for claims, and they were therefore resentful of the snooping agents. Their duties, as described by President Aldis, were "to file the petition, submit the application to take testimony, examine the depositions when received, and brief and submit the case for decision."[50] Since they usually had offices in Washington, they were on hand at all times to keep in touch with the progress of the case and to press for an early hearing.[51] They were familiar with the rules and practices of

---

[47] For the record of this trial, see File on the Commissioners of Claims, Papers of the House of Representatives, 44th Cong., 1st and 2d Sess., Box 1, Manuscript Division, Library of Congress. The trial opened on May 24, 1875.

[48] *Ibid.*

[49] In 1874 the House of Representatives called on the commissioners of claims to produce, for the inspection of the Committee on Claims, all of the complaints which had been filed against the agents and commissioners. The bundles of protesting letters, together with the reply of the accused employee of the commission, were turned over to the House at this time, and are preserved in *ibid.*

[50] Aldis' statement about the duties of the attorneys appears in an opinion rendered in response to charges brought by Liberty Bartlett against Gilbert Moyers. Aldis ruled it was "due to Attorney Moyers to say that in all his business before the Commissioners he had been diligent and industrious in a marked degree," and that the described services had been properly performed.

[51] In some cases the attorneys were negligent, although usually their own interests were carefully linked with the promotion of the case. One unfortunate attorney, however, was charged with "delay and neglect" when it was found that he had applied for a hearing for the case "after it had been for some time reported to Congress as allowed and published." See case of Daniel H. Pender, Warren County, Mississippi [claimed $12,024, allowed $6,452 in 1873], C. of C. No. 6933, GAO files.

the commission and could often advise claimants about their rights, especially as to what, in the eyes of the commission, constituted stores and supplies taken for army use: a distinction which the claimants themselves seem never to have quite understood.

The chief criticism brought against the attorneys was that of their exorbitant fees. Although no general rule seems to have applied, the most common practice was to split the award, allowing 50 per cent to the claimant and 50 per cent to the attorney. In such cases, however, this generous fee was usually made because the attorney agreed to bear most of the expenses connected with hearing the case, an accommodation which was sometimes the only way in which impoverished Southerners could have received any reimbursement at all for their losses.

The attorneys also served as solicitors in informing the Southern Unionist of his right to file a claim, in the period when this right hung often on a single decision of a judge or a department head. Usually at least one member of the law firm traveled throughout the South, seeking and sorting out eligible claimants who were unaware of their rights, and offering to prepare the case for a proper hearing. In addition, the best-known firms had printed booklets which were distributed throughout the area, outlining the laws of Congress and the decision of the courts, and describing the types of claims which could most hopefully be presented.[52]

---

[52] Typical of these leaflets is a small book entitled "Laws and Information Relating to Claims Against the Government of the United States," printed in Washington in 1866 for the firm of Chipman, Hosmer and Company, whose members appeared on behalf of many claimants before the Southern Claims Commission. The pamphlet deals with bounties, pensions, back pay, revenue, patents, and "Claims in the South." Although it advised that, at that moment, claims for quartermaster and commissary supplies were not eligible for hearing, it called attention to a "Report of the Committee on Claims, made in the early part of the last session" which acknowledged these claims but held that they were so extensive as to bankrupt the government and should therefore be dismissed as losses due to military necessity. Chipman and Hosmer went on record, however, "notwithstanding the conclusion reached by the Committee," as expecting that "as the equities of the various claims . . . are further developed and considered, favorable legislation will be extended to all portions of the country." Meanwhile, they advised claimants in the South to preserve their evidence, looking forward to that day.

CHAPTER VI

THE TEST OF LOYALTY

"Voluntary residence in an insurrectionary State during the war is *prima facie* evidence of disloyalty, and must be rebutted by satisfactory evidence. . . . It is a fact to be established by proof, and is not to be presumed." With this forthright statement the commissioners of claims set forth, in 1871 in their first Annual Report, the test of loyalty which was to guide them for ten years as 22,298 Unionists from the South passed in review before them.[1] From the first, therefore, a claimant was aware of the fact that, in the minds of the commissioners, he was guilty of disloyalty unless he could prove his innocence. His Unionism was, moreover, to be tested for its duration as well as for its degree. The evidence must show that each professed Unionist was opposed to secession not only before the war but also for the period of occupation by Union troops. He must have been genuinely loyal during the early period of Confederate military successes as he was in the later and less hopeful period of defeats. In addition, the commissioners were not satisfied that disaffection with the Confederacy in itself constituted authentic Unionism.

At the same time, they recognized the difficulty of proving overt acts of loyalty under war conditions, since "[t]ruly loyal persons in the rebellious States, except when within the lines of the Union Army, or in special localities, were obliged to be silent, to say nothing and do nothing for the Union cause."[2] Any outspoken friends of the Union were, the commissioners believed, liable to expulsion from their homes, confiscation of their property, imprisonment, and even perhaps death "by law or lawless violence." The commissioners also realized, however, that they must "bear in mind that it is easier and more profitable to be loyal now than it was during the war, and that much of the proof of disloyalty has perished, or been forgotten in the lapse of time."[3]

The commissioners were in effect modifying the wartime doctrine of constructive treason in the light of prevailing opinions on what constituted loyalty. Presidential proclamations of pardon during the late 1860's had run almost directly counter to the ever-more-restrictive acts on Capitol Hill. Johnson's proclamation of December 25, 1868, had, for example, promised full pardon and amnesty to "all persons engaged in the late rebellion," in direct defiance of Congress which a

---

[1] 1st Gen. Rept. of the C. of C., *House Misc. Docs.*, 42d Cong., 2d Sess., No. 16, p. 2.
[2] *Ibid.*, p. 3.
[3] *Ibid.*

year earlier (January 21, 1867) had repealed the war power given the President to issue such proclamations. The courts were immediately involved, since the action of Congress in 1867 had followed by just seven days a decision of the Supreme Court which held that the President's power of pardon was not subject to legislation, and that "Congress can neither limit the effect of his pardon nor exclude from its exercise any class of offenders."[4]

Even with Grant in the White House, the Supreme Court carried forward its policy of gradual liberalization. Four important decisions of the period may here be inserted in their chronological order, as they show the contrast between the views of Congress and the commission on the one hand, and those of the courts on the other. In the December, 1869, term, the Supreme Court ruled in the case of *Nelson Anderson* v. *United States* that Southern Unionists were public enemies of necessity, by reason of their residence, but as such they were objects of public sympathy. They were therefore entitled to reimbursement, not only on these grounds, but because Congress (March 13, 1863) had distinguished between loyal and disloyal citizens in the South and had provided that awards would be made to loyal men.[5] In the same term the Court made another important distinction, in the case of *United States* v. *Padelford,* setting the time when the loyalty test would begin to apply. The act of taking the prescribed oath of pardon and amnesty, according to this decision, amounted to full reinstatement within the Union, and evidence of "aid and comfort to the enemy" could disqualify a claimant only if voluntary acts of this nature could be shown to have occurred after the oath had been given. In the words of the decision, "the law makes the proof of pardon a complete substitute for proof that he gave no aid or comfort to the rebellion. A different construction would, as it seems to us, defeat the manifest intent of the proclamation and of the act of Congress which authorized it."[6]

Such was the climate of legal opinion on March 3, 1871, when the Southern Claims Commission was established. By December of that year, almost at the same time that the first Annual Report of the commission outlined its exacting rules respecting loyalty, the Supreme Court had handed down a series of decisions in which it held that any Southerner not barred by the statute of limitations was due his

---

[4] Reference without citation in *United States* v. *Klein,* 13 Wallace 141.

[5] The claims arising out of the Captured and Abandoned Property acts furnished the basis for all the decisions on loyalty here cited, and for most of the Supreme Court decisions bearing on this question. The loyalty provisions of this act appear in 12 *U.S. Stat. at L.,* 591.

[6] 9 Wallace 543.

portion of the funds held in the Treasury for disposal under the Captured and Abandoned Property Act, regardless of his conduct during the war. Although this decision was most completely outlined in the case of *United States* v. *Klein,* the Pargoud case, decided in the same term, furnished the test for this position. In the other cases, including the Klein case, counsel for the claimants had invariably argued that their loyalty had been established either by their records throughout the war or by the act of taking the oath of pardon and amnesty. In the Pargoud case, however, the claimant was a professed Confederate who made no pretense to having been loyal to the Union. On this ground the Court of Claims had denied his claim as being beyond their jurisdiction, since loyalty was held to be a requirement for reimbursement. Furthermore, with Justice Nott dissenting, this court had ruled that there was no appeal from its decision.

Pargoud's attorney had nevertheless obtained a hearing before the Supreme Court on a writ of mandamus, and the Supreme Court reversed the decision of the lower court and ordered that the claimant be paid. In so doing it held that the President's amnesty proclamation of December 25, 1868, "relieves claimants of captured and abandoned property from proof of adhesion to the United States during the late civil war."[7] Furthermore, the President's proclamation was held to be "a public act of which all courts of the United States are bound to take notice, and . . . to give effect." The Court of Claims had "erred" in not giving the petitioners the benefits of the proclamation, the opinion concluded. One important requirement of the act of March 12, 1863, had, however, been stressed. The Court took particular care to point out that claims reviewed under this act must be limited to those which had been filed within the two years, immediately following the war, allowed by the act. Therefore, the liberality of these decisions applied to a limited number of persons and was, perhaps, influenced in some degree by the fact that the statute of limitations applied.[8]

In the case of quartermaster and commissary claims before the Southern Claims Commission, on the other hand, a new category of claims from the South was being admitted for review. Even the courts had questioned the grounds upon which these claims were founded. For, in spite of the fact that orders for obtaining supplies from Southern Unionists had been given by the Quartermaster and Commissary departments, and that receipts and vouchers had been issued in good faith, both the Court of Claims and the Supreme Court had held that such

---

[7] 13 Wallace 156.
[8] *Ibid.;* see also *Armstrong* v. *United States, ibid.,* p. 154.

transactions could not be considered contracts, either real or implied. In the Frémont Contract cases, for example, the Court of Claims had given its opinion that "the authority of a general commanding a military department to bind the Government by *express* contract in time of actual hostilities and of great public danger, must be derived from the Constitution and laws of the United States, and is not an incident of the war-power." The judgments in these cases were later confirmed by a tie vote of the Supreme Court.[9]

The rigidity of the commissioners' test of loyalty was no doubt due to their operating more as a quasi-legal extension of a committee of Congress than as a court. Moreover, no statute of limitations could be held to apply in these cases. Therefore, the set of interrogations prepared by the commissioners to "show the general tenor of our inquiries,"[10] required exacting details on loyalty or disloyalty. The first forty-three questions asked of the claimant himself, and the additional set of sixteen questions asked of every witness, probed deeply into the claimant's professed Unionism. Eight additional questions were included to "be put to all male claimants . . . who were not less than sixteen years of age when the war closed."

Acts of disloyalty, which normally disqualified a claim, consisted of "voting for the ordinance of secession, holding civil or military office under the confederacy, furnishing aid or supplies to the rebel service, or to persons about to enter it, giving information to aid the rebels in their military operations, and engaging in a business whose object was to supply munitions of war or army supplies to the confederate government. . . ."[11] Claimants whose evidence of Unionism was limited to the period which began with occupation by Union troops, were called upon to produce facts which would show sustained loyalty from Bull Run to Appomattox, or to acknowledge that loyalty had not been proved.

However, some allowance was made for the fact that conditions had not, at best, been too conducive to the preservation of reliable evidence. During the period of the 'sixties, when Congressional policy had seemed to promise no restitution at all, much valuable evidence had been lost or destroyed. Often, witnesses who could have furnished important testimony, either for the claimant or for the government, had died or had moved. Realizing that it was not always possible, under these cir-

---

[9] 7 Ct. Clms. 82.

[10] 1st Gen. Rept. of C. of C., in *House Misc. Docs.*, 42d Cong., 2d Sess., No. 16, p. 3.

[11] These questions are given as revised and reissued on July 1, 1874, and published in the 4th Gen. Rept. of the C. of C., in *House Misc. Docs.*, 43d Cong., 2d Sess., No. 17, pp. 38–42. For the original set of questions, see 1st Gen. Rept. of C. of C., in *House Misc. Docs.*, 42d Cong., 2d Sess., No. 16, pp. 27–30.

cumstances, to produce the desired evidence, the commissioners attempted to evaluate the assembled data in the light of the adverse conditions.

The "large and doubtful" claims received the most thorough examination, both because more evidence was usually required for men and women of property, and because the commissioners were jealous guardians of the public purse. The oral examination in Washington required for the larger cases worked a severe hardship on the claimant, especially as it increased his expenses, but it seems to have helped him in one way. Face to face with a man who had been ostracized by his community, made an object of plunder and sometimes of persecution by the Confederates, and who had then sustained great losses at the hands of the Union army, it was less easy for the commissioners to adhere to positive and irrevocable conclusions as to proper and sustained Unionism than it had been when the first rules were prepared in the absence of actual claimants. The early convictions of the commissioners as to proper loyalty were, in this way, tested and tempered by the evidence they accumulated in the sessions in Washington.

An example of the modifying effect of time appears in two paragraphs in the fourth Annual Report to Congress wherein the commissioners discussed the problem of arriving at an equitable decision in terms of policy. Some misapprehension had apparently arisen, they wrote, "as to what in our judgment constitutes the proof of loyalty and disloyalty." It was a mistake, for example, to conclude that such seemingly obvious evidence of disloyalty as service in the Confederate army, furnishing a substitute, holding civil office under the Richmond government, or furnishing munitions of war, supplies, cotton, or money to aid its cause would "necessarily and in all cases require us to reject the claim." Such acts were rather prima-facie evidence of disloyalty which would "require the rejection of the claim unless explained and shown to be not the voluntary acts of the claimants, but done under duress, from necessity, or through personal fear of danger to life, family, or property."[12]

Claimants who had served in the Confederate army had appeared before the board, the commissioners continued, and their claims had been allowed. But in these cases, proof had been furnished that such service was involuntary, that they "were conscripted, served for a short time, deserted at the first opportunity, enlisted in the Union Army, served one, two, or three years, and were honorably discharged." Such

---

[12] 4th Gen. Rept. of C. of C., *House Misc. Docs.*, 43d Cong., 2d Sess., No. 18, p. 3.

proof, the commissioners asserted, "must satisfy every fair mind that the service in the confederate army was not voluntary, and that the party was really loyal to the Union cause." In all cases where disloyal acts appeared, similar reasoning applied. And, since "no two cases are alike," it had become "impossible to lay down a general rule as to the weight of evidence, and what is and what is not satisfactory proof that the disloyal act was done voluntarily or not." In arriving at a decision, they concluded, "the circumstances are *all* to be weighed; the *whole* evidence is to be considered; and it is only by so doing that a reasonable judgment can be formed."[13]

From time to time in the Summary Reports on individual cases, the commissioners freely expressed their growing awareness of the injustices which loyal Southerners had frequently encountered. In the case of Thomas L. Van Fossen, of Carroll Parish, Louisiana, for example, they showed righteous indignation at the "wanton and wholly unjustifiable" destruction of his property by the Union soldiers. Van Fossen had presented an impressive record to sustain his claim to loyalty. An old-line Whig, he had voted for Bell and Everett. A member of the Home Guard in New Orleans, he had, at the beginning of hostilities, voted against converting it into a "permanent organization to enter the Confederate service . . . [thus] incurring obloquy & some personal risk," and had left the company, refusing to enter the army. This action was, he admitted, prompted in part by the fact that he was at that time engaged, and "had promised the lady who was herself opposed to secession that he would not engage in the war." When the Confederate sequestration laws were passed, Van Fossen refused to pay his indebtedness to Northern merchants into the hands of the Confederate commission appointed to receive the money, and "in defiance of the order purchased a draft of 10,000 pounds ($50,000) & sent it North and paid his debts." In March, 1862, he withdrew from his partnership in the mercantile firm of C. A. Barriere & Co. He married and retired to his plantation in Carroll Parish in order to avoid any participation in the attempt to overthrow the Union.

During the entire period in which he lived under the Confederate government, Van Fossen had "remained on his place & awaited the approach of the Union army telling his wife 'if they come they will find me here at home attending to my own business & they will satisfy themselves about my character here.'" He had refused to sell his cotton to the Confederate government and, as a result, 552 bales had been burned by Beauregard's army. But when, at last, the Federals arrived,

---

[13] *Ibid.*

"they took the jewelry & ten years supply of clothing," appropriated all livestock and plantation supplies, and stripped the fields. Finally, a "party there in command of an officer set fire to his carriage house which burned with 13 double houses & a single house."

Under these circumstances, Van Fossen frankly admitted that his feelings underwent a change. "I believe I would have been glad to have seen the Confederacy succeed," he told the commissioners. And they, in turn, reported to Congress, "We are not disposed to hold Mr. Van Fossen accountable for such a feeling . . . after the wicked wrong done him by those who should have protected him. The provocation was too great for weak humanity." They concluded their endorsement of his claim by commenting on "the favorable impression which he made when on the witness stand. . . . He told the whole story & . . . it was not a cunningly devised tale framed for the occasion, but the straightforward manly statement of an honest man."[14]

At the same time, President Aldis was equally outspoken when he encountered a claimant with less worthy motives. In his report to Congress on one case, he wrote:

He . . . swore to his loyalty from the opening to the close of the war as of the most ardent and enthusiastically patriotic character. His sympathies for the Union never failed; his patriotic devotion to the flag and Government of his country glowed all the brighter during the dark days and nights in which the storm of battle and of blood lowered over the land. After he had sworn to his loyalty . . . several letters were exhibited to him, some of which he had written to officers of our Government since the war, and others to the rebel authorities during the war. He swore to the signature of these indiscriminately as his own, but finally his eye caught the address of the rebel secretary of war on one of them, and he commenced to equivocate and multiply his perjured falsehoods. He soon improvised a line of defense, and swore that those letters were concocted by certain enemies, who had plotted his destruction and secured the aid of his confidential clerk, now dead; thus adding to his treason and perjury the villainy of defaming character and blackening the reputation of the dead as well as the living in his brazen attempt to swindle and rob the Government.[15]

[14] Summary Report in the case of Thomas L. Van Fossen, Carroll Parish, Louisiana [claimed $59,471, allowed $19,038 in 1874], C. of C. No. 16762, GAO files. The plantation consisted of about one thousand acres for which, Van Fossen testified, "we were offered the year before the war . . . $125 cash, in gold, an acre by three different parties." It was originally the property of Mrs. Van Fossen, but the investigation into title revealed that it had been "incumbered to a considerable amount, and Mr. Van Fossen paid the incumbrances, purchased mules & other property, and to some extent renewed the stock, made purchases, & carried on the plantation in his own name." Mrs. Van Fossen had died when the claim was presented and, although it was originally filed in Van Fossen's name alone, the claim was later amended to include his wife's three children by a previous marriage, of whom the eldest was nine when the war began.

[15] Summary Report of the commissioners in the case of Jones Levy, Wilmington, New Hanover County, North Carolina [claimed $10,000, disallowed in 1871], House File Room, House of Representatives.

It may be added that this claimant's brother had served as a commodore in the United States Navy throughout the war, a fact which in no wise influenced the commissioners.

In the hearings in Washington, the commissioners allowed considerable latitude in the material presented by the claimants, who usually appeared with their attorneys. The petitioner was permitted to present his case in the form of a brief if he wished, and he then submitted to questioning, which was taken down in shorthand. The commissioner who had been in charge of the preliminary investigation and was familiar with the case usually conducted the questioning, but either of the other two members could interrupt at will.

Specifically, the commissioners questioned the applicant as to whether he had ever been in the "service or employment of the United States Government" at any time during the war; whether he had any relatives in the Union army or navy; whether he had ever been threatened or injured for his Unionist sentiments; whether his property had been confiscated by the Confederates; or whether he had ever been arrested and, if so, how he obtained his release. Finally they asked if he had taken the "iron-clad" oath, and if so, "when and on what occasions?"

Such Unionism as he could show was then, with the same type of questions, tested against his record of participation within the Confederacy. For example, he was asked if he had ever contributed to the raising, equipment, or support of Confederate troops; if he had been engaged in building gun boats, or had assisted with relief funds or subscriptions for the families of Confederate soldiers. Had the claimant himself or any of his near relatives served in the Confederate army, the commissioners asked. If he had not, they inquired into the nature of his service, business, or employment as it was related to supplying the Confederate forces. For example, in one case the witness swore that he had refused to make cartridge boxes for the Confederacy, but the questioning revealed that he had made saddles, bridles, lead lines, bands, breast chains, breechings, harnesses, knapsacks, and canteen straps for the cavalry, and his claim was disallowed.[16] In another instance involving a clothing merchant in New Orleans, the commissioners had been concerned with deciding whether the clothing seized from him and distributed to the destitute Negroes who followed the Federal army could be classified as "stores or supplies" used by that army, until they discovered that he had been engaged, before the

---

[16] Summary Report in the case of William H. May, Chatham County, Georgia [claimed $18,568, disallowed in 1879], C. of C. No. 10995, Justice Department, National Archives.

Union occupation, in supplying gray Confederate uniforms. This "disloyal" act disqualified his claim.[17]

If the property under consideration was a boat or marine equipment of any kind, or if the claimant was a merchant, careful inquiry was made to determine whether blockade-running or "running through the lines" was involved, since such activities were classed as "aid and comfort to the enemy." Subscription to any loans of the Confederate government, ownership of any bonds or securities of central or state governments, or even the sale of any cotton or produce to civil or military branches of that government was regarded with suspicion, especially if Confederate or state bonds or securities were received in payment. Here, again, the modification of early attitudes, under the influence of time and experience, may be illustrated by the records. Two reversals of decision in the case of Eugenia P. Bertinetti illustrate this process. In their first report to Congress on December 14, 1871, Mrs. Bertinetti's claim was recommended by the commissioners for allowance in the amount of $11,860, on the ground that she had demonstrated her loyalty. But two days later, in a hasty message to the Committee on Claims, the case was recalled, since Confederate treasury records showed that the claimant, under a former name, had purchased $8,500 worth of Confederate 7 per cent coupon bonds in May, 1863.[18] Two years later, however, the claim was again reported to Congress for allowance, on the ground that Mrs. Bertinetti had shown that the bonds had been purchased by her agent and that she had not known of the purchase until the close of the war "when the bonds were worthless." At the same time additional evidence of her loyalty had come to light. Memoranda from President Lincoln, General Grant, and President Johnson were produced. The records of the War Department showed that a special military board was appointed to assess her losses because of her loyalty, and that she was adjudged loyal by the Court of Claims and received an award of $16,200 for cotton, under the provisions of the Captured and Abandoned Property Act.[19]

---

[17] Summary Report in the case of Charity R. Lyons, executor of Lewis W. Lyons, deceased, Orleans Parish, Louisiana [claimed $12,322, disallowed in 1879], C. of C. No. 17354, Justice Department, National Archives.

[18] For a report of their action, see "Additional Report from the Commissioners of Claims upon the claim of Madam Eugenia P. Bertinetti," Dec. 20, 1871, in *House Misc. Docs.*, 42d Cong., 2d Sess., No. 21, pp. 1–3.

[19] At the time she filed her claim, Mrs. Bertinetti was the "wife of Commander Joseph Bertinetti, Envoy Extraordinary and Minister Plenipotentiary of his Majesty the King of Italy, near the Court of his Majesty the King of the Netherland." Her letter, written from the United States Legation in the Hague, explaining the circumstances surrounding the purchase of these bonds, is dated January 7, 1872. On November 24, 1873, she appeared before the commission and described her con-

Although the purchase of Confederate bonds continued to constitute strong prima-facie evidence of disloyalty, this disloyalty could be disproved—as it could also with Confederate military service—either by the weight of other evidence showing overt loyalty or on proof that the bonds had been accepted for cotton under duress. When the purchase had been voluntary, however, a different principle applied. A typical policy statement appears in the case of James M. Chiles, of Hinds County, Mississippi, who, in November, 1862, had sold thirty-two bales of cotton to the Confederacy, taking bonds in payment. "The sale appears to have been voluntary," wrote the commissioners, "and was direct aid to the rebellion, the transaction having occurred under the provisions of an act of the confederate congress, designed to raise money abroad on the credit of the stock of cotton in the hands of cotton planters and factors of the South. The disloyal character of this transaction has not been rebutted, and the claim is accordingly disallowed."[20]

The case of Kinchen W. King, of Marshall County, Mississippi, who had two sons in the Confederate army, is a good example of a ruling which excused the acceptance of Confederate money on the ground that duress was in evidence. King, an old man during the war and formerly an ardent Whig, was bitterly opposed to secession. He had voted for Bell and Everett and for Union delegates to the Mississippi convention. After the war started he had urged his three sons to go North, and the fact that he had induced one of them to go convinced the commissioners that his two older sons had served in the Confederate army against his wishes. The evidence showed further that he had at

---

versation with Judge George W. Stone. "I asked him to take charge of some moneys . . . & to invest them in the best manner possible," she testified. "I told him, though, to invest this money in cotton—far from the river so that it would not be exposed & be taken; and to guard it for me, until I could sell it. . . . I never told him to invest in bonds:—on the contrary I told him not to invest in bonds. . . . I told him to buy cotton, or to invest it in real estate: but you know at that time there was no real estate being sold because Confederate money had lost its value, & no one wanted to sell real estate for Confederate money." See the case of Mrs. Eugenia P. Bertinetti, Washington County, Mississippi [claimed $22,235, allowed $11,860 in 1873], C. of C. No. 154, GAO files.

[20] Summary Report in the claim of James M. Chiles, executor of Lewis B. Holloway, deceased, of Terry, Hinds County, Mississippi [claimed $10,136.25, disallowed in 1880], C. of C. No. 7128, Justice Department, National Archives. These produce loans, it will be recalled, were instituted as early as 1861, the cotton being given to the government in exchange for Confederate bonds, in a series of produce loans—known as "the hundred million dollar loan"—which provided that twenty-year, 8 per cent bonds were exchangeable for produce. The purpose of this plan, which continued into 1862 and 1863, was to store up cotton in the hands of the Richmond government, which could then make agreements with Europe for its future delivery. See J. C. Schwab, *The Confederate States: A Financial and Industrial History* (New York, 1901), pp. 12, 24–25.

first refused to take money from the Confederacy and had yielded only when he "was arrested and frightened into it." His loyalty was held to have been proved.[21]

The commissioners drew a clear distinction between conscientious objection to war and loyalty.[22] In the case of James C. Owens, a Campbellite of Williamson County, Tennessee, the commissioners regretted "that Mr. Owen, who is shown to be an honest man, could not place himself within the provisions of the law which would entitle him to relief." Owens explained his position by saying, "I was at all times willing and ready to be a law-abiding man and to obey the laws of the Government. I was not willing to take an active part on either side. I wished to and did simply remain quietly at home attending to my own private affairs. I did not wish and would not have done otherwise for either side." He could not rejoice over the success of either side in battle and he consistently refused to sell any of his property to either side for war purposes. As such, he was classified as a "neutral" and his claim was disallowed.[23]

The loyalty of Rev. Milton S. Shirk, a Baptist of Shreveport, Louisiana, was not established by his statement that he had refused to pray for Jefferson Davis, since he added that he had prayed only "that the war might come to a close and that instead of hostility peace might reign." It is of interest that Shirk, who chose to support only the cause of peace, "preached every Sunday during the war at four churches," without any objection arising as to his Northern birth or Unionist

---

[21] Summary Report in the case of Edward King, administrator of Kinchen W. King, N. Mt. Pleasant, Mississippi [claimed $11,246, allowed $4,353.58 in 1877], C. of C. No. 21933, GAO files.

[22] See Edward Needles Wright, *Conscientious Objectors in the Civil War* (Philadelphia, 1931), *passim*, for a description of the role adopted by the Friends, the Mennonites, and similar groups in the North and in the South. Although no exact figures are available, the author uses the estimate of a total of 406 conscientious objectors in the North who registered during the eight months when they were subject to draft. In the South, the total was 515, which covers a longer period of the draft but at the same time applies to a smaller total army force. This figure for the Confederacy, which is from a report, in February, 1865, of J. C. Breckinridge, the secretary of war, is broken down by states to show that Virginia had a total of 107 objectors, North Carolina 342, and East Tennessee 66 (pp. 181–182). For comparison, the author also includes figures for the First World War which show that "the ratio of men professing conscientious objection in the camps to the total inductions into the army was as 3,989 to 2,810,296 or .0014 per cent" (p. 244).

[23] Summary Report in the case of James C. Owens, Williamson County, Tennessee [claimed $16,293.50, disallowed in 1877], C. of C. No. 7043, File Room, House of Representatives. The commissioners added that "it is refreshing to read the depositions in a case, including those of the claimant and his witnesses, and feel perfectly certain that they are all testifying honestly, truthfully, and conscientiously ... [but] conscientious adherence to his religious convictions placed him in a position which now excludes him from the list of those who are receiving pay for property taken by the Federal Army through recommendations of this commisison."

sentiments.[24] Miss Sarah M. Thomas of Natchez spoke for the laymen of like conviction, whose claims were not allowed, when she said, "I regarded the war as a great calamity, regretted the unnecessary loss of life, and prayed that God would end the war in his own time and was glad when it ended."[25]

When, however, a minister in the South refused to pray for Jefferson Davis, or particularly if he had dared to pray for the President of the United States, the commissioners considered that a degree of loyalty had been shown. Because of its liturgy, the Episcopal church faced a problem in this regard. Rev. Frederick W. Boyd, of Carroll County, Louisiana, insisted on the familiar form of the prayer for the President of the United States. On one occasion, he said, he offered the prayer in the presence of his bishop, "although I received his animadversions on that account." But, he testified, "I told my bishop frankly that when the prayer book was altered by any proper authority I should consider the matter [of praying for the president of the Confederacy], but not until then."[26]

The doctrine of constructive treason applied almost as rigidly to Negro claimants as it did to church officials. The commissioners ruled, "While there exists a legal presumption of loyalty in favor of the condition of slavery, it does not extend to the complexion and apply in favor of free colored people, especially if they were like many in Louisiana, reputable citizens and large planters."[27] A very small number of claims were filed by former slaves, for the obvious reason that during the war years they were virtually a propertyless class. Most of their claims, therefore, were disallowed for lack of a clear title, or for fradulent transfer of title by former masters on the approach of the Federal army.[28]

---

[24] Testimony of Rev. Milton S. Shirk, Washington, Oct. 25, 1872, in his own case, Shreveport, Louisiana [claimed $125,602, allowed $5,205 in 1872], C. of C. No. 8308, GAO files.

[25] Summary Report in the case of Sarah M. Thomas, Natchez, Mississippi [claimed $16,305.12, disallowed in 1875], C. of C. No. 11829, File Room, House of Representatives.

[26] Testimony of Frederick W. Boyd, executor of James Railey, Carroll County, Louisiana [claimed $30,958, allowed $7,800 in 1874], C. of C. No. 1151, GAO files.

[27] Summary Report in the case of Alphonse St. Armand, Waterloo, Point Coupee Parish, Louisiana [claimed $2,290, disallowed in 1874], C. of C. No. 10614, File Room, House of Representatives.

[28] For typical examples see Summary Report of the commissioners in the case of William and Louisa Ferguson, Fairfax County, Virginia [claimed $150, disallowed in 1877], C. of C. No. 19994, File Room, House of Representatives; Summary Report in the case of Charles F. Norris, Jackson, Hinds County, Mississippi [claimed $1,000, disallowed in 1876], C. of C. No. 11996, *ibid.;* Summary Report in the case of Charles A. Moseley, Holly Springs, Marshall County, Mississippi [claimed $405, disallowed in 1876], C. of C. No. 8559, *ibid.;* Summary Report in

The free Negroes of Louisiana frequently owned slaves in their own right, and this economic identification with the South sustained their allegiance to the Confederacy. An exception was Cornelius Donato, a slaveholder, who testified he "had been very glad . . . to see the war because we all thought the war would enfranchise us and give us our rights as citizens & abolish slavery and all that & put every man on an equal footing as citizens." As free Negroes, he explained, they had been able to hold their own property as citizens of the state, but socially and politically the colored Creoles were regarded as Negroes. Donato and his stepfather, Dubreul Olivier, were stock raisers and joint owners of about three thousand head of cattle and a large number of horses, which they pastured on the public lands in St. Landry Parish.[29]

Similar shadings in the strict application of guilt-by-residence were made in cases involving those groups which Clement Eaton calls the "extraneous elements in Southern society," namely the foreign stocks, such as the Germans, the Irish, and the French around New Orleans. The number of claims from these groups was also small, but the incidence of Unionism was high. The Confederate government required a special oath of allegiance from all foreigners, and the commissioners in turn were impressed by those petitioners who had refused to comply.[30] A common refrain is echoed in the statement of one claimant that he "could not take two oaths; that he had taken an oath of allegiance to U. S. Government, and he did not intend to violate that oath."[31]

None of the claimants born in Germany was a slaveholder, and not one was sympathetic to the institution of slavery. They reflected the opinions of Carl Schurz and the German groups in Missouri which had played such an important role in preventing the secession of that state. Representative of their attitude was the claim of John H. Herman, a practicing physician and owner of a large mill in Arkansas. At the time of the vote on secession, he ordered all work at the mill to stop and urged "every man in his employ to go to the polls & vote

the case of Thomas Shaw, Duckport, Madison Parish, Louisiana [claimed $700, disallowed in 1874], C. of C. No. 17339, *ibid.;* Summary Report in the case of Henry Gorman, Lamar, Marshall County, Mississippi [claimed $729.75, disallowed in 1876], C. of C. No. 21322, *ibid.*

[29] Testimony of Cornelius Donato in Washington, Dec. 8, 1876, in his own claim, St. Landry Parish, Louisiana [claimed $33,125, allowed $15,750 in 1877], C. of C. No. 19763, GAO files.

[30] Ella Lonn, *Foreigners in the Confederacy* (Chapel Hill, 1940), p. 392.

[31] Testimony of Michael Lynch before Special Commissioner John L. Conley, in his own claim, Fulton County, Georgia [claimed $1,330, allowed $665 in 1873], C. of C. No. 6326, GAO files.

against secession (i.e.) against holding a convention & for delegates pledged to the union."[32] After Arkansas seceded, Herman's mill became a center of Unionist activities, serving as a hide-out for runaway Negroes and for refugees fleeing North. In 1862, when the Confederate general, R. C. Price, issued an order forbidding any assistance to the Unionist Cherokees, under penalty of death, Herman "issued meal & flour to Indian women openly."[33] As a result the "rebel half-breed Indians" decimated his livestock. Under Confederate pressure, he was finally forced to flee the state and "his mill [worth] between $15,000 and $20,000 including residence and carding machine was burned by the rebels." After the Federal army crossed the property "the plantation was returned to a state of nature."[34]

In a similar vein, Thomas W. Skelly, a naturalized Irishman who was a school teacher in Scriven County, Georgia, refused a position on Beauregard's staff and a commission in Governor Brown's militia. Driven from his home, he became a martyr to the Union: one night, while returning from a Federal camp to which he had delivered intelligence materials, "he was shot and killed by a federal picket." His wife, who had inherited the plantation from which the claimed articles were taken, was subsequently dispossessed for having furnished "important" information to the Union army.[35]

The rigid loyalty requirements were thus modified by an exacting process of trial and error. And Unionism was not a negative quality. Abstract ideals had to be translated into concrete actions, ranging in degree from passive resistance to open subversion, as noted above. Loyalty oaths, exacted by the commissioners, required documentation of resistance to Confederate authority, or they were pronounced fraudulent. To the yeoman Democratic Unionists of the Appalachian highlands and the inland centers of dissent belong the bulk of the deeds of dramatic valor aimed directly at the military sinews of the Confederacy. Southern supplies were burned, bridges dynamited, troop

---

[32] Memorandum of the commissioners of testimony taken by Special Commissioner Harris, 1874, in the claim of John H. Herman [claimed $10,895, allowed $4,555 in 1878], C. of C. No. 11955, GAO files.

[33] An interesting letter from Albert Pike to D. N. Cooley, commissioner of Indian affairs, describing this miniature war, is reproduced in Annie Heloise Abel, *The American Indian as Slaveholder and Secessionist* (Cleveland, 1915), pp. 134 n.–140 n. The letter is dated at Memphis, Tennessee, February 17, 1866, and describes Price's trip through the Indian country while acting as a commissioner for Robert Toombs. Price describes his interview with the Cherokee leader John Ross, and also his negotiations with Stand Waite, who headed the so-called "Southern Party" among the Indians.

[34] Testimony of John H. Herman, as cited in footnote 32, above.

[35] Summary Report in the case of Anne J. Skelly, trustee, Gordon County, Georgia [claimed $10,698.33, allowed $5,121 in 1872], C. of C. No. 13015, GAO files.

movements reported, prison breaks organized. Men and women participated in these activities. Some were killed; others were imprisoned, tried for treason, and banished or executed. In such cases, after verification of the facts, decisions as to loyalty were clear-cut.

The large planter Unionists provided a more complex problem. Tied to their estates, possessing a slave labor supply, influential in the intellectual life of the community, they lacked the mobility of the disaffected yeomanry, and were more subject to impressment of supplies and financial levies. Under surveillance of Confederate authorities, civil and military, they followed a line of passive resistance, while opposing conscription, assisting Unionist refugees, hiding deserters from the Southern army, adding fuel to the war of ideas, and frequently observing the dictates of the Lincoln administration. From the tangled web of records and testimony, it was difficult to follow the elusive skeins of loyalty across half the continent, through war-damaged files and misted memories and obliterating years.

However, since the entire account of the Washington hearings is preserved in shorthand notes, exactly as it occurred, a clear report is available of the questioning and cross-examination by the commissioners as they sought to resolve contradictions. Mrs. Anna Fitzhugh, an aunt by marriage of Robert E. Lee, testified: "I felt sympathy for my own people ... for they were my friends ... [but] from the beginning to the end I never felt a moment's hesitation or change.... As large as this country was, I thought it better to have it under one government than under two...."[36] Henry Jackson, a Negro hack driver of Alexandria who appeared in the case as a government witness, contended simply: "Why she was on Beauregard's side. I don't have to think about it at all; I know that."[37] Conversely, Colonel John S. Mosby testified that he, with two of his men, had slept one night among the pines of her estate but decided not to seek breakfast at her house because, "I understood she was on the Union side ... a great many of my men were from Fairfax County, and I heard it from them."[38]

The parade of witnesses, as they appeared in these large cases, included men and women from all walks of life. Mrs. Marie Evans of

---

[36] Testimony of Mrs. Anna Fitzhugh before the commission, Alexandria, Virginia, Jan. 3, 1873 [claimed $375,000, disallowed in 1875], C. of C. No. 14013, Justice Department, National Archives.

[37] Testimony of Henry Jackson, Washington, Dec. 11, 1872, in *ibid*.

[38] Testimony of John S. Mosby, Feb., 1889, in an appeal of the decision of the commissioners heard by the Court of Claims, in *ibid*. Mosby identified himself as the leader of the famous Mosby's Raiders. At the time of his appearance before the court he was a practicing lawyer in San Francisco, California.

Louisiana, for example, produced letters from such well-known Union men as Reverdy Johnson, E. B. Washburne, and General B. F. Butler—then in Congress—certifying to her loyalty. Judge George F. Shepley, military governor of New Orleans, was a witness in her behalf.[39] On December 10, 1872, General William Tecumseh Sherman appeared before the commission to testify regarding the loyalty of Mrs. Leonora Williamson, of Memphis, Tennessee. Sherman described his frequent visits to the Williamson home while he was in command at Memphis, covering a period of about five months, commencing in July, 1862. "Their home was a beautiful one," he said, "surrounded with flowers & gardens, & they were always extremely polite & hospitable." Mr. Williamson was "as good a citizen as you would meet in any country." Mrs. Williamson, who seemed to be "engaged in business on her own account," spoke to him frequently about the war, "and always in good taste & in good spirit. She had negroes & lands that she inherited, & we always understood she was a good kind mistress." He added, "all we asked of the people of Memphis was to remain quiet & mind their own business and [the Williamsons] . . . assuredly did that."[40]

Resistance to conscription took a variety of forms, and was weighed by the commissioners to determine whether it was "merely aversion to military service or genuine Unionism." One claimant explained that he had been able to avoid service because a Confederate commodore was boarding with him at the time. "I found out that by not charging him any board and dividing what little stimulants I had, I could obtain his influence, and with his influence I got exempted," he testified. Such avoidance, the commissioners ruled, did not demonstrate "any real adherence to the Union cause."[41]

In contrast, Joseph Freshley, of Lexington County, South Carolina, described the persistent efforts of his son to flee northward and enlist in the Union army. "Forced into the Confederate Army," the boy deserted and returned home to be harbored and concealed. A Confederate "dog company" organized in his area to hunt down deserters and refugees with bloodhounds, followed his tracks and finally located him "in a tree." Father and son were taken away to the "Lexington county jail where they kept my son a day and a half and then sent

---

[39] 4th Gen. Rept. of C. of C., *House Misc. Docs.*, 43d Cong., 2d Sess., No. 18, Pt. 2, p. 7.

[40] Testimony of William Tecumseh Sherman, Washington, Dec. 10, 1872, in the case of Leonora Williamson, Memphis, Tennessee [claimed $82,185, allowed $19,250 in 1872], C. of C. No. 8849, GAO files. For an example of the commissioners' technique of analyzing the conflicting evidence in parallel columns, see Appendix C.

[41] Testimony of the claimant William Coolidge, Savannah, Georgia, in Washington, March 15, 1872, in his own case [claimed $16,001.75, disallowed in 1871], House File Room, House of Representatives.

him away to join his regiment. . . . They kept me there about 7 days locked up in jail." Subsequently the son deserted again, and was on his way north to join the Federal forces when the war ended.

The arrival of Sherman's army within the week brought about Joseph Freshley's release, but in common with so many of the claimants, liberation by the invading army led directly to his ruin. When the Federals descended upon his two plantations, which "were large and well stocked," they "took all he had." In view of these great losses and of the fact that each item claimed was not only "well proved" but that the claimant had brought his price "down to a low figure," Commissioner Aldis recommended an allowance for each item claimed: a rare occurrence in any large claim. Except for two of the ten items listed, however, all were reduced as to quantity, and of $18,587 claimed, only $4,381 was allowed.[42]

One of the most subtle, troublesome, and recurrent loyalty issues was voluntary military service to the Confederacy by children of Unionist parents. Mrs. Susan V. Whitehead of Greene County, North Carolina, was able to discourage one son but unable to convince another. Her youngest son, at seventeen, "did not want to go to the Army nor did I want him to go," Mrs. Whitehead testified. He was kept out first by the purchase of a substitute, later under the "twenty-Negro law," and finally, when that was repealed, was sent to West Virginia with the purpose of "trying to get him on a railroad." When that plan failed, Mrs. Whitehead was "perfecting arrangements for him to go through the lines," when word came that Sherman's army was approaching.

An older son, on the other hand, had volunteered for the Confederate army at sixteen, although "opposed by his father and myself." Three months later the boy died in the service. "I often thought," Mrs. Whitehead said sadly, "I ought to have coerced him and made him stay . . . [but] he was unyielding in his disposition and threatened to run away unless allowed to go." Questioned as to whether she had assisted the boy in any way while he was in the army, she had replied with spirit, "I sent my son a box of eatables. I would have furnished him that under any circumstances because he was my child, not because I wished to encourage the rebellion."[43]

---

[42] Summary Report of the commissioners in the case of Joseph Freshley, Lexington County, South Carolina [claimed $18,587, allowed $4,381 in 1876], C. of C. No. 22195, GAO files.

[43] Testimony of Susan V. Whitehead before Commissioner E. W. Woods, Chapel Hill, North Carolina, March 19, 1874, in her own case, Greene County, North Carolina [claimed $10,000, allowed $7,838 in 1875], C. of C. No. 844, GAO files. See also the Summary Report in the same case.

Assistance to the Federal army when it arrived was frequently introduced into the testimony as evidence of active aid for the Federal cause. But it was carefully investigated, also, for its real motives, and then admitted or rejected according to the surrounding circumstances. The commissioners had found, for example, that some men were "regarded as a good rebel when in rebel lines, and a good Yankee when in Yankee lines."[44] On the other hand, when, as in the case of Mrs. Matilda A. Harbison of Arkansas, it was shown that "she, with her daughter, visited the Federal hospitals in Little Rock & ... [were] the only ladies of that city who did so," good Unionism was held to be in evidence.[45]

Because Unionists of substantial property usually lived in large homes, they frequently offered shelter to the disabled soldiers of both armies. Sometimes these homes were converted into temporary hospitals. Dr. Hugh Morson of Port Royal, Virginia (a cousin of James A. Seddon, the Confederate secretary of war, but himself an open Unionist), converted his home into a hospital and volunteered his services for the sick and wounded. The commissioners allowed the amount claimed for "500 lbs pork, 392 lbs flour, poultry, vegetables &c for hospital uses," in full.[46] E. E. Malhoit, of Assumption Parish, Louisiana, formerly a state senator, turned his large home into a hospital in October, 1862, when "a battle took place near Labadieville & within about ¾ mile of Mr. Malhoit's house," and payment was allowed for such items as "bed and bedding ... actually used for wounded soldiers of whom there were about one hundred in the house."[47]

Such men as Thomas Kersey of Arkansas, who "helped Union men out of the country into the Federal lines," and aided "Union refugee families" in escaping to Kansas,[48] and such women as Margaret Menly of Texas, who "aided and assisted all Unionist refugees ... who frequently called at our Rancho on the Pintos Creek in the night for pro-

---

[44] Testimony of John O. Conner, postmaster at East Baton Rouge, Louisiana, in the case of Marie Evans of Orleans Parish, Louisiana [claimed $493,335, disallowed in 1874], C. of C. No. 3107, printed with the 4th Gen. Rept. of C. of C., *House Misc. Docs.*, 43d Cong., 2d Sess., No. 18, Pt. 2, p. 7.

[45] Summary Report in the case of Matilda A. Harbison, Pulaski County, Arkansas [claimed $14,500, allowed $1,236.50 in 1877], C. of C. No. 9868, GAO files. Additional evidence of the loyalty of this family appears in the statement that Mrs. Harbison "married a Union man & her 2 daughters married Union officers."

[46] Summary Report in the case of Hugh Morson, Port Royal, Virginia [claimed $13,461.50, allowed $7,067 in 1872], C. of C. No. 11613, GAO files.

[47] Summary Report in the case of E. E. Malhoit, Assumption Parish, Louisiana [claimed $11,315, allowed $3,980 in 1872], C. of C. No. 1057, GAO files.

[48] Testimony of Thomas Kersey taken by Special Agent Liberty Bartlett in Greenwood County, Arkansas, in his own case [claimed $8,641.60, allowed $3,285 in 1874], GAO files.

visions and information as to the Movements of Confederate troops . . . in pursuit of persons Escaping by way of Mexico," were held to have demonstrated satisfactory loyalism.[49] William W. Jones, of the United States Secret Service, who had maneuvered himself into an appointment as captain on the staff of the Confederate general, Philip D. Roddy, had documentary proof of the service of many Unionists to the intelligence work of the United States Army.[50]

Equally telling evidence was supplied by the warnings dispatched by military officers of the Confederacy to suspected Unionists. On October 27, 1862, a note from General P. D. Roddy warned John C. Goodloe, of Colbert County, Alabama, that he was "represented as frequently passing from your residence inside our lines to Corinth & elsewhere inside of the Enemy's lines." Roddy added a sharp warning, " . . . if I learn that you avoid our pickets again it will cost you your liberty and the sentries have been ordered to shoot you on sight."[51] On the Virginia border, Colonel Angus W. McDonald addressed an official letter to Mrs. Jacob Craigen informing her that "the course of your husband to his native state has caused all his real and personal estate to be forfeited and none of either now within Virginia, can ever be claimed by him. Respect for your sex Madam," McDonald continued, "prevents me from putting you to the inconvenience of being suddenly deprived of your household goods, but it is my duty to notify you that you must immediately quit the land which now belongs to the Confederate States."[52]

Efforts were made by some Unionists to comply with shifts of policy in Washington that affected the South, and such efforts were introduced as evidence of substantive loyalty. John Fox, of Fauquier County, Virginia, furnished his own answer to the riddle of slavery by emancipating all of his 113 slaves and leaving a portion of his property, real and personal, to apply for the benefit of his slaves who were to be removed to the North, and to be located on land to be purchased

[49] Testimony of Margaret Menly before Special Commissioner Joseph Fitzsimmons, Nueces, Texas, March 31, 1875, in her own case [claimed $15,020, allowed $1,115 in 1878], C. of C. No. 12035, GAO files.
[50] Deposition of William W. Jones, Colbert County, Alabama, before Special Commissioner Richard S. Watkins, Dec. 16, 1873, in the case of Henry Gargis [claimed $415, allowed $210 in 1873], C. of C. No. 5195, GAO files. The Gargis plantation consisted of about twenty-eight hundred acres, of which one hundred acres were in cultivation.
[51] Letter from General P. D. Roddy, commanding general, Confederate army, dated in the field Oct. 27, 1862, in the case of John Goodloe, Colbert County, Alabama [claimed $27,218, allowed $7,446 in 1872], C. of C. No. 4348, GAO files.
[52] Letter from Angus W. McDonald, colonel, C. S. A. Command, dated Green Spring Run, Virginia, Oct. 5, 1861, in the case of Jacob I. Craigen [claimed $22,974.50, allowed $2,187 in 1872], C. of C. No. 8607, GAO files.

for their benefit. Before his death he had gone with his servants to
Ohio and Indiana and seen to their resettlement.[53] Although Fox died
before his claim was filed, the commissioners were willing to assume
loyalty on the evidence of his will.[54]

Catherine S. Minor, of Natchez, described the dilemma of many
Southern loyalists when, in response to questions about her attitude
toward slavery she said, "I was always an abolitionist at heart, but
I am afraid not a philanthropist. I did not know how to set them free
without wretchedness to them, and utter ruin to myself."[55] Mrs. Martha
E. Fitz, of Issaquena County, Mississippi, conformed with the Proclamation by making agreements with forty-seven of her slaves "for their
manumission, and they were thereafter to work her plantation upon
terms mutually advantageous. . . ."[56] In Marshall County, Mississippi,
Gray W. Smith and Richard Parham refused to "run off their negroes
further South on the rumored approach of the Union army," as their
neighbors had done, because they believed that proper terms of compromise could be obtained in Washington.[57] To this end, they circulated
a petition asking that slaveholders of the occupied territory in Mississippi be allowed to retain their slaves pending their proof of loyalty,
thus placing them on the same footing as the exempted slaveholders
in loyal territory.[58] Harriet J. Carey, of Hinds County, Mississippi,
testified: "My ideas of loyalty are not opposed to secession merely, but
an approval of the acts that established the freedom of the slaves. . . .
I owned slaves & concluded if I was merciful & humane to them I
might just as well own them as other Persons . . . [but] I had an in-
stinctive horror of the institution." She added, "We did not dare call
ourselves an abolitionist—but those were my sentiments, always."[59]

---

[53] Testimony of Eli Taggett before the commission in Washington, in the case
of the John Fox estate, Wm. M. Hume, administrator, Fauquier County, Virginia
[claimed $24,561, allowed $7,545 in 1873], C. of C. No. 14803, GAO files. Taggett
said that he had run the plantation "for many years" before his master's death
and had taken charge of the mill on the place.

[54] Summary Report of the commissioners in *ibid.*

[55] Testimony of Catherine S. Minor before the commission, Washington, Oct. 23,
1872, in her own case [claimed $64,155, allowed $13,072 in 1879], C. of C. No. 7960,
GAO files.

[56] Testimony of Mrs. Martha E. Fitz before Special Commissioner Enos Clarke,
St. Louis, Missouri, Nov. 9, 1874, in her own case, Issaquena County, Mississippi
[claimed $19,500, allowed $7,135 in 1874], C. of C. No. 10510, GAO files.

[57] Testimony of Gray W. Smith taken at Lamar, Mississippi, Dec. 1, 1877, by
Special Agent R. B. Avery, in Smith's own case [claimed $10,000, allowed $7,000
in 1878], C. of C. No. 4686, GAO files.

[58] Testimony of Richard H. Parham, Benton County, Mississippi, before Special
Commissioner Henry F. Dix, Jan. 9, 1873, in his own case [claimed $12,479, al-
lowed $8,467 in 1873], C. of C. No. 360, GAO files.

[59] Testimony of Harriet J. Carey, Hinds County, Mississippi, in her own case
[claimed $9,995.50, allowed $413.50 in 1873], C. of C. No. 12758, GAO files.

In Halifax County, Virginia, Rev. John T. Clark, who was forced
to leave his pastorate in an Episcopal church because of his Union
sentiments, retired to his plantation where he gave most of his time
to the instruction of his slaves. "I opened a School in my own house
and devoted myself to teaching," he said, "while preaching occasionally to the white people; but mostly to my own slaves, one hundred
& sixty (160) in number, & other slaves in the Neighborhood, in a
house on my own land, which I had built for a schoolhouse & Church."
He complied with the Emancipation Proclamation and after Appomattox continued his school, "at first gratuitously, but beginning with
June 1866, I received a small Salary from the Committee in New York,
of the Freedmen's Commission ef the Protestant Episcopal [Church],"
he added. "And now in my reduced cimcumstances, I support myself
in part [through the school]—with the addition of a very small salary
from the Church ... & am the same law abiding & loyall Citizen that
I have been all my life."[60]

The loyalty of other slaveholders, who had maintained that the problem could be settled by constitutional or legal means, dissolved before
the vexations of emancipation. Wilson F. Dillon, of Hinds County,
Mississippi, who had been an outspoken adherent of the Union cause,
with many overt acts of loyalty to his credit, said frankly, "After the
proclamation of President Lincoln in 1862 I thought it a most unjust
measure to thousands of Union men who were in the South. I then
did not care what the devil became of the country. I did not have a
constant sympathy with the cause of the United States during the late
rebellion."[61] Richard Fletcher, of Pulaski County, Arkansas, likewise
found his "Unionism strained by the Emancipation Proclamation,"
and admitted that he had run his seventy slaves off to Texas, fearing
they would be captured if they remained in Arkansas.[62]

The political and intellectual antecedents of the propertied claimants were probed, as a test of loyalty, to expose the ideological foundation of each claim. Devotion to the Constitution and the Union was
especially apparent in the old-line Whig strongholds in Mississippi

[60] Signed statement of John T. Clark, rector of Christ Church, Halifax, Virginia,
Feb. 10, 1873, in his own case [claimed $8,532, allowed $5,255 in 1873], C. of C.
No. 13330, GAO files.
[61] Testimony of Wilson F. Dillon before the commissioners, in his own case, Hinds
County, Mississippi [claimed $9,660, disallowed in 1879], C. of C. No. 6955, Justice
Department, National Archives.
[62] Summary Report of the commissioners in the case of Richard Fletcher, Pulaski
County, Arkansas [claimed $18,515, disallowed in 1872 and a petition for rehearing
filed July 15, 1873, returned on May 7, 1875], C. of C. No. 2270, Justice Department,
National Archives.

and Louisiana, and in parts of Tyler's Virginia. O. C. Brooks, a large planter and landowner of Warren County, Mississippi, was readily identified as a "follower of Webster's constitutional arguments on secession."[63] Mrs. Mary Boyd, of Carroll County, Louisiana, drew her loyal sentiments from her father, who "was largely interested in the Colonization Society ... that was a great point between himself and Mr. Clay. At the time of my father's death," she added, "he was laid in Mr. Clay's family vault.... They were bosom friends."[64] Thomas Bacon, of Alexandria County, Louisiana, concluded his testimony with the statement, "My convictions and sympathies were altogether with the power of the U.S. as being the only lawful one, & I considered the other a usurpation, which possibly might be successful, but in whose success I wanted no part."[65]

In these and many other ways, the origins and the durability of Unionist sentiments were tested. Exposed to two fires, the loyalist had to steer a course through the treacherous waters of Confederate pressures and Federal indifference and despoilation. A few representative cases suggest the cumulative problems and contributions of the minority of dissent within the Confederate home front, the final yardstick of loyalty. Only the most hardy were able to emerge unscathed at the war's end to face the rigors of reconstruction and to be measured for the Procrustes' bed of the commissioners of claims.

In Mississippi, Judge William L. Sharkey was a constant problem for the Confederate authorities. Before the war, Sharkey had served for many years as chief justice of Mississippi. He was a member of the Baltimore convention of 1860, and later on had refused two cabinet posts. According to E. P. Jacobson, United States attorney for the Southern District of Mississippi in 1874, "Jefferson Davis not only hated him because of his sentiments but feared his great influence, but for which Judge Sharkey's life would have become one more offering on the altar of the Union."[66] His refusal to sell goods to the Confed-

---

[63] Summary Report of the commissioners in the case of Mary A. Brooks, Warren County, Mississippi [claimed $26,280, disallowed in 1877], C. of C. No. 10826, Justice Department, National Archives.

[64] Testimony of Mrs. Mary Eliza Boyd before the commission, Washington, Oct. 12, 1874, in the case of Frederick W. Boyd, executor of James Bailey, Carroll County, Louisiana [claimed $30,958, allowed $7,800 in 1874], C. of C. No. 11551, GAO files.

[65] Testimony of Thomas S. Bacon, Washington, March 12, 1873, in his own case, Alexandria, Louisiana [claimed $13,500, allowed $3,050 in 1874], C. of C. No. 4041, GAO files.

[66] E. P. Jacobson to Asa O. Aldis, Jackson, Mississippi, Nov. 16, 1872, in the case of William L. Sharkey, Jackson, Mississippi [claimed $3,655, allowed $1,920 in 1872], C. of C. No. 2635, GAO files.

erate authorities during the war was, according to one of his witnesses, "seized upon as a pretext to arrest the Judge and give him a good deal of anxiety and trouble to get released."[67]

In the first siege of Jackson, Mississippi, Sharkey turned over the first floor of his home to General James B. McPherson for the General's headquarters, thus sustaining the losses of property at the hands of the Union army which entitled him to his claim before the Southern Claims Commission.[68] After the war, he served as provisional governor of Mississippi under Johnson, and subsequently made perhaps his greatest contribution, in the assistance he furnished in the preparation of those cases before the Supreme Court designed to restore the rights of citizenship in full to Southerners.[69]

In the Natchez area, William Minor and Josiah Winchester, having made their strong stand against secession in 1860–1861, dug in for the duration to await the arrival of the Union army. Winchester had served as a delegate to the secession convention for his state, and was one of the fifteen men who signed the attestation clause rather than the ordinance itself.[70] Minor, according to his wife, "considered secession as the most stupendous act that the world had ever seen . . . was violently opposed to it . . . and did all in his power to prevent it." He wrote to the governors of all states before the vote was taken, urging them "to pause on the subject, & not to do it." He visited the states of Louisiana and Mississippi, stopping at various points on the way to try to reason with public men. During the war, Union officers, aware of his sentiments and of his wealth and prominence, sought him out for advice and assistance. General Benjamin F. Butler urged him to go to Washington for a conversation with Lincoln, and offered to furnish a gunboat for the purpose, but, according to Mrs. Minor, her husband

[67] Testimony of John W. Robb, an attorney of Hinds County, Mississippi, Washington, March 13, 1872, in *ibid.*

[68] Signed statement of Judge William L. Sharkey, June 20, 1871, and Summary Report of the commission, in *ibid.* Among the items which the commissioners could not make allowance for were "2 dozen knives, 2 dozen Napkins and 2 Table clothes, 2 Chafing dishes, 2 English Tea Kettles, 4 stew pans, waffle irons & tea kettle, 6 Goblets, and sundry other articles which had disappeared during McPherson's visit." According to Judge Sharkey, "My wife told me that all the Dining articles were [taken]—a part loaned to Gen. McP & never returned & the remainder taken by the Genl's servants."

[69] For Sharkey's able assistance in the attempt to obtain a ruling of the Supreme Court on the validity of military government in the time of peace (April 5, 1867), see Charles Warren, *The Supreme Court in United States History* (Boston, 1923), III, 177–178, 180; and for his arguments in the McCardle case, see p. 188.

[70] Testimony of Josiah Winchester, Washington, Dec. 24, 1872, in the case of Stephanie M. Chotard, Concordia, Louisiana [claimed $57,172, allowed $13,800 in 1875], C. of C. No. 7125, GAO files.

"was advised not to do it, fearing it would tend still more to injure his family around Natchez."[71] General Lorenzo Thomas arrived in Natchez with advance information as to the influence and reliability of the Minor family, and sought them out at his first opportunity.[72]

In the Red River country in Louisiana, William Bailey and Dr. James B. Sullivan, both veterans of the war of 1812, made their stand together, after losing in their active fight against secession. Sullivan was subsequently arrested by the Confederates for having, on the advice of General Godfrey Weitzel, "remained upon his plantation, neither making sale of his accumulated crops of cotton nor removing any property of any kind whatever from his premises, notwithstanding the solicitations of Confederate agents so to do." Under the protection of Union officers, he was subject to Confederate depredations, lost some of his horses and four hundred bales of his cotton. With the sudden retreat of the Federals on April 25, 1864, his Unionism was most severely tested when the fleeing Union troops, "after partaking of the hospitality of your petitioner . . . as they marched in front of and through his plantation, collected and gathered together all of his stock, consisting of horses, mules, oxen, cattle, sheep, and hogs," set fire to all of his houses and buildings, and burned three crops of cotton, "utterly consuming the whole even to the fencing."[73]

Thus reduced in a few hours from affluence to comparative poverty, and with some 170 of his former slaves made free, Dr. Sullivan went to the Union headquarters in Alexandria, counting on the support and protection of the higher officers. But there, to his dismay, "he saw his horses in the artillery, his mules in the transportation trains constructing the dam across the Red River, and the army consuming his cattle, yet he failed *from the confusion consequent upon the recent*

[71] Testimony of Mrs. Rebecca A. Minor, Washington, April 21, 1874, in the case of Catherine S. Minor, Natchez, Mississippi [claimed $64,155, allowed $13,072 in 1879], C. of C. No. 7960, GAO files. See also J. Carlyle Sitterson, "The William J. Minor Plantations: A Study in Ante-Bellum Absentee Ownership," *Journal of Southern History*, IX (1943), 59–74.

[72] In a letter to Stanton written October 24, 1863, General Thomas comments at some length on the Unionist sentiment in Natchez. "I find several of my old friends who are Union men, men who have been so from the beginning," he wrote. In a discussion of the prospect of bringing the area back under the Federal government, he also mentions Judge William Sharkey as a logical leader since he is "the person of most influence." See *Official Records*, Series III, Vol. III, pp. 916–917.

[73] Summary Report of the commissioners in the case of Dr. James B. Sullivan, Rapides, Louisiana [claimed $24,515, allowed $13,463 in 1872], C. of C. No. 250, Justice Department, National Archives. See also his petition "praying for compensation for property referred to the Committee on Claims December 20, 1870, thence to the Comm's of Claims on March 15, 1871," in *ibid*. In addition to his houses, the burned items included a corn mill, cotton gin stands, stabling and shed for two hundred head of horses, mules, and oxen.

defeat of the army, to recover any of his stock, or to obtain receipts therefor."[74]

Tired, discouraged, and ill, he returned to his home where, at midnight on May 23, 1864, he was arrested by a squad of Confederate soldiers. In Alexandria, he was put in prison "not with the citizen and political prisoners, but by a special order of the Confederate commander, engendered by malice for . . . [his] adhesion to the Federal Government, confined with 287 Jayhawkers, negroes, and yankees in a single room." For seventy hours he remained there, without blanket, mattress, or food, in a situation "obnoxious beyond conception by the filth and vermin of such a number crowded together." When food arrived, it was "brought upon a barrow used in cleaning out stables." Twenty days later, a military court charged him with acting as a spy and with disloyalty to the Confederacy. Under a guard of forty men, he was removed to Shreveport, where the Confederate authorities, including Governor Henry Watkins Allen, tried him for treason.[75]

The large supplies furnished by General Bailey had saved the army of General Nathaniel P. Banks "from utter demoralization" during the second Red River campaign. The army's supplies from New Orleans were, at this time, "completely cut off for 6 or 7 weeks," when on a single afternoon General Taylor captured 250 army wagons. Loyal Confederates had drawn off or secreted their stock, according to orders, and only Unionists, such as Bailey, came forward to assist. In addition to the importance of the supplies he furnished, Bailey's military experience made him of use to General Charles P. Stone, for whom he furnished information on the campaigns in Texas and on the Red River. Bailey, a former Whig, and "one of the wealthiest planters in Louisiana," once a friend of Henry Clay, made no secret of his Union sentiments. Born in Virginia in 1800, he moved west to the rich lands of Louisiana in the middle 1830's. By 1861 his plantation, consisting of a little over fifteen hundred acres, of which some thirteen hundred acres had been cleared was, according to J. F. Mollere, a Union secret service man, "as nice a plantation as I had ever seen in the south, well stocked—everything was plentiful about the place."[76] But by May of 1864, "when the Army left . . . not a hoof, a pig, a chicken, or a peck of Corn, was obtainable, except from Arkansas, & at fabulous prices."

---

[74] Petition of James B. Sullivan, *ibid.*

[75] *Ibid.*

[76] Testimony of J. F. Mollere, a United States detective in the secret service of the army under General Charles P. Stone, Washington, Nov. 14, 1871, in the case of William Bailey, Rapides, Louisiana [claimed $104,492.40, allowed $45,161.72 in 1873], C. of C. No. 980, GAO files.

All of the fencing was gone, and according to Mollere, "You could see where the soldiers had ditched around their tents, & they had taken rails & filled up the furrows with them, & covered them with cotton to make beds. The fencing, corn-cribs, & everything was taken."[77]

Robert E. Scott, of Warrenton, Virginia, whom General John A. Spillman called "the leading man of all this country and whose influence was all in favor of the Union and against secession," suffered the most tragic fate of any of these leaders, when he was shot upon his own threshold by a group of Union stragglers. Brought up by his father, Hon. John Scott, "in the old Whig doctrine," he was always "a believer of 'Straitest Sect' in the power and blessings of the Constitution and the Union, to regard it as the Palladium of liberties, peace, and prosperity of the States." Through the "unhappy struggle," both Scott and his sister had therefore been *"firm and uncompromising"* Unionists. The sister, Mrs. Margaret G. Lee, moved into his home at the time of Scott's death, to care for his orphaned children. In a letter written to General John H. Patrick in 1865, she described the property losses subsequently suffered by the family. "I have been loyal throughout to the United States and I ask remuneration from 'my Government' for the losses I have sustained from the occupation of my farm by troops and armies of the United States," she wrote. "Worth at the outbreak of the war One hundred thousand dollars, I am now reduced almost to want and scarcely able to obtain the necessaries of life." Her fencing had been entirely destroyed, her stock driven off, her buildings pulled down, and her wood cut; in fact, a "fine & valuable estate made ... common and valueless."[78]

Against such contentions the 949 claims in excess of $10,000 filed with the commission were examined by the commissioners.[79] For purposes of the accompanying chart and the tables in chapter ix, the following breakdown has been made. The act of June 15, 1878, barred 272 of these claims for nonprosecution, and they have been eliminated.[80]

[77] Roderick McKee to the commissioners, Jan. 6, 1873, in *ibid.*

[78] Mrs.Margaret G. Lee to General John H. Patrick, April 29, 1865, in her own case [claimed $48,343, allowed $13,467 in 1871], C. of C. No. 1673, GAO files. Mrs. Lee herself died in 1866 and, by her will, left her entire estate to Scott's daughters. The will as probated included as assets her claim against the government, and lands in Illinois and Missouri, as well as the Warrenton farm.

[79] 3d Gen. Rept. of C. of C., *House Misc. Docs.*, 43d Cong., 1st Sess., No. 23, p. 2. Of this number 50 claims exceeded $100,000, and 145 exceeded $50,000.

[80] 20 *U.S. Stat. at L.*, 566. This act extended the time of taking evidence until March 10, 1879, but barred any except rebutting evidence after that date. It further provided that "all claims wherein the evidence of the claimant or claimants is not so filed in the office of the Commissioners of Claims, and which have not been submitted to the Commissioners for decision within the time herein limited, shall be barred forever thereafter."

This left 677 claims in excess of $10,000 reported to Congress with a Summary Report as allowed or disallowed. In the final accounting 263 claimants in the over-$10,000 bracket failed to appear in person before the three-man board. With the consent of the commissioners, 198 of these 263 claimants filed amended petitions reducing their claims below $10,000 to avoid the expensive process of appearing in Washington with their witnesses. The remaining 65 cases were disallowed for fraudulent title, by recommendation of the special agents on the basis of field investigations alone. These 263 cases, however, are included for purposes of this study. There were in addition 24 cases for $10,000 even, and these claims have been included with the 677 in excess of $10,000, making a total of 701 cases for $10,000 and over acted on by the commission with specific recommendations.

Though the commissioners did allow amended petitions reducing the total amount claimed, these reductions are not indicated in their annual statements to Congress. The initial face value of the claims as originally filed was used in calculating their Summary, Annual, and Final reports. For this reason the figures in the original application were retained in preparing the following table and throughout the footnotes of this study. Men and women from Louisiana, Mississippi, and Virginia, in that order, accounted for most of these large claims, with a total of 436, or about two-thirds of the cases heard. These states predominated because of their greater concentration of wealth and because the Federal armies had been active in these areas, either in battle or in camp. All of the seceded states, however, were represented in reasonable proportion, as table 3, prepared from the cases involving $10,000 and over, shows:[81]

[81] Prepared from the "Register of Claims," included in the records of the commission in Treasury Section, National Archives, Record Group 56, in which each claim was listed as it was filed.

TABLE 3

State	Total claimed		Total disallowed cases		Total allowed cases		
	No. of cases	Total amount claimed	No. of cases	Total amount disallowed	No. of cases	Total amount claimed	Total amount allowed
Alabama............	33	$ 780,482.30	23	$ 487,034.85	10	$ 293,447.45	$ 58,128.00
Arkansas...........	68	1,844,570.26	51	1,535,118.45	17	309,451.83	63,160.24
Florida............	7	174,767.50	2	108,708.00	5	66,053.50	32,580.00
Georgia............	60	1,689,011.41	52	1,474,674.98	8	214,336.43	30,523.66
Louisiana..........	164	8,099,469.17	134	6,190,172.04	30	1,909,297.13	418,765.58
Mississippi........	152	3,824,063.04	108	2,650,404.77	44	1,173,658.27	270,421.27
No. Carolina.......	11	167,233.90	7	122,025.90	4	45,208.00	15,124.00
So. Carolina.......	12	890,203.17	8	564,768.42	4	325,434.75	13,047.89
Tennessee.........	65	1,912,727.23	52	1,497,678.93	13	415,048.30	141,318.52
Texas.............	6	129,946.25	3	45,847.00	3	84,099.25	44,574.25
Virginia...........	120	3,031,351.59	69	2,008,745.17	51	1,022,606.42	261,749.39
W. Virginia........	3	38,603.01	1	14,050.00	2	24,553.01	6,230.00
Totals........	701	$22,582,422.83	510	$16,699,228.49	191	$5,883,194.34	$1,355,622.80

CHAPTER VII

THE TEST OF PROPERTY

THE ACT creating the commission described its responsibilities in regard to property in two brief phrases. Its jurisdiction was limited to "stores or supplies" which must have been "taken or furnished . . . for the use of the army."[1] In their first report to Congress, which appeared in December of 1871, the commissioners listed the commodities to be considered. Horses and mules, wagons and grain, were clearly quartermaster stores; hogs and cattle, cured bacon and molasses were among the main items of subsistence stores which appeared in large amounts in the petitions, and could usually be classified easily. The phrase "for the use of the Army," however, frequently called for close decisions following the procedures established by the military departments of the government.

The printed petitions outlined the information to be set forth "clearly, concisely, fully . . . and not argumentatively."[2] Space was provided for an itemized account of each article claimed, "excluding any and all items of damage, destruction, and loss (and not use) of property, or unauthorized or unnecessary depredations by troops or other persons upon property, or of rent or compensation for the use or occupation of buildings, grounds, or other real estate." Further, the petitioner was called upon to swear that the goods had been taken for "the actual use of the Army and *not* for the mere gratification of individual officers or soldiers already provided by the Government with such articles as were necessary or proper for them to have." A breakdown of the customary supply lines often created a shortage where a local requisition was "so useful, beneficial, or justifiable as to warrant or require the Government to pay for it."[3]

In distinguishing between the meaning of the words "taken" and "furnished," the commissioners were guided by the opinion of Attorney General A. T. Ackerman, who stated:

The difference seems to signify such appropriations as were essentially involuntary on the part of their owners; there was an exertion of force in cases of *taking*, which did not exist in cases of *furnishing*. The giving of receipts in the latter and the failure to give receipts in the former indicates, in the one case, a ready submission by the owner to the capture of his property, which is wanting in the other.[4]

---

[1] 16 *U.S. Stat. at L.*, 524.
[2] 2d Gen. Rept. of C. of C., *House Misc. Docs.*, 42d Cong., 3d Sess., No. 12, p. 41.
[3] 1st Gen. Rept. of C. of C., *ibid.*, 42d Cong., 2d Sess., No. 16, p. 20.
[4] A. T. Ackerman, attorney general, to George S. Boutwell, secretary of the Treasury, April 6, 1871, reproduced in the Washington *Daily Morning Chronicle*, April 10, 1871, Vol. IX, No. 136, p. 1.

In one ruling on a minor point, however, the commissioners adopted a more generous interpretation which had been used in the War Department. The act of March 3, 1871, had used the words "stores or supplies" more broadly than had the act of July 4, 1864, and the intent of Congress to include under their surveillance all stores and supplies was thus held to include claims for medical and hospital stores and supplies for the engineer's department.[5] In actual fact, however, this seeming liberalization had little effect on the total amount of goods claimed or allowed.

Printed on four pages of legal-size paper, the petition furnished space for the listing of the articles taken and their quantities, together with their estimated value at the time taken. In general, men of substantial holdings presented an average of about twenty-five items, of which the most common were corn, fodder and hay, hogs, horses, beef cattle, and mules. Occasionally over a hundred items were listed, representing almost a complete inventory of the supplies on a plantation or in a store.[6] In an age as yet unconditioned to forms, the entries themselves were often phrased in the familiar terms which suggest the individuality of plantation life. In specifying quantities, there was no uniformity of measuring units. Corn was listed in bushels, barrels, cribs, or acres; bacon in pounds, sides, barrels, or casks; and livestock was familiarly described as "fine carriage horses," or "blooded stallions."

Wiley J. Davis of Hardeman County, Tennessee, listed 261 items, in the longest petition filed. His list reported the completely stripped plantation which the army left behind it. In addition to substantial numbers of hogs and shoats, beef cattle and heifers, and large quantities of corn and fodder, wood and seasoned lumber, Davis gave such plantation equipment as log-chains, hemp bagging, blind-bridles, picks, poleaxes, and nails. Household items include "delf dishes," "britannia candlesticks," a piano cover, a "large patent coffee mill," "4 yards Irish linen," and even "24 bottled Dr. Lowery's alterative,

---

[5] 1st Gen. Rept. of C. of C., *House Misc. Docs.*, 42d Cong., 2d Sess., No. 16, p. 4.

[6] The petition of Asa B. Daniel, of Aberdeen, Monroe County, Mississippi, for example, lists fifty-seven items taken from his drug store, including asafetida, balsam copaiba, chloroform, extracts of aconite, belladonna, colocynth, digitalis, sarsaparilla, cod-liver oil, sassafras, iodine, and quinine. See claim of Asa B. Daniel, Aberdeen, Monroe County, Mississippi [claimed $11,556.80, disallowed in 1872], C. of C. No. 5355, Justice Department, National Archives. The commissioners noted that most of the items "were taken on a raid from claimant's drug store lawlessly, and without authority or necessity. . . . The whiskey, liquors, and tobacco appear to have attracted the soldiers there, and a lieutenant, to cover up the lawless plundering and pillage, said it was for army use."

24 bottles, pint, Dr. Lowery's liniment," and "12 one-quart bottles of catsup."[7]

Equally revealing as to losses sustained, however, is the statement of Arthur Middleton Blake of Charleston County, South Carolina, who, contrary to the instructions which required a separate listing for each article, filed his claim with a single entry which read: "To the deprivation of the services & labor due to him of 401 slaves, and to the buildings, furniture, objects of virtue & taste, books, pictures, linen, wines, and various buildings, mills, cotton gins, threshed rice & crops not harvested destroyed or used by the Federal Army... $400,000.00."[8] Blake, who filed his claim from London, explained through his attorney, Benjamin H. Rutledge, that the losses for the services of his slaves were not named in the petition with the purpose of "claiming payment for them as property," but rather "to show the position of wealth and affluence of the claimant before the late civil war in contrast with the absolute ruin to which he was reduced thereby... from all which the said claimant's loyalty... to the cause of the Government and the Union, should have protected both him and his property."[9]

In another section, the printed instructions called for exact detail as to the circumstances surrounding the transfer of the goods, including, when possible, the name, rank, and regiment, corps or station of the Federal troops involved, and the place to which the property was removed. Also, the claimant was required to name two sets of witnesses. One group included those persons through whose testimony he could prove the quantity, quality, and amount of the goods he had lost; the other those persons who could swear "that from the beginning of hostilities against the United States to the end thereof, his sympathies were constantly with the cause of the United States."[10] This state-

---

[7] See claim of Wiley J. Davis, of Bolivar, Hardeman County, Tennessee [claimed $25,457.18, disallowed in 1871], C. of C. No. 5453, Justice Department, National Archives. The claim was disallowed by the Commissary and Quartermaster departments under the provisions of the joint resolution of June 18, 1866, which had extended the jurisdiction of these departments, under the act of July 4, 1864, to Tennessee.

[8] See claim of Arthur Middleton Blake, Charleston County, South Carolina [claimed $400,000, disallowed in 1873], C. of C. No. 4222, House File Room, House of Representatives. This claim was disallowed chiefly because "the inquiries of our special agent lead us to believe that a battle was fought in the near vicinity of the claimant's house & that at that time his house, buildings & a large part if not all of the property for which compensation is asked were burned or destroyed by the federal forces."

[9] Petition of July 6, 1871, of Arthur Middleton Blake, by Benjamin H. Rutledge, attorney in fact, to the commissioners, in *ibid.*

[10] 1st Gen. Rept. of C. of C., in *House Misc. Docs.*, 42d Cong., 2d Sess., No. 16, pp. 22–23.

ment, properly sworn to and signed by the claimant and his attorney, was then filed, registered, given a number, and placed on the waiting list for a hearing, with the proviso that it could not be taken from the custody of the clerk except by special order of the commissioners.[11]

Such tangible evidence as would establish the validity of the petition was also filed at this time, including, if possible, the vouchers, reports of army boards, letters from army officers familiar with the circumstances, receipts, letters, and lists to show supplies on hand when the Union army arrived, and numerous sworn affidavits and depositions which had been prepared for the claimant. Where army records or letters were incomplete or missing, the commissioners accepted as evidence any lists which the claimant had prepared at the time of the taking, in preference to accountings made from memory. At times, however, when these lists seemed to be too exact, they had the effect of creating a suspicion in the mind of the examining commissioner as to their authenticity. In one case, for example, Commissioner Ferriss challenged with a vigorous indictment the incriminating circumstances surrounding the late appearance of such a list. In his first appearance before the board, the claimant swore that he had mislaid his list and gave an oral accounting of his losses. Shortly thereafter, he forwarded what he described as a "true copy of the original list." When it was discovered, however, that this list corresponded exactly "in numbers of barrels, tierces, boxes, sacks, hhds & bushels & in prices & amounts, with the items in his petition though the latter he claims was made up entirely from recollection," Ferriss commented tersely that this was "truly . . . an unparalleled feat of memory!"[12]

The difficulty of furnishing exact proof for each item claimed often presented an insuperable task to the claimant. The stories told in the records illustrate why a complete accounting was not always demanded. In the case of John C. Goodloe, of Colbert County, Alabama, the notations of the commissioners for each item claimed (indicated in brackets), illustrate the various ways in which the transfer of goods could be made, especially if the plantation lay in a long-contested battle zone. The excerpt from the Summary Report reads as follows:

Items 1 and 2 ["8 mules @ $200 and 7 No. 1 horses @ $175"] were taken by a Lieut. & 5 or 6 men under Rosenkrans Sept. 9, '62.

---

[11] No. 18, in "Rules and regulations of the commissioners of claims appointed under the act of Congress of March 3, 1871," in *ibid.*, pp. 17–19.

[12] Summary Report in the case of Christopher White, Chatham County, Georgia [claimed $60,746, allowed $1,297 in 1877], C. of C. No. 13994, GAO files.

Item 3 ["2 fine Jacks @ $1500 each"] One of the Jacks was only 2 years old. The other was returned to the clmt & afterwards taken by a Soldier as we think obviously without authority.

Items 4 & 5 ["4 No. 1 Mules @ $200 and 5 fine horses @ $175 each"] These were taken by Col. Sweeny when preparing for Straights' raid, & Gen'l Dodge refused to give them up.

Items 6.7.8.9 & 10 ["36 head beef cattle, 16,200 lbs @ 5¢, 150 sheet @ $4. each, 10 fine mules @ $200, 6 head good horses @ $175, and 6000 lbs Bacon @ 25¢ per lb."] These items proved by a voucher given claimant by Genl. Dodge who was in command of the U. S. troops. It is dated May 5, '63 & states the taking as the date of Apl. 30, '63. No amounts . . . stated in the receipts. . . . We allow . . . at the fair market price at the time as we find it. . . . Item 10 . . . it is alleged was stored in a house on the mountain & taken by our troops, but nobody saw it taken—the proof of it was missing when our troops were camped about 3 miles off. The wagon tracks led from the house to the nearest point of road. If taken by the troops it must have been taken Ap. 30. . . . We disallow the 6000 pounds & the whole of item 11 ["1500 bu Corn @ $100"] standing on the same proof.

Items 12, 13 & 14 ["13 beeves 6500 lbs @ 5¢, 112 Sheep @ $4.00, 329 hogs, 150 lbs ea. 49,350 lbs @ 10¢"]—Taken by Genl. Blair's command. See exhibit No. 10 signed by A. O. Morton, Lt. Col. & C[hief] of C[ommissary] S[ubsistence] dates Nov. 5, '63 by order of Genl. F. P. Blair. We allow the beeves at 300 lbs each—sheep at 3.00 each—hogs at 100 lbs each & 5 cents per lb.

Items 15.16.17 ["6 good mules @ $175 each, 1 thoroughbred Peytona mare 8 yrs. and 1 Thoroughbred Morgan Stallion, 5 yrs."] are not sufficiently proved. Claimant knows nothing as to their taking. The testimony of the colored witness (Washington Johnson) is both too vague & unreliable to satisfy us when not otherwise corroborated.[13]

The experience of Mrs. Martha E. Fitz, of Issaquena County, Mississippi, may be recounted in some detail to illustrate the discouragement and delay in securing a settlement. Mrs. Fitz had little difficulty in establishing her loyalty. She had been a ward of Andrew Jackson in her youth and "from him imbibed an undying devotion to the Federal Government."[14] During the early part of the war she had, because of her outspoken Unionist sentiments, been "made to feel the displeasure of the Confederates by special depredations and needless spoilations upon her property."[15] In one instance a detachment of Confederate

---

[13] Summary Report of the commissioners in the case of John C. Goodloe, Colbert County, Alabama [claimed $27,218, allowed $7,446 in 1872], C. of C. No. 4348, GAO files. The view of Goodloe's loyalty shows an equally detailed examination into that aspect of the claim. The commissioners concluded that "the Exhibits filed in the case & marked from A to Z & from 1 to 8 fully show that he was well known to Union officers & confided in by them as a true Union man. He gave valuable information to Buell & Dodge & is highly praised by Genl. Woods & Genl. R. D. McCook. He was distrusted, watched & threatened by the Confederates. See especially Exhibits H. D. Q & Y. . . . We find him loyal."

[14] Handwritten petition of Mrs. Martha E. Fitz, Issaquena County, Mississippi [claimed $19,500, allowed $7,125 in 1874], C. of C. No. 10510, GAO files.

[15] Summary Report of the commissioners in *ibid*.

soldiers was sent to her house because she "insisted upon keeping the United States flag floating on her premises." The officers ordered her to "burn it or take the flag down over the door which," she added, "I did not do." As a result, the "house was searched from top to bottom," and her son "was fired at four times."[16] Finally she was forced to leave her plantation, and proceeded to Lake Providence which, in May of 1863, was occupied by Union troops.[17]

Mrs. Fitz agreed to sell a large quantity of corn to the United States. Brigadier General H. T. Reid appointed two officers to get the corn. They "measured the cribs and examined the corn and gave the claimant a certificate" for between 9,000 and 10,000 bushels in "good merchantable condition." General Reid agreed on a price of 75 cents per bushel, took the certificate issued, and said he would arrange for payment for the corn and have it removed. Later, when Mrs. Fitz's agent visited him at Cairo, Illinois, he confirmed the story and assured the agent that "there would be no trouble in getting paid" by the quartermaster at Vicksburg, who had a general knowledge of the claimant and knew that the corn had been removed to that city by boat. The agent proceeded to Vicksburg, from which point he regretfully reported that he had been "unable to find the Quartermaster responsible."[18]

As a refugee at Lake Providence, which was occupied at the time by part of Grant's army, she was able to obtain letters of credence from the chief of staff and the adjutant general. From Grant himself she obtained a pass for free transportation for herself, her son, and nine Negroes whom she had freed at the time of the Emancipation Proclamation. The party reached St. Louis in a destitute condition, but, with her credentials, they were able to obtain rations from General W. K. Strong, the post commander.[19]

Peter Clark, auditor for the Quartermaster Department, was impressed with her "culture, information, and refinement," and accordingly set himself to assist her in obtaining her due. He first wrote the quartermaster general in Washington who, however, replied that Mrs. Fitz would have to wait until some law might be passed in favor of such claims. Clark then applied to President Lincoln, through Senator O. H. Browning, but according to Clark's testimony, "the same diffi-

---

[16] Testimony of Mrs. Fitz before Special Commissioner Enos Clarke, St. Louis, Missouri, Nov. 9, 1874, in *ibid.*

[17] Summary Report of the commissioners in *ibid.*

[18] *Ibid.*

[19] Testimony of Peter Clark before the commissioners of claims, Washington, May 6, 1874, in *ibid.* Clark, who was seventy-two when he appeared before the commission in 1874, was a practicing lawyer in New York City at that time.

culty occurred there. Mr. Lincoln, although he appreciated her condition, thought he could not interfere specially, & we would have to
wait."

Still determined, Clark saw Salmon P. Chase, the secretary of the
Treasury, having heard that some provision had been made by that
department to assist loyal refugees in returning to and carrying on
their plantations. "Mr. Chase," said Clark, "gave me a very warm letter
to Mr. Mellen, his agent, but nothing could be done. Mrs. Fitz, in fact,
was entirely destitute, & she could not go down there."

Clark then arranged to lease her premises to "a very excellent man
from Illinois," who went South with a large stock of provisions and
farming implements. But shortly afterward, the Union force at Skip-
with's Landing was withdrawn and "raids were made, so that he had
to escape with his life, & lost everything he put there." Clark then
visited the plantation himself and saw that everything was gone. As
a result of her losses, and with the "maturing of a large debt for the
purchase of quite a number of slaves," the plantation, which had been
obtained by her father-in-law by a patent from the government in 1828,
was sold under a judgment.[20] By 1874, when she appeared before the
commissioners, Mrs. Fitz had still received no payment for her corn.
Her claim was finally allowed in their Annual Report in December
of that year, and, after filling out the necessary forms, she finally
received some reimbursement for her losses, from which she had to
deduct witness fees and expenses for her attorneys.[21]

The huge quantities of corn, wheat, cattle, and grains which appeared
on the petitions filed for the larger claims from the Mississippi and
Louisiana areas, tend to substantiate the evidence that cotton and
sugar acreage had been materially reduced during the war years in
favor of standard foodstuffs. They emphasize as well the self-sufficiency
of a large plantation. The petition filed by Mrs. Adelia E. Casson, of
Alexandria, Rapides Parish, Louisiana, reports the wholesale despoilation of another plantation as a result of the visit of Federal troops.
Mrs. Casson's list, with her evaluation of her losses, reads as follows:[22]

10 miles fencing, planks and posts	$ 3,960.00
5 miles fencing	1,980.00
200 mules and horses	40,000.00
200 hogs	2,000.00
150,000 bricks	1,800.00

[20] *Ibid.*
[21] Summary Report of the commissioners in *ibid.*
[22] Summary Report in the case of Adelia E. Casson, Alexandria, Rapides Parish,
Louisiana [claimed $278,315, disallowed in 1874], C. of C. No. 9357, GAO files.

60 hogsheads sugar	7,800.00
50 barrels molasses	1,000.00
6 wagons	1,200.00
60,000 pounds bacon	21,000.00
130 sheep	365.00
1 saw mill	5,000.00
20,000 bushels corn	20,000.00
1 steam cotton-gin, press, grist-mill, &c.	12,000.00
48 double cabins	12,480.00
1 overseer's house	3,000.00
1 cook-stove	500.00
1 nursery	3,000.00
1 hospital	4,000.00
Wheelwright, cooper, and blacksmith shops	2,000.00
Blacksmith's dwelling	3,000.00
Gardener's dwelling	1,500.00
Bridge over Rayour Rapides	3,000.00
5 corn-cribs	1,500.00
1 fodder-house	150.00
1 sugar-house, furnace, machinery, &c.	100,000.00
1 railroad and fixtures	10,000.00
18 double cabins	4,680.00
1 overseer's dwelling	2,500.00
1 hospital	1,500.00
3 corn-cribs	900.00
1 cotton-gin house and fixtures	5,000.00
1 cotton-house	1,500.00
Total	$278,315.00

The commodity most frequently listed was corn. The amount was tested against the report of witnesses and then against the capacity of the plantation to produce such a crop. The Negroes on the plantation were often the most reliable witnesses on losses, and the commissioners frequently placed final confidence in their reports. The testimony of Reuben Atkinson, which describes the arrival of the soldiers at what he called the "home place" in Greene County, North Carolina, gives the sort of evidence these former slaves, thoroughly familiar with the plantation, could supply. The soldiers, Atkinson said, arrived in the night: "I reckon there were between five hundred and a thousand men ... they filled the big road for a mile." When the corn was taken he was about one hundred yards from the cribs, and he watched the soldiers filling their wagon beds with the corn. Questioned as to the amount of corn so taken, he replied:

There were six cribs which would hold about two hundred barrels each. They were all full. There was also a barn holding about four hundred barrels which was also full. I know they were full for I helped to fill them. There were three other barns near the great house filled with corn. They were about three hundred *yards* from the other cribs. The Six cribs at the overseers house was full when the Yankees come. The Years allowance for the Stock was put in the barn near the overseers house. We had been feeding out of this barn. The six cribs would hold about two hundred barrels each. Two of the barns at the big house would hold two hundred and fifty barrels each and the other one would hold from one hundred and fifty to two hundred barrels of corn. . . . I cut the logs for the crib and they told me what size to cut them. I recollect distinctly of his [the overseer] telling me the cribs would hold two hundred barrels. I reckon we raised about twenty five hundred barrels of Corn a year. We sometimes run about twenty five plows. Sometimes we had as many as twenty five men on the farm besides women and children . . . the soldiers kept taking the corn as long as they stayed in camp which was about three weeks.[23]

Such exact information was not, of course, always available. Sometimes the petitioner was not sure himself how much corn he had, nor certain of its quality. One case from Fauquier County, Virginia, includes the evidence of a witness who testified that Pope's troops had "used a field of growing corn of about 20 Acres and a large quantity of old corn from the Corn house." He thought about half of the 200 bushels claimed came from the corn house. But the commissioners reasoned that the green corn claimed "must have been taken by Pope, for the Corn would not be called green in Nov[embe]r when the fed[era]l troops returned. . . . We are satisfied from the testimony . . . that corn was taken in Nov[embe]r . . . & allow for 400 bushels at 70 cents. The charge for Green corn we reject."[24]

Conflicting evidence appears in the Summary Report of an Alabama claim wherein the claimant had testified that he had two fields of corn, of over forty acres each, near town. The claimant described having seen the corn taken by General Samuel R. Curtis' command, who were cutting it and feeding it to the stock. Another witness could identify the cornfields, but did not see the corn taken. Still another witness said there was no Indian corn there that year but a patch of sweet corn. In this instance the commissioners drew on evidence respecting his farm equipment to conclude that the petitioner had neither hands nor teams on the "home place" to put in and cultivate such a crop of corn. And if he had, they held, he should have had other witnesses than himself to the taking.[25]

[23] Testimony of Aaron Whitehead in the case of Susan V. Whitehead, Greene County, North Carolina [claimed $10,000, allowed $7,838 in 1875], C. of C. No. 844, GAO files.

[24] Summary Report in the case of Mary E. Jennings, guardian of her minor children, Fauquier County, Virginia [claimed $13,165.20, allowed $1,906.14 in 1875], C. of C. No. 18470, GAO files.

[25] Summary Report in the case of Thomas A. Hough, Woodruff County, Alabama [claimed $21,692.50, allowed $2,540 in 1876], C. of C. No. 11332, GAO files.

When they had satisfied themselves as to the quantity of goods involved, there remained the problem of determining the proper price. Usually it was less than the price named by the claimant. Standard prices were developed for the different areas and, if the price charged by the claimant was low, the established price was allowed. In one Tennessee claim, for example, the commissioners wrote: "For corn in cribs in Nov. '62 we have always allowed 50 cents per bus. & we do so here though the receipts estimate it at only 25 cents. Mr. Cossit is entitled to that fair price which in all other cases has been allowed claimants."[26] Further examination of this claim revealed that the plantation contained 1600 acres, of which about 1000 acres were cultivated. Witnesses had established the fact that there were about 600 acres in corn. Deducting what "was trodden down by the Army," the commissioners ruled that at least "400 acres had been gathered by the troops."[27]

In arriving at these standards, the claimant's figures were compared with prices in the area and in newspaper and market reports. The Quartermaster and Commissary departments gave frequent advice as to amounts paid by their officers in a given locality at a given time during the war. Thus, on October 17, 1871, the Quartermaster's Office reported that the "price of Mules at Nashville Tenn in 1862 was $115.00 in the second quarter, $120.00 in the third and $125 in the fourth quarter."[28] On November 14, the official returns from several officers on the lower Mississippi in March, 1863, were consulted for a proper price for fodder, hay, and corn, which was found to be 51 cents per bushel for corn, $20.00 per ton for fodder, and $27.00 per ton for hay in February of 1863. At Helena, Arkansas, in May of the same year, hay had advanced to $31.50 per ton. Meanwhile, at Baton Rouge, Louisiana, corn was selling at $1.00 per bushel and hay at $30.00 a ton.[29]

The Subsistence Office usually replied most precisely to requests from the commission. A letter of May 10, 1871, gave the fair contract price for fresh beef in western Virginia between September, 1861, and January 1, 1862, as 6¼ cents per pound net. The contract price of potatoes at Washington, D.C., was 60 cents per bushel in 1861, 72 cents in October, 1862, and 76 cents in 1863. The department added a note of warning about the proper prices to govern the payment for subsistence

---

[26] Summary Report in the case of Franklin D. Cossitt, Fayette County, Tennessee [claimed $31,620, allowed $14,102.77 in 1875], C. of C. No. 20459, GAO files.
[27] *Ibid.*
[28] Record Book D., "Letters Sent, Claims," 1871, Quartermaster General's Office, Record Group 92, War Department, National Archives, p. 547.
[29] *Ibid.*, Record Book C., 1871, p. 571. Reports cited were those of Captain H. B. Noble and Captain R. B. Hatch from Helena, and Captain F. B. Perkins from Baton Rouge, Louisiana.

stores. The "incidentally high prices—usually based upon the locally estimated value of confederate currency—at the various places where stores were taken," the note read, had seldom proved dependable. Instead "the prices governing at some healthy market approximately near and fairly supplied with similar articles, and where the currency of the United States was the medium for estimating values," was chosen as a guide. "This is a very important point," the letter added, "and it would be very serviceable to this Dept., if the Commissioners of Claims would determine and settle upon some judicious course in its determination."[30]

In addition to the spot prices, the Quartermaster and Commissary departments furnished printed lists of prices prevailing in those Northern centers which were the chief sources of supply for the Federal army. For the Quartermaster's Department, "prices paid under contract . . . for leading articles of quartermaster stores, each month, during the war of 1861–1865," show a wide price range for most items listed. For example, cavalry horses in 1862 brought $116.00 in Baltimore, $96.00 in Chicago, $109.42 in New York, and $114.37 in Washington, D.C. Corn was purchased in April of 1863 at $2.00 per hundred pounds in Baltimore, 92 cents in Chicago, $1.42 in Cincinnati, 91 cents in Davenport, and $1.60 in New York and Washington. The chief markets were Baltimore, Chicago, Cincinnati, Detroit, Indianapolis, Louisville, St. Louis, New York, and Washington.[31]

The prices listed on the claims for specific items likewise varied greatly. A spot survey of amounts claimed and allowed in Louisiana cases in 1863, for example, show the prices claimed per bushel of corn ranging from $1.00 to $1.50, and the amounts allowed by the commissioners from 75 cents to $1.00. Beef cattle were listed at such prices per head as $40.00, $17.00, $30.00, $60.00, $75.00, $20.00, and $35.00, and the corresponding allowances of the commissioners in amounts of $19.00, $12.50, $20.00, $20.00, $35.00, $25.00, $14.00, and $20.00. Prices allowed for bacon ran consistently at 10 cents a pound; for flour, $10.00 a barrel; and for hay and fodder, $20.00 a ton. Hogs valued by the claimants at 8 cents, 2 cents, 4 cents, and 10 cents per pound were

[30] Letter Book 95, Subsistence Office, United States Army, Record Group 192, National Archives, p. 341.

[31] "Statement showing prices paid under contract by the Quartermasters Department for leading articles of quartermaster stores, each month, during the war of 1861–1865, at points in the United States, mentioned," bound with "Claims for Quartermasters' Stores and Commissary Supplies of Loyal Citizens in Loyal States," Court of Claims library. The corresponding list of prices paid by the Subsistence Office for the same period was published in the Annual Report of the commissary general of subsistence for 1867.

paid for by the commissioners at an average price of 5 cents. The great-est variations in prices appeared, of course, in the case of livestock, especially horses and mules.

Fence rails, the commissioners wrote, had usually been taken by the army for use as fuel. As a result, the Quartermaster's Department had admitted them for allowance for their value as fuel rather than for their value as fence rails, at the rate of one hundred rails per cord and at a price usually of $3.00 per cord. Obviously the damage to the owner, the commissioners commented, was "more than this, for rails are worth more than wood, and without fences the farmer loses to a great extent the use of his land." Furthermore, since the country was being "denuded of wood," by reason of the occupation and action of the army, they recognized that he "had to pay an increased price to replace them."[32]

The summary report on Mary E. Jennings, of Fauquier County, Virginia, called for payment for a total of 42,640 fence rails and some 300 cords of wood cut from standing timber. In their review of the case, the board concluded that Pope's army had undoubtedly taken "a great many rails during their week's stay on the place," as they were in retreat after the battle of Cedar Mountain. And when Meade's army camped in the vicinity and on the farm between November, 1863, and May, 1864, they had "doubtless burned what rails Pope left." The fence rails were, therefore, allowed as losses.

But in regard to the standing wood consumed during these periods of occupation, it was "difficult to determine how many acres of wood were cut over for fuel." A surveyor's map, attached to the case, showed that about seventy-seven acres of woodland had been cut down, but it was "not proven that all was cut over by our troops." A witness for the claimant estimated that only fifty acres had been so denuded. The petition had charged $9,000 for the wood on seventy-seven acres. This amount, according to the report, was "grossly Exaggerated," since it would constitute a payment of $116 per acre "when wood, land & all" sold commonly in the region for from $30.00 to $40.00 per acre. They therefore allowed for the wood $1,200, and for the fence rails $859.20, the last item representing payment of the full amount claimed for "2864 Panels Fencing, 10 Panels, 28640 rails," for losses during Pope's occupation of the farm.[33]

---

[32] 1st Gen. Rept. of the C. of C., *House Misc. Docs.*, 42d Cong., 2d Sess., No. 16, pp. 6–7.
[33] Summary Report in the case of Mary E. Jennings, guardian of the minor children of J. L. Jennings, deceased, Fauquier County, Virginia [claimed $13,165.20, allowed $1,906.14 in 1875], C. of C. No. 18470, GAO files.

In the case of Josiah De Loach of Memphis, Tennessee, the military importance of woodlands had a bearing on the decision regarding a tract of timber "slashed down by the army to prevent Rebels from hiding in it," and subsequently used for fuel and fortifications. In this case the commissioners found that since it was "in evidence . . . that cleared land in that vicinity is worth about as much as timber land, we infer that timber for fuel was not very valuable," and their allowance of $1,500 for the $6,000 claimed for "Timber on 200 acres" seemed to them a "liberal compensation."[34]

Wood used in building fortifications, or as converted into lumber, presented similar compensation problems. Of some one hundred thousand feet of lumber appropriated in a mill yard belonging to Joseph H. Risley of Georgetown, South Carolina, the evidence showed that "some lumber was used for bunks, some boards and scantling were used for fences, and some for fuel." Admitting "all that is urged as to the scarcity & high price of lumber," the commissioners set a price of $25.00 per thousand feet as a "liberal allowance" for the wood used as lumber, and allowed the regular rates for fuel for the lumber which had been so used.[35]

Witnesses were adroitly cross-examined to establish the productive potential of each plantation or farm, as the best means of discounting inflated quantities and valuations. Benjamin T. Sellers, manager of Hobonny, a rice plantation in Beaufort, South Carolina, explained that the plantation contained eight hundred acres of rice land and six hundred acres of "upland," and the general practice was to cultivate "about six hundred acres of the rice land each year," and rest "about two hundred acres." Three hundred Negroes, of whom about one hundred were field hands, were required to operate the plantation. The average yield on the river was about forty bushels per acre, "although," Sellers added proudly, "I never made less than forty-five there in my life." The fifty acres of rice raised on Hobonny in 1862 and 1863 was "shipped to Charleston and sold." In 1864, the year the Union army arrived, five hundred acres yielded between fifteen thousand and twenty thousand bushels of rice.

Prompted by the commissioners, Sellers elaborated on the operation of a rice plantation. "Sometimes the 'volunteer' rice gets in with it," he said, "which is very injurious to the crops & we rest the land that

---

[34] Summary Report in the case of Josiah De Loach, Memphis, Tennessee [claimed $13,430, allowed $3,700 in 1872], C. of C. No. 8063, GAO files.

[35] Summary Report in the case of Joseph H. Risley, Georgetown County, South Carolina [claimed $235,865.50, allowed $879.89 in 1880], C. of C. No. 11844, GAO files.

year, & then it will bring sixty or seventy bushels to the acre. We plant it in potatoes, oats, or something to eradicate the 'volunteer' rice, & then the next year it yields largely." He added, "I never used an ounce of manure on rice in my life." All of the enriching of the land was accomplished "by irrigation & the overflow." As to the harvesting of the crop, Sellers explained, "we cut it in the fall with sickles; we then stack it in small stacks for a few days: we then take & put it in flats, and flat it up in the barn yard or general depositor for the crop, where it is put up into larger stacks, called ricks, & there it remains until it is threshed." When Commissioner Ferriss pressed him for details of the threshing, Sellers continued, "It is not necessary for it to remain in [the stacks] . . . at all: it is fit for threshing as soon as we get it out of the field. . . . The threshing machine is in the mill, which is filled with bins to put the rice into. After it is threshed the rice is dry and is put right into the bins." He estimated that between eight hundred and twelve hundred bushels a day could be threshed in this way.[36]

Cornelius Donato, of St. Landry Parish, Louisiana, explained to the Washington board the difference between the "creole cattle" described in his petition and Texas cattle which, he said, "are larger than our stock and they let them get old before they bring them to market, too." With the Creole strain, the custom was to sell them "on the place there from $20 to $22.50, and when we shipped them to New Orleans we got as high as $25 a head some $30 and some as high as $35." The Union army, however, had generally paid only $10.00 a head. Donato estimated that he had, when the army arrived, "about three thousand head by the quantity of calves with brands . . . beeves, cows & some young cattle two-year-olds, & a few one-year-olds." Questioned as to what he considered an adequate price for the 125 horses he had claimed, Donato could not reply so readily, since, as he explained, "we didn't generally sell horses much: we were raising them for our own use. We branded from a thousand to eleven hundred and fifty calves [a year] and we had to use that many. We never fed horses: we had to keep them on grass. . . . Sometimes a man will have to ride six or seven horses a day to catch and brand calves."[37]

---

[36] Testimony of Benjamin T. Sellers before the commission, Washington, March 15, 1872, in the case of Edward Middleton, Beaufort, South Carolina [claimed $14,703.00, allowed $12,240.00 in 1873], C. of C. No. 10531, GAO files. Middleton, a graduate of Annapolis, served with the United States Navy throughout the war; his brother, who sided with the Confederacy, remained at home and operated the plantation.

[37] Testimony of Cornelius Donato, Washington, Dec. 8, 1876, in his own case [claimed $33,125, allowed $15,750 in 1877], C. of C. No. 19763, GAO files.

Animals loved and prized by their owners were taken from the plantations, along with the grazing stock. These horses are described with affection and by name both by their owners and by the Negroes who were brought to Washington as witnesses. Mrs. Frederick W. Boyd, when asked to price the horses taken from her plantation in Carroll County, Louisiana, replied that Cinderella was "a blooded mare brought from Kentucky," for which her father had paid $1,200 in 1860. Kate, a saddle mule purchased during the war, had cost $250, and Mrs. Boyd added that "she was a fast mule." In the fall of 1863, after the capitulation of Vicksburg, five more family horses had been taken, including the carriage team, Julia and George, "large Kentucky horses," for which her mother had paid $1,500. "They were worth all that for cavalry horses," she added, "and Duke, the saddle horse, was worth $500."

The circumstances of the seizures were vivid in Mrs. Boyd's mind. "They took the mare from me when I was riding and took the mule from my servant," she said. "I was going to my mother's across the road." She appealed to General Walter Gresham, who had asked her to identify the men "and he would have them handled." General Gresham had assured her "they had no right to do it . . . they had done it without orders." When she had succeeded in identifying them, they were sent to Vicksburg for judgment, and the General then "sent a man from the barracks with me to search in every one of the corrals for them, they could not be found—neither of them." She had never seen any of them again, she concluded wistfully, except Julia and George; she saw them some time later in a detachment of Union cavalry.[38] The commissioners noted that the "horses were stolen—gross & shameful depredation," but added that they could not allow for the prized animals, since they were obviously not taken by subscribed army procedures. "A pair of very heavy & fine carriage horses taken for the Artillery," could, however, be admitted, since General George C. McKee, who appeared in Washington as a witness for Mrs. Boyd, had seen them "in the Artillery & says such horses then were allowed at from $160 to $200." Regarding this item, the recommendation concludes: "We allow $160. Each. None but very heavy & superior horses were taken for Artillery use."[39]

---

[38] Testimony of Mrs. Frederick W. Boyd, Washington, April 20, 1872, in her own case [claimed $30,958, allowed $7,800 in 1874], C. of C. No. 10551, GAO files.

[39] Summary Report in the case of Frederick W. Boyd, Carroll County, Louisiana, in *ibid*. General McKee appeared before the commission in Washington on April 20, 1872, and identified Mrs. Boyd, who had taken the oath of allegiance before him and whose loyalty was "never disputed." McKee, who was provost marshal at Natchez from July through October, 1863, had served as a major in the 11th Illinois Infantry, and was, when he testified before the commission, serving as a congressman from Vicksburg.

In Mrs. Boyd's case, an entry for two hundred tons of cotton seed, valued at $4,000, could not be allowed, since "cotton seed was of no use to the Army." Allowance could, however, be made for "60 pounds of coffee ($30.00); 50 pounds of Sugar ($10.00); I barrel of Flour ($10.00); and 30 lbs Soap, Salt &c ($10.00)," since they had been "taken from Mrs. Boyd's storeroom on 9. July '63 in Govt wagons & with the knowledge & under the directions of Genl Greshham to the Camp." Six dozen chickens and two dozen turkeys, which disappeared while the army was in camp, could not be admitted, but twenty-five hogs, valued at $100 by the claimant, were found to be "fat hogs taken off in Govt wagons on 9 July '63," and were consequently allowed at $4.00 per head.

For a total of 37,500 bushels of corn charged at $10,000, only $6,000 was allowed, since evidence showed that part of the corn had been raised on the Carondolet plantation, which belonged to Mrs. Boyd's brother, Otey Railey, "who was in the rebel Army." The rest of the corn was admitted, however, on the basis of "testimony of Genl Clark & Capt. Jones (who were in the Q^r H^r Dept.) & had the business of furnishing Genl McPherson with forage." The examination before the commission revealed that about five hundred acres had been planted in corn, which the army "began to take" in February or March of 1863. Allowing for what was used on the plantation and otherwise, the commissioners estimated that "at least ⅔ds of the Crop was taken for Army use," and added that "most of it was gathered from the fields— some from a large corn crib." Summing up the evidence for this item, the report concluded:

Mr. Harris, whose farm joined this plant^n estimates the corn on both the Railey plant^{as} at from 40,000 to 50,000 bus.—Henry Bells a colored man who had charge of the hands gathering the corn says there were sometimes 15 or 20 wagons drawing away the Corn—they hauled it to the forts 2 miles off—& were so employed 2 or 3 weeks—Some of the witnesses say that 600 acres were planted. Genl Clark & Capt. Jones speak of the plantations as being very rich & fertile & in excellent condition. We think that probably twelve thousand bushels of corn were taken from the Raleigh plantation—and that the value of corn, as most of it was in the field standing, was about 50 cents per bus. at that point & time—We allow for the corn $6000.00.[40]

The requirement that all items must have been furnished for "army use" was rigidly adhered to and disqualified innumerable claims where the loyalty of the claimant was not at issue. The petition filed by Dr. Webster M. Raines, "a physician of the botanic or Thomsonian school"

---

[40] *Ibid.*

who had "a large laboratory for the preparation of medicines," illustrates the extensive aid given sick, wounded, and imprisoned soldiers by many Unionists whose supplies did not meet the property tests prescribed by Congress. It reads:

Furnishing eleven United States officers with provisions four months, and twelve mattresses	$1,500.00
Taking care of twenty-three United States officers thirty-five days, and furnishing provisions for same	800.00
Boarding John Bains, a United States soldier, six months	180.00
One suit clothes furnished John Bains	100.00
Confederate money furnished John Bains	175.00
Paid out in confederate funds to save John Bains from being shot	5,570.00
Boarding John Bains till close of war	840.00
Board of thirty United States officers and soldiers three months, & furnishing same with blankets and clothing	1,500.00
Furnishing provisions and clothing at different times to fifteen hundred escaped prisoners	5,000.00
2 cases clothing and provisions furnished Andersonville prisoners	8,000.00
Supplies furnished three brigadier generals, thirty-five colonels, and nine majors, United States Army	10,000.00
Total	$33,665.00

The commissioners were impressed with the services performed by Dr. Raines, who "did all he could, often at great peril of his life, to help escaping prisoners . . . and to provide medicines, clothing, and comforts to Union prisoners . . . in the confederate hospital at Macon." But precisely because they were "charities, kind and humane acts" voluntarily rendered, they could not be "regarded as furnishing stores or supplies for the use of the Army . . . for which this act of Congress was . . . enacted."[41]

Although 82 per cent of the claims filed for over $10,000 represented losses from Southern plantations, as has already been noted, these larger claims also furnished a side light on the increase in Southern manufacturing which began to make itself felt during the decade preceding the war. The demands of the war itself tended to stimulate interest in manufacturing, especially of the much needed ordnance, and the war also checked the migration of skilled technicians and labor from the North to the South. Seacoast and siege guns were made at the Tredegar Iron Works at Richmond, and armories at Richmond, Fayetteville, and Asheville produced about twenty-eight thousand small

---

[41] Summary Report in the case of Webster M. Raines, of Washington, District of Columbia, for property taken at Macon, State of Georgia [claimed $33,665, disallowed in 1873], C. of C. No. 11744, Justice Department, National Archives.

arms during 1863.[42] From Alabama, Governor John G. Shorter wrote enthusiastically to Richmond of the development in his state which forecast the industrial empire in Alabama today.[43]

Although the rules of the commissioners did not admit the claims of corporations, the commissioners were called upon, from time to time, to distinguish between property claimed by individuals and property owned by corporations. In such cases, they assembled available evidence and reported on it in some detail to Congress, because, as they wrote regarding the claim of the Mount Savage Iron Company, "We have thought proper to make this statement . . . in case Congress was disposed to compensate the claimant. The claim being made by a corporation, we have no jurisdiction in the premises. It is therefore disallowed."[44]

Similarly, a claim for $85,145 worth of coal belonging to the firm of McCloskey, Cosgrove & Co., of Pittsburgh and New Orleans, was disallowed on the ground that the firm had no title to the property when it was taken by the army. This coal, it may be briefly said, was shipped from Pittsburgh "on or about the 20th of April, 1861," after Louisiana had seceded and after Lincoln's proclamation of April 15, 1861, "in order to take advantage of the spring rise in the water of the Ohio, without which coal-laden barges could not get over the shallows and sand-bars." James McCloskey, the New Orleans partner, was described as "an active rebel," whereas John S. Cosgrove and John McCloskey, in Pittsburgh, were "truly loyal . . . active and liberal in their voluntary contributions to the Union cause." The coal was first captured by the Confederates in November, 1861, but was subsequently released, "doubtless by the activity and influence of James McCloskey," the commissioners judged. Finally, in December, 1862, it was taken by the Federal authorities. The final disallowance of the claim centered about the fact that, on October 29, 1863, the firm having failed, the rights of the New Orleans members were assigned to the reorganized Pittsburgh firm and "such assignment of the claim as against the United States was wholly void." The commissioners concluded their

---

[42] *Official Records*, Series IV, Vol. III, p. 733; Vol. IV, pp. 956–957.

[43] *Official Records*, Series I, Vol. LII, Pt. 2, pp. 480–481.

[44] See claim of the Mount Savage Iron Company [claimed $18,018.00, disallowed in 1874], C. of C. No. 21691, in Justice Department, National Archives. When the claim was filed, the corporation had been dissolved, its assets having passed into the hands of Franklin N. Delano and John A. Graham, both of New York and both directors of the original company. The president and directors were, the commissioners pointed out, "both loyal and solvent." Delano was one of the founders of the Union League Club of New York City, and Graham was "one of the parties who originally built the Monitor, & he built several other iron clads."

report: "We have repeatedly decided that such assignees were not entitled to allowance for claims so assigned; that it was our duty to regard such assignments as void as against the United States. We cannot depart from these our decisions in this case."[45]

The skilled artisans or tradesmen from the North who had migrated to the South during the 'fifties seldom received allowances as Southern Unionists, since they had usually become engaged in the ordnance or munitions industries during the war, and were thus considered to have assisted the Confederate cause. Daniel B. Ladd, of Fulton County, Georgia, is typical of such men. Born in Ohio, he had come to the South in 1850, selling lightning rods. In the course of a few years he had acquired coal mines and boats for transporting coal "on the Tennessee River between Shellmound and Whiteside." During the war these boats had assisted in the escape of Union men, and when the Federal army set out from Nashville for Atlanta, Ladd had provided maps of the roads and the distance, which had rendered such valuable service that "General Garfield has those papers now." But the commissioners rejected his claim, on the basis of his coal mining operations in 1861. "He must have known from the situation of the mines and the necessities of the Confederate Government and the requirements of that service," they reasoned, "that the working, enlargement and development of those mines would inure to the benefit of the Confederacy, and he put himself into a position at that time where it would become imperative for him to render aid."[46]

The problem of determining legal ownership occurred in a simpler form in the case of C. T. Weston, who had moved to Front Royal, Virginia, from Pennsylvania in 1853 and was, during the war, the proprietor of a large flour mill there. His property was confiscated at first by Confederate and then by Federal authorities, and finally, in 1864, the mill itself was burned by the Federal troops. Since this loss, estimated by the owner at $44,163, was due to destruction, it was not allowed. The question of ownership arose, however, not in connection with the mill but over the proper title to some three thousand bushels of wheat held in the mill. During the war it had become a custom, because of the inflated currency, for farmers to deposit five bushels of sound wheat at the mill for which they would receive one barrel of

---

[45] Summary Report in the claim of Rhodes & Bagley, assignees of McCloskey, Cosgrove & Co., of New Orleans, Orleans Parish, Louisiana [claimed $85,145, disallowed in 1873], C. of C. No. 412, Justice Department, National Archives.

[46] Summary Report in the claim of Daniel B. Ladd, Fulton County, Georgia [claimed $15,710, disallowed in 1876], C. of C. No. 22004, Justice Department, National Archives.

flour in return. The problem as it was seen by the commissioners, therefore, was to determine whether the wheat taken from the mill by the Federal soldiers belonged to Weston or to the farmers who had deposited it with him. The claim was finally disallowed, without a final decision on the division of the wheat, since the commissioners decided that most of it had disappeared through looting by individual soldiers who "rolled off the barrels and traded them for vegetables and eggs."[47]

The substitution of a system of commodity exchange for transactions which would normally involve currency, appears frequently in the records. Even confirmed Unionists were often forced to convert produce into Confederate bonds, which sometimes caused the commission to disallow their claim. The case of Priscilla W. Burwell brought to light a use of commodities in lieu of cash which was a maze of complications. Mrs. Burwell asked reimbursement for "135 Hogsheads of fine sugar 100 lbs each, at 25 per lbs.," and "14 boxes Sugar 400 lbs each at 25 per lb.," for a total of $35,150. The loyalty of her husband, Armistead Burwell of Vicksburg, was "fully proved," as was his share of ownership in the firm of Cobb, Manlove and Company of that city.[48] Manlove, the leading and active partner of the firm, was a confirmed Confederate. In the spring of 1861, Burwell, because of his openly avowed Unionism, was forced to leave Vicksburg. At the time, the firm owed him $30,000, and he directed that the funds be remitted to him at St. Louis. Meanwhile Manlove, having nothing but Confederate money, bought sugar in an amount sufficient to cover the debt, with the purpose of shipping it to St. Louis where Burwell could convert it into the cash which would liquidate the debt. But before it could reach St. Louis, the sugar was appropriated by Federal troops.

The commissioners at first disallowed the claim, holding that without more definite evidence that the sugar actually belonged to Burwell rather than to Manlove, the amount could not be granted. Ownership, by this ruling, rested on the fine point of whether Burwell knew, when the sugar was captured, that it was his property. Testimony was brought forward to show that an agent of the Manlove firm had, in advance of shipment, crossed the Union lines and proceeded to St. Louis, bringing "in his shoe a bit of paper from Manlove on which these words were written, 'Sugar stored for you.'" But the paper had been lost.

By March of 1879, however, Congress referred the claim back to the commission for further investigation and report. Depositions filed

---

[47] Summary Report in the case of C. T. Weston, Warren County, Virginia [claimed $58,767.40, disallowed in 1875], C. of C. No. 2255, Justice Department, National Archives.

[48] See chap. xi for an account of the revealing letter which Burwell wrote to Lincoln.

from Duff Green, C. A. Manlove, and the claimant's son, Charles B. Burwell, established the fact that the sugar had been stored in Burwell's name. On reconsidering the case, but still without the actual evidence previously required, the commissioners accepted the circumstantial reports and ruled that, since Burwell could not communicate with Vicksburg and could not go there or even "send and take the Sugar," his acceptance of the Manlove offer might be assumed.[49]

The quantity of supplies found by the Union army indicates that estimates of the productive capacity of the Southern states may have been underestimated. This contention is supported by the files of the commission and by contemporary accounts. As early as 1861, governors, state legislatures, and President Davis requested that foodstuffs which had customarily been shipped in from the North be raised at home, thus building self-sufficiency.[50] As the war progressed, however, the army and urban dwellers began to suffer for want of food; this is shown by notations which appeared in army records as early as October, 1862.[51] In an agrarian economy such as that of the South, these shortages were localized. The lower South, for example, where the land was easily tillable and two or three crops of vegetables could be produced within a year, never suffered from inflation and short supplies as seriously as did the Atlantic seaboard states.

As late as January, 1864, General D. H. Maury wrote to General Polk that plenty of meat was being cured in Alabama.[52] In the same year, General J. K. Jackson estimated that Florida would produce annually twenty-five thousand head of cattle (ten million pounds); one million pounds of bacon; and one thousand hogsheads of sugar, fruit, and other provisions.[53] And in December, 1864, General Lucius B. Northrop of the Confederate Bureau of Subsistence reported to Secretary James A. Seddon that there had been no complaint of lack of subsistence in the armies outside Virginia; "the territories from which

---

[49] Summary Report in the case of Priscilla W. Burwell, executor, Vicksburg, Mississippi [claimed $35,150, allowed $11,248 in 1879], C. of C. No. 111, GAO files.

[50] In his message to the Confederate Congress of November 18, 1861, Davis outlined the policy designed to build self-sufficiency within the Confederate states while using the cotton supply to hasten recognition abroad, since, he noted, "for every laborer who is diverted from the culture of cotton in the South, perhaps four times as many elsewhere . . . will be forced also to change their occupation." See Richardson, *Messages and Papers of the Confederacy* (Washington, 1905), I, 143. For the entire message see *ibid.*, pp. 136–144, and for earlier emphasis of the importance of abundant grain crops see *ibid.*, pp. 81, 123, and *Official Records*, Series IV, Vol. II, pp. 476, 700.

[51] *Official Records*, Series I, Vol. XIX, Pt. II, p. 605; Vol. XXV, Pt. II, p. 730; Vol. XXXII, Pt. 3, p. 679.

[52] *Ibid.*, Series I, Vol. XXXII, Pt. 2, p. 552.

[53] *Ibid.*, Series I, Vol. XXXV, Pt. 2, p. 606.

they draw have been undesolated by the enemy." Meanwhile, in Richmond there were only twenty-five days' rations for one hundred thousand men.[54] The effect of invasion was later apparent in Mississippi; here there was an abundant supply until 1864, but with the removal of slaves and the impressment of horses and mules by the Union army, the state's resources were rapidly exhausted.[55]

When Sherman left Chattanooga for Atlanta late in the war, Governor Joseph E. Brown, in a series of appeals, called upon all Georgians to remove all provisions and Negroes, burn all bridges, and block all roads.[56] But in spite of these admonitions, Sherman wrote to his wife from Savannah, "we came right along living on turkeys, chickens, pigs, bringing our wagons loaded as we started with bread, etc."[57] Governor Zebulon Vance of North Carolina regarded Sherman's invasion as evidence of "the utter demoralization of the people." With a base line of communication of 500 miles "in Sherman's rear, through our own country, not a bridge has been burned, not a car thrown from its track, nor a man shot by the people whose country he has desolated." This circumstance demonstrated, he said, "what I have always believed, that *the great popular heart* is not now, and never has been in this war! It was a revolution of the *Politicians,* not the *People.*"[58] And on March 26, 1865, the Richmond *Examiner* protested indignantly that "this is a beautiful commentary upon the liberality and policy of our people—when General Lee calls for provisions to feed his army, we are told that this man and that have given them all, but when the Yankee raiders come along, they find meat-houses and corn cribs or cellars filled with abundance."[59]

Hoarding, speculation, transportation difficulties, and illicit trade with the Federal government, all doubtless contributed to the final capitulation of the Confederacy.[60] The propertied Unionists had a hand in this economic sabotage, and the vast reservoir of supplies disclosed to the Court of Claims and the commissioners of claims shows the economic resistance of the loyalists as well as the administrative deficiencies of the Davis government.

---

[54] *Ibid.*, Series IV, Vol. III, pp. 931–932.
[55] *Publications of the Mississippi Historical Society,* Centenary Series, VII, 204.
[56] *Official Records,* Series I, Vol. LII, Pt. 2, pp. 673–674.
[57] M. A. De Wolfe Howe, *The Home Letters of General Sherman* (New York, 1909), p. 316. The letter was dated in Savannah on December 16, 1864.
[58] Quoted in Cornelia Phillips Spencer, *The Last Ninety Days of the War in North Carolina* (New York, 1866), pp. 27–28.
[59] "Plenty of Provision," in the Richmond *Daily Examiner,* March 24, 1865.
[60] James W. Silver, "Propaganda in the Confederacy," *Journal of Southern History,* XI (Nov., 1945), 487. The impact of wartime shortages on the Confederate population is treated by Mary Elizabeth Massey in her study, *Ersatz in the Confederacy* (Columbia, 1952).

CHAPTER VIII

REFINEMENTS AND RESTRICTIONS
OF POLICY

IN ADDITION to the paramount problems of loyalty and property, the commissioners had to formulate policies for the claims of aliens and corporations; to decide on the eligibility of minors or of disloyal heirs of loyal claimants; to classify tobacco and cotton when they had occasionally been used as quartermaster stores; and to deal with matters of rent and bankruptcy.

The use of the word "citizens" in the act of March 3, 1871, led to a ruling which was outlined on the first page of the first Report to Congress. By this interpretation, aliens "domiciled here," but not naturalized, were excluded from the jurisdiction of the board. Peter Klaine, a subject of France living in Franklin County, Arkansas, whose loyalty to the Union was clearly shown, served as a test case. The commissioners ruled that since he "never was naturalized, and never took any steps toward naturalization; [and] admits that he . . . owns allegiance to France, though domiciled in this country," his claim was not admissible for review or allowance.[1] By a strict construction of the word "citizen," they could decide that when a claimant "was an alien when the claim accrued, his naturalization since the war does not remove his disability."[2]

This ruling followed the will of Congress rather than the more liberal policy of the Court of Claims and the Supreme Court. In the case of *Byrnes* v. *United States*, the Court of Claims held, in its term of 1867–68, that a resident alien filing a claim under the Captured and Abandoned Property acts was not required "to establish positive sympathy or loyalty, but simply to prove that 'he has never given any aid or comfort' to the rebellion."[3] Only a few months later, however, Congress

---

[1] Summary Report in the case of Peter Klaine, Franklin County, Arkansas [claimed $50,910, disallowed in 1872], C. of C. No. 482, Justice Department, National Archives. Klaine had previously presented his claim through the State Department and the minister of France, to the House of Representatives, and to the War Department. In 1907 the case was still unsettled when it reappeared before the Court of Claims where, on December 19, 1913, it was dismissed for nonprosecution.

[2] 1st Gen. Rept. of C. of C., *House Misc. Docs.*, 42d Cong., 2d Sess., No. 16, pp. 1–2.

[3] Ct. Clms. 195. In the case of *Waltjen* v. *United States*, decided in the same year, the court further held that "a resident alien who proves to the satisfaction of the court his complete neutrality during the rebellion may recover for cotton captured." See *ibid.*, p. 238. In the case of *Carlisle & Henderson* v. *United States*, the court ruled that "the well-established rule that an alien while domiciled in a country owes to it a local and temporary allegiance, which continues during the period of his residence, in return for the protection he receives; and that, for a breach of this

in the act of July 27, 1868, specified that aliens could not maintain suits against the United States unless their own governments accorded corresponding rights to citizens of the United States.⁴ But the court maintained its ground and again in 1869 reaffirmed its previous stand by holding that "a naturalized citizen was, at the time of the passage of the act of July 27, 1868, prohibiting suits by aliens under the Abandoned or Captured Property Acts, entitled to sue in the Court of Claims."⁵

Since their ruling represented a departure from legal precedent, the commissioners explained their position at some length. Loyalty during the war, they reasoned, could not reasonably be interpreted as meaning less than that relationship from which the government might have required military service. And since the United States had "uniformly directed" that foreigners be discharged from the service if they claimed exemption on that ground, it followed that loyalty was not required of a foreigner. Further, the government had held that an alien in the South was doing his whole duty if he remained strictly neutral. But according to the commissioners' rules respecting loyalty, neutrality during the war on the part of any citizen did not constitute loyalty.

This decision was designed to limit their own jurisdiction rather than to establish a legal precedent, for the commissioners called attention to the fact that foreigners "domiciled and remaining here during the war" had no right to require their own governments to interfere on their behalf for losses sustained as a result of the war. But in the view of the law of domicile, and the well-established policy of Congress which held that neutrality did not constitute loyalty, they con-

---

temporary allegiance, he may be punished for treason, extends to aliens who were domiciled during the rebellion within the insurrectionary district and within the confederate lines." See 8 Ct. Clms. 153. The Supreme Court subsequently affirmed this ruling (16 Wallace 147).

⁴ 15 *U.S. Stat. at L.*, 243. In the case of *Brown* v. *United States*, decided on May 22, 1871, the Court of Claims had taken occasion to comment on the results of the qualification provided in this act, which applied to the policy of foreign governments toward citizens of the United States. The cases heard before them, the justices revealed, had yielded some surprising results, especially to those "popular orators and writers [who] have impressed upon the public mind the belief that in this republic of ours private rights receive unequalled protection from the Government. . . . The laws of other nations have been produced and proved in this court, and the mortifying fact is judicially established that the Government of the United States holds itself, of nearly all governments, the least amenable to the law." See 5 Ct. Clms. 271.

⁵ 4 Ct. Clms. 395. See also in *ibid.*, p. 471, the case of *Mintz* v. *United States*, in which the court held that "a claimant naturalized after bringing his action, and before the passage of the act of 1868, is not affected by its provisions, and may maintain an action in the Court of Claims."

cluded: "We think Congress intended to reserve exclusively to itself the consideration of the rights of foreigners to compensation."[6] In this group of cases which they subsequently reported to Congress as beyond their jurisdiction, the commissioners revealed that they were influenced by the fact that an alien within the Confederacy had been exempt from military service and therefore his loyalty or disloyalty was not determinable.[7]

Another restriction of jurisdiction outlined in the first Annual Report ruled out all cases which asked allowance for *"rent* and the use of real estate," on the ground that they did not come under the definition of the term "quartermasters' supplies." In this ruling, the commissioners followed precedents which had been established both by the Quartermaster Department and by the courts. But there were earlier precedents, as well, for admitting them. Claims for rents arising in Tennessee during the war had been favorably considered up to June 12, 1865, when Stanton made what came to be known as the "Murfreesborough decision." The secretary of war upheld the opinion of the quartermaster general that since "Murfreesborough was a hostile town captured by our troops from an enemy who did not surrender on terms, but was driven out by force of arms," everything in the city was a prize of war. Rent claimed for buildings occupied "for shelter and troops, and for sick and wounded soldiers" could not, therefore, be allowed after 1865.[8]

New Orleans had been another exception. When the city was first occupied, general army policy classed the rent of buildings in captured towns as not allowable, by the same reasoning which disallowed claims for destruction, by the march or occupation of troops, of property, fences, and crops in hostile districts.[9] But after the President's proclamation of April 2, 1863, when the New Orleans district was held to be outside the insurrectionary region, claims for rent based on certified accounts issued on the authority of accounting officers of the Treasury had been paid up to August 20, 1866, the official date of the end of the war. On February 21, 1867, however, Congress had passed

<hr>

[6] 1st Gen. Rept. of C. of C., *House Misc. Docs.*, 42d Cong., 2d Sess., No. 16, p. 2.

[7] In the case of Bernardo Garcia, a resident of Atlanta, the commissioners pointed out that he was exempt from military duty in the Confederacy because he professed to be a Spanish citizen. See Summary Report in the case of Bernardo Garcia, Atlanta, Georgia [claimed $17,035, disallowed in 1874], C. of C. No. 5715, Justice Department, National Archives.

[8] "Memorandum for government officers charged with the consideration of claims from hostile districts," from M. C. Meigs, quartermaster general, dated Washington, D.C., June 12, 1865, reproduced in part in *House Rept. No. 134*, 43d Cong., 2d Sess., p. 253.

[9] *Ibid.*, p. 250.

another in its series of prohibitory acts, in this case forbidding "the settlement of any claim for the occupation or injury to real estate when such claim originated during the war for the suppression of the southern rebellion in a State or part of a State declared in insurrection."[10] The Supreme Court, in 1869, upheld the legality of this principle, where no valid contract existed, in the case of *Filor* v. *United States.*[11]

The Filor case, which was subsequently placed before the Southern Claims Commission, had been something of a test case with respect to rent allowances, again because the loyalty of the petitioner was never in question. James Filor, a resident of New York, had first filed his claim for rent of a wharf in Key West, Florida, leased from his agent by Federal officers. In 1866, the judge advocate general refused to pay the rent since the wharf had been sold to Filor by a Confederate: a transaction which, he maintained, merely put the wharf into the hands of loyal men. The lease itself was held to be invalid since it was not approved by the quartermaster general. Furthermore, the rent bargained for ($6,000 a year) was called excessive.[12] In 1867, the Court of Claims sustained this opinion and recommended disallowance both because rent was involved and because the Federal officers who signed the lease were held to be lacking in authority so to implicate the government.[13] The Supreme Court, in 1869, upheld this decision, holding further that "an 'appropriation' of real property by the army under the act of 1864 extends to all cases where the occupancy is not in pursuance of a *valid* contract. . . . If the petitioners are entitled to compensation for the use of the property," the Court concluded, "they must seek it from Congress."[14] When the Filor case appeared before the commissioners, they could cite the precedent of the courts, and the Filor case was accordingly returned to its attorney without investigation.[15]

In their ruling on rent, the commissioners were influenced by the "abundant and decisive" opinions of the judge advocate general. Moreover, the "uniform usage" of the Quartermaster Department in considering rent claims from the North which had been filed with them

---

[10] 14 *U.S. Stat. at L.,* 397.
[11] 9 Wallace 45.
[12] See case of the estate of James Filor, William Pinckney, and William Curry, Court of Claims, Congressional No. 11135, Justice Department, National Archives.
[13] 3 Ct. Clms. 25.
[14] 9 Wallace 45.
[15] Case of Emily J. Filor and William Pinckney, New York City and Key West, Florida [claimed $36,000, disallowed in 1876], C. of C. No. 706, Justice Department, National Archives.

under the act of July 4, 1864, had been to reject them. "We think this usage must have been well known to Congress," President Aldis con-cluded. "However just claims for rent and the occupation of land may be, if it had been intended to submit them to this board, they would have been named in express words in the act. Claims of loyal citizens at the North and the South must stand on the same basis, and be governed by the same rules of construction."[16]

The use of the word "citizens" in the enabling act formed the basis for a third restrictive ruling, which has interesting implications for the legal arguments which have grown out of the "due process" clause. Forty-three churches, lodges, colleges, and corporations, or quasi corporations, had prepared claims for damages incurred when their buildings were used as hospitals or their property appropriated by the army. But instead of ruling that these claims were beyond their jurisdiction because stores and supplies were not usually involved and neither rent nor damage could be allowed, the commissioners held that such groups, as corporations, were not "citizens."

This view was well expressed in the Summary Report on the claim of Edward Fitzgerald, the Catholic Bishop of Arkansas, wherein the commissioners held that the church corporation, rather than the bishop, was the party beneficially interested in the claim for timber and fence rails. "We have decided in numerous cases," the commis-sioners wrote, "that we will not consider and report on claims filed by corporations or associations, for the reason that the law limits the claims to 'citizens' whose loyalty or disloyalty may be established by evidence. We hold that it does not include church corporations or re-ligious associations of any kind or character."[17] Again, in a similar report involving the Indiana Methodist Church of Portsmouth, Vir-ginia, they stated simply, and without any investigation, that "a corporation has no standing before this commission. It can not prove 'loyalty' and is not a 'citizen.' The claim is therefore disallowed."[18]

Here the commissioners seem to have arrived at an interpretation of a single word in the act of March 3, 1871, which ran counter to the prevailing philosophy of both the courts and Congress but which, at the same time, carried out Congress' intent to limit payment of claims. The Court of Claims ruled in 1870 that "proof by a corporation that

---

[16] 1st Gen. Rept. of C. of C., *House Misc. Docs.*, 42d Cong., 2d Sess., No. 16, p. 4.
[17] Summary Report in the claim of Bishop Edward Fitzgerald, Little Rock, Pulaski County, Arkansas [claimed $17,385, disallowed in 1873], C. of C. No. 12037, Justice Department, National Archives.
[18] Claim of the Indiana Methodist Church, Portsmouth, Virginia, [claimed $500, disallowed in 1873], C. of C. No. 1223, Justice Department, National Archives.

it was incorporated for a lawful purpose, and never applied any of its funds in aid of the rebellion, sufficiently shows its loyalty."[19] In the view of Congress, the doctrine of "over-ruling necessity" sometimes produced times and circumstances when it became the "right and duty of the Government to seize and occupy the property of corporations to aid in suppressing the rebellion and in preserving the territorial integrity of the nation and the unity of its people." At such times, corporations, like citizens, could be held to be within a zone of war and, since property was involved, could be suspected of making their own contributions toward the "sinews of war."

In a report issued by the Committee on Claims in Congress in 1875, this reasoning is carefully substantiated. The report quotes Cornelius van Bynkershoek in holding that "a corporation, like a tree, is known by its fruits. A corporation which encouraged men to make war—to convert pruning hooks into spears, and plowshares into swords—is by no means loyal." In taking this stand, the committee recognized that there was a time when it was held that a corporation could not commit a trespass, but pointed out that "that doctrine has long since been exploded. A corporation acts by its agents. Their authorized acts within the scope of the corporate authority are the acts of the corporation. The maxim applies *qui facit per alium facit per se*. A corporation may be guilty of disloyalty."[20] By the same reasoning, corporations chartered by foreign governments or by authority of the seceded states could claim no protection beyond that accorded to other enemy property, since the property, because of its location, could be classified as a means of giving strength to the rebellion.[21]

The numerous claims filed with the commission on behalf of churches and philanthropic or educational institutions were the subject for debate in Congress, especially as they were entitled to certain immunities under conditions of war. General Order No. 100 specified that property belonging "to churches, or hospitals, or other establishments of an exclusively charitable character, to establishments of education, or foundations for the promotion of knowledge . . . " could

[19] *Hebrew Congregation* v. *United States*, 6 Ct. Clms. 241. The Supreme Court subsequently held that "corporations created in the Southern States before or during the war of 1861, may sue under the Abandoned or Captured Property Act, and make proof that they never gave aid and comfort to the enemy. The act makes no distinction between natural and artificial persons." *United States* v. *Home Insurance Company*, 22 Wallace 99. See also 10 Ct. Clms. 145 for that court's similar ruling on the same case.

[20] *House Report No. 134*, 43d Cong., 2d Sess., pp. 244–245 n.

[21] *Ibid.* See also *Planters' Bank* v. *Union Bank*, 16 Wallace 483, and *House Rept. No. 777*, 43d Cong., 1st Sess., for the claims of book agents of the Methodist Episcopal Church South.

not be appropriated or sequestered by the victorious army, as could public money and public movable property, but they could be "taxed or used when the public service may require it."[22] In theory, at least, only urgent necessity was held to justify such use. But the number and variety of claims filed by institutions offered ample evidence that immunities had not always applied.

On January 12, 1869, Senator Charles Sumner had made a plea on behalf of educational institutions. "Even amid the struggles of the [Revolutionary] war, as early as 1779, the Reverend Dr. Witherspoon was allowed $19,040 for repairs of the college at Princeton damaged by the troops." Similar allowances were made to an academy in Wilmington, Delaware, and to a college in Rhode Island, on the recommendation of "Mr. Hamilton while Secretary of the Treasury, as 'affecting the interests of literature.' " On this account, Sumner concluded, "they were treated as exceptional."[23] But in similar cases Congress had decided that the decisive question was whether or not the school was "loyal."

The College of William and Mary, for example, sought indemnity for the destruction of buildings and property by "disorderly soldiers of the United States during the late rebellion," but Congress denied the claim.[24] A bill making an allowance for damages to the buildings of East Tennessee University, used for occupation by United States troops, was vetoed by Grant on January 30, 1873,[25] but an almost identical claim from Kentucky University was allowed on January 17, 1871,[26] largely because this university was situated in loyal territory. The decision regarding the two Southern schools was finally made on the ground that such institutions were a source of strength to the Confederacy, since they were engaged in inculcating the sentiment of rebellion. To withdraw them from "a work so destructive of public interests," could, therefore, be deemed a "military necessity."

The decision on bankruptcy, which affected a larger group of persons than any of the above rulings, was not announced until 1874. The commission held that claimants who had availed themselves of

[22] Section II, No. 34, General Orders No. 100; *House Exec. Docs. No. 100*, 43d Cong., 1st Sess.

[23] Charles Sumner in *Cong. Globe*, 40th Cong., 3d Sess. (Jan. 12, 1869), p. 301.

[24] For House proceedings and debates, see *Cong. Globe*, 42d Cong., 2d Sess. (Feb. 2, 1872), pp. 784–785, 940–943, 1190–1195.

[25] For Senate proceedings see *Cong. Globe*, 42d Cong., 2d Sess. (April 9, 1872), p. 2288; and House proceedings in *ibid.*, 42d Cong., 3d Sess. (Jan. 18, 1873), p. 697.

[26] See Senate proceedings, *Cong. Globe*, 41st Cong., 2d Sess. (May 2, 1870), pp. 3145, 5538; and House proceedings in *ibid.*, p. 678. The allowance was approved January 17, 1871. 16 *U.S. Stat. at L.*, 687.

the bankrupt law surrendered all rights to any allowance. Attorneys in such cases argued strenuously that at the time of action in bankruptcy the claim could by no reasoning be considered an asset, since there was then no tribunal before which it could be adjudicated or enforced and no true liability on the part of the government to pay the claim. It followed, therefore, that since the right to the claim did not exist as an asset subject to assignment, it could not pass to the assignees in bankruptcy. Instead, the attorneys insisted, the dormant claim would fall under the classification of "mere naked, intangible rights, invested with no attributes of property, and not the subject of assignment or transfer."[27]

But the commissioners ruled that the fourteenth section of the bankrupt law had clearly specified that the property to which an assignee is entitled includes not only all real and personal property and choses in action, but "all rights in equity." The act of March 3, 1871, they said, had not created the claims. Such claims had been paid at the beginning of the war, and it had required affirmative legislation to "suspend" their payment. The establishment of the commission had, therefore, merely recognized the claims and provided a tribunal for their adjudication and settlement. Thus, by a backhanded acknowledgment that the act of July 4, 1864, was in effect an outright repudiation by Congress of an existing obligation, the commissioners ruled out the claims of any Southerners who had been forced to undergo bankruptcy while they were waiting for the claim to be acknowledged. Finally, in overruling the lawyers' contention that assignment or transfer of the claims could not be part of the bankruptcy action, they referred to an established practice of allowing claims filed by loyal heirs of loyal claimants. "If this is true, we have erred in recommending payments to heirs and legatees," the commissioners wrote. "If they pass by will, then assuredly they pass in bankruptcy."[28]

This declaration placed hundreds of claims outside the jurisdiction of the commission. The claim of Washington G. Campbell, of Memphis, Tennessee, is illustrative. The agent assigned to investigate this case uncovered Campbell's certificate of bankruptcy, dated December 7, 1867, and filed in the District Court of the United States for the District of West Tennessee. The court record also showed that Campbell was adjudged a bankrupt on November 27, 1868, and discharged from bankruptcy on February 21, 1872. "By these proceedings," the

[27] 4th Gen. Rept. of C. of C., *House Misc. Docs.*, 43d Cong., 2d Sess., No. 18, Pt. 2, p. 4.
[28] *Ibid.*

commissioners held, "it will be perceived that Mr. Campbell's claim against the Government . . . passed to his assignee in bankruptcy, and was invested in that officer at the time his claim was filed April 15, 1871, and the claimant has never been reinvested with the title or ownership of the claim."

Campbell had, moreover, produced proofs in an affidavit that no one other than he had any interest in the claim because of the bankruptcy proceedings. But the commissioners insisted that "his creditors have an interest in that claim, whatever he may aver under oath." This interest persisted even though they failed to prove their rights before the register in bankruptcy, since "their omission to do so was undoubtedly for the reason that they saw no assets in the hands of the assignee." The report concluded: "Had Mr. Campbell stated in his schedule of assets that he had a claim against the Government of the United States for $13,000, which at that date was a 'right in Equity,'" his creditors would "no doubt have proved their claim."[29]

Another example of the variety of complications which could develop in bankruptcy appears in the Thomas Mackie case. The agents' investigations uncovered the fact that the claim had been listed as an asset in bankruptcy proceedings but had subsequently been sold by the assignee to one J. A. Willard, in 1869. Since such a sale was prohibited by law, an agreement had been reached whereby Willard transferred the claim back to the original owner, with the understanding that he would get 25 per cent of anything collected from the government. When this "nice little arrangement" was discovered, the commissioners took considerable satisfaction in disallowing the claim, not only on the basis of the bankruptcy ruling, but because the proof had by no means satisfied them that the claimant had "remained throughout the war an adherent of the Union cause."[30]

The important ruling regarding the eligibility of heirs, which was noted in the foregoing decision on bankruptcy, applied to cases which were accepted for review as falling within the jurisdiction of the commission. A surprisingly large number of the claims which reached their office represented estates: presumably in part because the opportunity to prove loyalty under their rules was increased for aged persons, who were more likely to have been nonparticipants in the war. In

[29] Summary Report in the case of Washington G. Campbell, Memphis, Shelby County, Tennessee [claimed $13,278, disallowed in 1877], C. of C. No. 181, Justice Department, National Archives.

[30] Summary Report in the case of Thomas G. Mackie, New Orleans, Orleans Parish, Louisiana [claimed $10,425, disallowed in 1874], C. of C. No. 8241, Justice Department, National Archives.

these estate cases it was extremely difficult to determine the proper interest of each heir, and the problem was not simplified by the ruling of the board which held that only loyal heirs were entitled to indemnity for the stores and supplies furnished the army. This ruling, it should be noted, was a contradiction of the practice of the Court of Claims which had held, as early as 1867, that "where the loyal owner of the property died after the capture [of his property], it is not necessary to show the loyalty of his distributees."[31]

In announcing their decision in this matter in 1872, the commissioners assumed that the original owner of the property claimed was loyal and living when the property was taken, but had since died. If he had been living, his claim would have been allowed. But his claim was now presented by his heirs who were disloyal during the war. The report read: "We construe the act to mean that the claimants who present the claim before us, that is, the heirs, must prove their loyalty—that it is not enough that the ancestor was loyal." When it was clear that some of the heirs were loyal and some disloyal, they continued, "We reject so much as would go to the disloyal and allow what should go to the loyal ones." One logical exception to this rule was made. When claims were presented "by one who is a mere representative of others, and who has no beneficial interest, such as an executor or an administrator," the loyalty test was not applied to the agent, "but he must prove the loyalty of those he represents—that is, the legatee or heirs."[32]

The complicated investigations and rulings required in order to reach final decision in many "estate" cases are suggested by the two paragraphs which concluded the Summary Report in the case of the heirs of James Mooring of Marshall County, Mississippi. An allowance of $5,982.50 to the Mooring estate was described as follows:

At the time this claim arose, its proceeds were divisible into eleven distributee shares,—According to our present audit the value of each of these shares was and is $547.50. We disallow the shares of Lavinia, Susan, Emily and John, children of the testator, because their loyalty during the war has not been shown. We disallow the shares of Cannon Patterson and David Pointer, grandchildren, who are dead, because their distributees are not fully shown and it is impossible to say what part of their shares go to such distributees as are known and were loyal. We disallow one-half of the share that would have gone to testator's son Freeman, had he lived, because it belongs to his widow, whose loyalty is not proved. We disallow six-ninths of the share of testator's daughter Lucy, because the

---

[31] *Aubert* v. *United States,* 3 Ct. Clms. 84 and *Mims* v. *United States,* 4 Ct. Clms. 521.

[32] 2d Gen. Rept. of C. of C., *House Misc. Docs.,* 42d Cong., 3d Sess., No. 12, p. 3.

distributees of that part were either disloyal or have not been disclosed, or it is impossible with the information before us, to determine the size of their shares. We allow one share each to Mrs. Willie R. Hardin, daughter of testator, to Mrs. Alie Parish, sole distributee of testator's son Jeremiah, and to Abbott Ragby, sole distributee of his own brother Clayton and his mother Leanda, who was testator's daughter. We also allow to each of them one-tenth of one half of the share of testator's son Freeman, and to each of them one-ninth of the share of testator's daughter Lucy. This makes the aggregate allowance to these persons $1907.14. We disallow the rest of the claim.[33]

Sometimes this practice of testing the loyalty of each beneficiary brought to light the split in families over the question of secession. An interesting example is the Gillespie case, filed from Hamilton County, Tennessee, which was concerned with property belonging to the four children and heirs of George L. Gillespie, who died in 1860. Two of the heirs, John M. Gillespie and his sister, Mrs. Anna Watkins, were not loyal. According to the report of Special Agent Brownlow, Mrs. Watkins was "an excellent woman but did not pretend to be loyal during the war." She willingly volunteered the information, for example, that her husband, a hardware merchant, had "sold large quantities of pistols and ammunition to the Rebels."[34] Her brother, John M. Gillespie, was likewise an outspoken advocate of the Confederacy. His feelings were made clear in the copy of a letter he had written on July 11, 1863, to James A. Seddon, the Confederate secretary of war, regarding some "petitions that have or will soon be sent on to President Davis, by some of our lukewarm Southerners to get some conscript Lincolnites released from service in the army, who are now and have been for some time lieing hid in it." Seddon was advised to "tell these fair weather Southerners and Lincoln hiders that before he [Davis] can act on any petition for release from service in the army they must show clearly to him that they have been with the South in word and action both before and since the passage of the Conscript law."[35]

On the other hand, the loyalty of another brother, Colonel George

---

[33] Summary Report in the case of Robert H. Malone, executor of James Mooring, Marshall County, Mississippi [claimed $15,485, allowed $1,907.14 in 1880], C. of C. No. 17257, GAO files.

[34] Report of Special Agent John B. Brownlow in the case of John M. and Col. George L. Gillespie, Hamilton County, Tennessee [claimed $25,911.30, allowed $5,485 in 1873], C. of C. No. 9879, GAO files. The Gillespie farm, which contained eleven hundred acres, was described by Brownlow as "altogether a large productive farm and [they] always kept a large amount of stock and it is reasonable to believe that they had the horses and mules charged in the account."

[35] John M. Gillespie to James A. Seddon, Confederate secretary of war, dated July 11, 1863, and filed in *ibid.*

L. Gillespie—and the extent of division in the family—was shown by his service in the Union army throughout the war; at the time the claim was filed, he was on General Sheridan's staff. Young Gillespie had been a student at West Point when the war broke out and had entered the United States Army directly from the school. The youngest member of the family, Elizabeth S. Gillespie, was still a minor at the close of the war, and, according to its custom, the commission ruled that she "was hardly old enough to have any opinions about the war," and therefore found her loyal. Of the $10,970 allowed as indemnity for property used by the army, the half which would go to the "disloyal" heirs, John Gillespie and Anna Watkins, was deducted. The $5,485 remaining was divided equally between George and Elizabeth Gillespie, who were found to be "loyal."[36]

The ruling on Elizabeth Gillespie demonstrates the practice of the commissioners which, in the case of certain minor children, took into account the legal principle concerned with "corruption of blood," or "nonage." If a deceased individual had, by the terms of his will, endowed his minor children with property rights of their own, they were considered to be loyal regardless of the convictions of the testator or of his executor or administrator. Representative of this type is the claim filed by Mrs. Martha Beasley, guardian of her seven children. Mrs. Beasley made no claim to loyalty, and explained to the commissioners that she "didn't know it was necessary to prove loyalty or anything of that kind" when she had filed the claim. But no proof was required of the loyalty of either of the parents, when it was established that Mr. Beasley, at the time of his death in 1862, had left the homestead farm of Puddleduck to his widow for life, with the provision that the children would receive $10,000 each when they came of age or were married, and that the estate would be divided equally among them on his wife's death. Mrs. Beasley, therefore, as guardian of the children, and with the consent of her husband's administrator, prosecuted the claim on behalf of her seven living children, and the five who were minors each received $500 of the total of $2,500 allowed.[37]

Claims from Louisiana, where the code had been established according to Roman law rather than in conformity with English common law, called for special rulings to bring them in line with state practice. The establishment of proper title to the property, in the case of Mrs.

---

[36] Summary Report in *ibid.*

[37] Summary Report of the commissioners, and testimony of Mrs. Martha E. Beasley, taken at Petersburg, Virginia, Jan. 10–12, 1878, by Special Commissioner Isaac P. Baldwin, in the case of Martha E. Beasley, guardian, Dinwiddie County, Virginia [claimed $29,715, allowed $2,500 in 1880], C. of C. No. 5066, GAO files.

Stephanie Chotard, hinged on a provision of Louisiana law with respect to the rights of women. Mrs. Chotard, who was the niece of Robert J. Walker, had well established her loyalty. Her husband, on the other hand, was held to be disloyal because he had served in the Confederate army. The allowance for property in the case thus rested upon proof of its ownership. Mrs. Chotard was able to establish that the plantation was "my own individual property, inherited from my father," and her husband had no rights to it, because "the only right they [husbands] have in Louisiana is the community property, which is only the increase of its value after marriage." When Mrs. Chotard demonstrated that the "property decreased after marriage, and there was no actual property belonging to my husband, and had not been for several years before the war," she was held to be its full owner, and the claim was allowed.[38]

Cotton and tobacco, the two items of property which received special rulings in the Annual Reports, raised questions only when their use by the army might be considered to have made them quartermaster supplies. Cotton, the commissioners found, was "taken in some instances to strengthen fortifications, but probably only in cases of emergency."[39] In these circumstances they decided to follow the ruling of the judge advocate general, who had held that cotton so destroyed must be regarded as "loss by casualty of war," and therefore was not subject to indemnity. On February 9, 1867, this ruling had been legalized when Congress passed the law prohibiting payment for property destroyed by the army.[40] On June 1, 1870, a private bill in Congress authorized payment to O. N. Cutler for cotton seized by General Grant for military purposes, but it was shown that this cotton had been grown under a contract with the government made under the Captured and Abandoned Property Act, and the allowance was made on this ground.[41]

The Quartermaster General's Office made allowance for cotton when it had been taken for beds in hospitals and could therefore be classified as "hospital stores." The commissioners decided to accept this

---

[38] Summary Report of the commissioners, and testimony of Mrs. Stephanie M. Chotard, Washington, Oct. 5, 1871, in her own case, Lake Concordia, Louisiana [claimed $57,172, allowed $13,800 in 1875], C. of C. No. 7125, GAO files.

[39] 1st Gen. Rept. of C. of C., *House Misc. Docs.*, 42d Cong., 2d Sess., No. 16, p. 7. The commissioners cited the Digest of Opinions of the judge advocate general, 97, 98, Opinions, Vol. XXVI, p. 2471. For a case in which cotton used for barricades was not allowed because "Judge Holt so decided during the war," see Summary Report in the case of Charles Delano, Madison Parish, Louisiana [claimed $78,636.74, disallowed in 1873], C. of C. No. 10243, Justice Department, National Archives.

[40] 14 *U.S. Stat. at L.*, 397.

[41] 16 *U.S. Stat. at L.*, 640.

ruling for their own adjudications,[42] but in the ten years of the commission's existence, the problem of making awards for cotton so used rarely arose. One case involving such payment, presented by Mary C. Lane, a native of Burlington, Vermont, describes the circumstances which allowed payment for cotton and sketches conditions in a Confederate community as well. For some three or four years before the outbreak of war, Miss Lane had been teaching school in the vicinity of Vicksburg. During this period she had accumulated about $1,800, which she had loaned to the residents of the Mississippi community. With the outbreak of the war, she had remained to complete her school term and then found that, since only Confederate money was available, she could not collect enough United States currency to pay her way north. In order to obtain payment of her loans, she had at length decided to accept sixty-seven bales of cotton "then in his gin house," from a Mr. Hobbs who owed her about $1,500. She had decided to "run the risk of keeping it & of exporting it . . . to discharge her debt agt. him." From another debtor she accepted eight more bales.

In May, 1863, when Grant crossed the Mississippi and took Jackson, Miss Lane's cotton was appropriated by the army, and she immediately filed the complaint. W. W. Van Ness, chief quartermaster of the 9th Army Corps, who investigated the loss, shortly reported that he had traced about sixty bales of her cotton "to the Hospitals, where it was used for beds for the sick & wounded of our Army." For as much of her cotton as could clearly be shown to have reached the hospitals, Miss Lane was, therefore, allowed 10 cents per pound for a total of $3,280 of the $18,150 she had claimed.[43]

The necessity for a ruling on tobacco, on the other hand, grew out of a special order, covering a limited period of time, which raised the question of whether tobacco became a commissary supply. The ruling was based on a special order of General Sherman who, when rations were short after the capture of Atlanta, had authorized the chief commissary of subsistence to take possession of all tobacco in Atlanta and issue it, in lieu of other rations, to make the "army contented, and, as far as possible, to make up to them for their usual rations."[44] In their first Annual Report, the commissioners noted that claims for tobacco taken under this order were pending before them, but added that "the examination of them is still going on, and they will be reported upon hereafter."[45]

---

[42] 1st Gen. Rept. of C. of C., *House Misc. Docs.*, 42d Cong., 2d Sess., No. 16, p. 7.
[43] Summary Report in the case of Mary C. Lane, Warren County, Mississippi [claimed $18,150, allowed $3,280 in 1871], C. of C. No. 306, GAO files.
[44] 3d Gen. Rept. of C. of C., *House Misc. Docs.*, 43d Cong., 1st Sess., No. 23, p. 3.
[45] 1st Gen. Rept. of C. of C., *ibid.*, 42d Cong., 2d Sess., No. 16, p. 7.

Meanwhile, President Aldis had made inquiry of the commissary general to learn that department's policy in the matter. The general explained, in the first place, that "tobacco was not by legal enactment furnished to the United States troops until after the publication of Gen'l Orders No. 64, of the War Dept., Adjutant General's Office, dated August 15, 1866 . . . which authorized and ordered the furnishing of Tobacco to enlisted men." Before that time, tobacco had not been allowed as a supply, with the one exception of the Atlanta cases covered by Sherman's order.[46] A claim submitted by George J. Stubblefield for 9,830 pounds of chewing tobacco, at $1.50 per pound for tobacco, so "taken by the order of General Sherman," had been allowed by Congress, and thus served as a precedent.[47]

By 1873 the commissioners were ready to report that they would follow the practice described by the commissary general. Claims for tobacco taken pursuant to Sherman's special order were therefore allowed when the petitioner also met the loyalty test and other tests required in the commissioners' investigation. But in order to avoid confusion in the minds of men from other parts of the South who had listed tobacco on their petitions, the commissioners stated emphatically, "The payment stands upon the ground that when an army is deprived of its usual rations the commanding general can, in his judgment, authorize an article not a supply to be taken and used for the time being as a supply and in lieu of other rations." Finally they added, "We have strictly followed this precedent and have not allowed for tobacco except when taken under this order."[48]

Again, only a small number of claims, some fourteen, were affected by this ruling. The largest allowance, $3,039 for a total of $16,010 claimed, went to David Young, an Atlanta druggist who had also served as a lay preacher for the Methodist Church, South. Young's strong stand as a Unionist and an Abolitionist, the evidence showed, had resulted in his ostracism from his church which, he told the commissioners, "simply ignored me, left me out. Did not call on me to do any service." He had acquired the tobacco just before Sherman's arrival, and had paid $20.00, $30.00, and $40.00 a pound for it in Confederate money.[49] His petition called for payment for 38 boxes

---

[46] Subsistence Office to A. O. Aldis, commissioner of claims, Washington, June 26, 1871, in Subsistence Office, United States Army, Letter Book 95, pp. 524–525, Record Group 92, War Department, National Archives.

[47] *Ibid.*

[48] 3d Gen. Rept. of C. of C., *House Misc. Docs.*, 43d Cong., 1st Sess., No. 23, p. 3.

[49] Testimony of David Young before the commission, Washington, Jan. 20, 1873, in his own claim, Atlanta, Georgia [claimed $16,010, allowed $4,039 in 1873], C. of C. No. 3035, GAO files.

of tobacco, 3,941 pounds at $2.00 a pound, which he held to be a fair price. If he had had $1,000 in gold at the time, he explained, he could have bought 1,000 pounds of tobacco "and more too I expect, because they were very anxious to get clear of it. They could not get transportation for it ... there was a good many things," he added, "that you could have bought very low at that time."[50]

Young's claim had reached the commissioners only after a long series of testings in the various government departments. On June 13, 1868, the commissary general had declined to recommend payment, holding that he was restricted by the act of July 4, 1864, inasmuch as Sherman's order specifying tobacco as an item of commissary supply had placed tobacco under the limitations of this act. By March 22, 1870, encouraged by "the more recent decisions of the Supreme Court," Henry Sherman, Young's attorney, had asked the Third Auditor's Office to reconsider the case on the ground that their previous limitations had been overruled by recent Court decisions "and this class of claims held to be susceptible of immediate adjustment by the Departments or Bureaus, ordinarily having jurisdiction of the same."

In a long brief, the attorney reminded Treasury officials that, except for Sherman's order, the tobacco could have been allowed under section two of the Captured and Abandoned Property Act, which named cotton, rice, sugar, and tobacco as the staples of the South held to be chiefly covered by the act. Further, he brought to their attention that, because of Sherman's order, Young had voluntarily surrendered his tobacco, with the full understanding that it would be accounted for on the reports of the subsistence officer, also by Sherman's order, and that reimbursement would be forthcoming. He cited the principle "laid down by Secretary (now Ch. Justice) Chase," on March 2, 1867, which held that cotton voluntarily surrendered, or its proceeds, would be restored to loyal persons, if the agent who received the property had certified to the voluntary abandonment and had furnished "assurance that the same, or its proceeds, would be restored on application to the Department."[51]

Young held such a receipt for his tobacco.[52] This receipt, counsel

[50] *Ibid.*

[51] Brief of Henry Sherman, attorney for the claimant in the case of David Young, Atlanta, Georgia [claimed $16,010, allowed $3,039 in 1873], C. of C. No. 3035, GAO files.

[52] The certificate or receipt filed with the case in *ibid.*, was dated September 10, 1864, Office Chief Commissary, Atlanta, Georgia, Headquarters Military Division of the Mississippi, and read: "I certify that I have this day taken possession of the following property for and in behalf of the United States for Government purposes—viz: 30 boxes tobacco weighing 3941 pounds.... Said property was

argued, carried with it a most specific authority, since it had been made
as a result of a "direct order of the General in Command" to issue
receipts for supplies which were actually consumed by the troops. The
Supreme Court, in the case of *Nelson* v. *United States*, had been particularly explicit on the right of Unionists in the South to prosecute
their claims at the first opportunity, he continued. In the Padelford
case the Court had further clarified the three principles which summed
up the whole view of the law, and these perfectly established Young's
rights in the matter, as follows:

"I. That the private property of the Petitioner (Padelford) was by the general
policy of the Government, Exempt from capture *after* the National forces took
possession of Savannah."

So also in the case of Claimant *after* General Sherman took possession of Atlanta.

"II. That this policy was subject to modification by the Government, or by the
Commanding General in the exercise of his Military discretion."

This modification made by General Sherman at Atlanta, was in protection of
the rights of private property & in favor of the claim of the present claimant.

"III. That the right of possession of private property, is not changed, in general,
by the capture of the place where it happens to be, except upon actual seizure in
obedience to the order of the Commanding General."

No such seizure was ordered or made by Gen. Sherman as to the property of
the present claimant. Hence his right to immediate payment therefor.[53]

In conclusion the attorney argued that, since Young's loyalty had
also been fully established, "or whether so otherwise established or
not, he is entitled at once to recover the amount of his claim. This
would be so even if his property had been subject to capture and
actually seized by order of the General in command, under this decision
of the Sup[reme] C[our]t."[54]

On May 20, 1870, with this brief before him, the commissary general had, however, repeated his opinion that settlement of the claim
was not authorized by law. And on December 21, 1870, the third auditor
had, therefore, refused to reconsider the claim.[55] The commissioners

---

found immediately after the capture of Atlanta by the forces of the United
States and is said to belong to David Young, a citizen of Atlanta, Georgia and
will be found duly accounted for on my return of Provisions for the month of
September 1864. . . . No payment has been made or tendered for said property.
J. M. Blair Capt. & C. S. V.

24 boxes Holland Empress very fine
4 boxes Page Hero very fine
7 boxes Masonic fine
3 boxes A. A. A. common"

[53] Brief of Henry Sherman in *ibid.*
[54] *Ibid.*
[55] Decision of third auditor, Dec. 21, 1870, in *ibid.*

allowed the claim, however, with the brief comment that "from the testimony of Capt. Blair who took his tobacco, of Mr. Markham a well known Union man, who was relied upon by Genl. Sherman to distinguish the loyal from the disloyal at Atlanta, and others, & the report of our Special Agent, Mr. Tucker we find him loyal. The tobacco was taken by Capt. Blair under Genl Sherman's order of Sept. 8, 1864. . . . For the tobacco we allow $3,039.00."[56]

The departures from legal precedents, described in this chapter, show the essentially Radical policy of the commissioners who, given a choice, usually made their rulings in line with the prevailing opinion of 1868 rather than with the more liberal views of the Supreme Court.

---

[56] Summary Report of the commissioners of claims, in *ibid.*

CHAPTER IX

THE DISTRIBUTION OF CLAIMS

WHEN THE commissioners of claims closed the doors of their offices in March, 1880, they had accounted for all of the 22,298 men and women who had filed petitions from March 3, 1871, to March 3, 1873. The petitioners were widely distributed and of every economic status. In the words of the commissioners, the testimony "presented a vivid and crowded panorama of the war in those sections that were the actual theaters of military operations," and included "every part of the country and ... every rank of society."[1] Claims were filed from 655 counties and from all of the seceded states. The total figures by states are as follows: Tennessee, 4,027; Virginia, 3,731; Georgia, 3,447; Alabama, 2,581; Arkansas, 2,396; Mississippi, 2,233; North Carolina, 2,209; Louisiana, 716; South Carolina, 555; West Virginia, 201; Florida, 111; and Texas, 91.

Of the $60,258,150.44 claimed, only $4,636,920.69 was allowed. The disparity between these two figures does not, however, indicate that only about 6 per cent of the totals listed in the petitions was allowable. The act of June 15, 1876, which barred all evidence not submitted by March 10, 1879, outlawed 5,250 claims, for approximately $15,000,000, and a total of fifty-seven cases had been withdrawn. Some padded or fraudulent claims, usually involving large sums, further distorted the figures. Likewise, the severe scaling down of prices, or the exclusion from the original claim of such items as rent, damage, depredation, or destruction sharply reduced the amounts allowed. In the final accounting, about 41 per cent of the 16,991 cases reported to Congress satisfied the rigorous examination of the commissioners with respect both to loyalty and to property. By way of comparison, it is interesting to note that whereas the Southern Claims Commission by 1880 had allowed $4,636,920.69 to loyal Southerners for quartermaster and commissary stores, the Court of Claims, in the ten years from 1864 to 1874, had allowed a total of $6,300,436.80 for cotton and contraband. This last amount represented a draft of only about $400,000 on the $20,910,-656.44 collected into the Treasury under the Captured and Abandoned Property acts. Of this total, $5,907,381.78 had been added to the original account since the end of the war. This sum came from two sources, listed as "Profits to Government arising from purchase and resale of

---

[1] 5th Gen. Rept. of C. of C., *House Misc. Docs.*, 44th Cong., 1st Sess., No. 13, p. 10.

products under section 8, act of July 2, 1864," and "Amount expended from the proceeds and returned."[2]

The data assembled on claimants of amounts of $10,000 and over, under examination in this study, contain a wealth of economic and social information with which to supplement other community and personal records of the South. A total of 701 of the 949 claims for $10,000 and over were reported to Congress.[3] These 701 Southern Unionists belonged to the group of landed men and slaveholders. To be exact, 575, or 82 per cent, of these claims were filed by planters or individuals combining plantation ownership with other occupations. The average number of slaves owned by them was 54, varying from 15 to 310. When it is recalled that in the whole South, in 1860, there were only 2,358 slaveholders who owned as many as 100 slaves, these 575 planter-Unionists represent a striking proportion.[4]

An analysis of the figures for the trades or professions of the 126 nonplanter claimants is arranged according to states. All the thirty-three claimants from Alabama were planters except three who were the owners of steamboats. The count for Arkansas shows a wider range, with fifty-four planters, three merchants, three physicians, three owners of steamboats or ferries, two ministers, two proprietors of woodyards, and one owner of a machine shop. Florida's seven cases were made up of five planters and two representatives of shipping interests. Of the sixty claimants from Georgia, thirty-two were planters, six were general merchants, three were bankers, two were owners of machine shops, two were physicians, three were druggists, two were saddlers or shoemakers, one was a butcher, one a grocer, one a cabinetmaker, one a dry goods merchant, one a hotel owner, one a steamboat owner, one a judge, one a livery stable owner, one an operator of a gristmill, and one a woodyard owner.[5]

In the $10,000-and-over group, Louisiana shows the largest number of claimants of any state, with 126 planters, five general merchants, two "speculators," two tanners, two doctors, two coal brokers, two ministers, thirteen steamboat, ferry, or dredge owners, one druggist, one

---

[2] The effect of the statute of limitations on subsequent allowances of the court is apparent in the fact that, by 1888, this sum had been increased by only about $3,500,000 for a total of $9,864,300.75. See J. G. Randall, *The Confiscation of Property during the Civil War* (Indianapolis, 1913), p. 50.

[3] For the table from which this figure is derived showing the breakdown by states, see chap. vi.

[4] L. C. Gray, *History of Agriculture in the Southern United States to 1860* (Washington, 1933), I, 483. These figures show that nearly one hundred thousand middle-class planters owned from ten to fifty slaves each.

[5] Tabulated from the material contained in the cases themselves.

grocer, one yacht owner, one commission merchant, one cotton merchant, one printer, one wholesale grocer, one hotelkeeper, one owner of a literary institution, and one owner of an ironworks. Of the claims from Mississippi, the next largest group, 137 were from planters in the rich riverbottom areas, four were filed by physicians, two by steamboat owners, two by leather merchants, and one each by a grocer, a druggist, a lumberman, a lawyer, a general merchant, a machinist and a schoolteacher. Third in the order of number came Virginia, with 109 claims filed by planters, three by physicians, two by steamboat owners, and the remaining six by a machinist, a merchant, a tinsmith, a lumberman, a whaler, and the absentee owner of an ironworks.

All eleven claims for $10,000 and over from North Carolina came from planters, except for one from the owner of a steamboat. Of the twelve claims from South Carolina, nine were filed by planters, one by a steamboat owner, one by a proprietor of a coalyard, and one by the owner of a wheelwright shop. Fifty-four planters from Tennessee filed claims, together with three steamboat owners, two physicians, one commission merchant, one cotton merchant, one hotelkeeper, one owner of a marble yard, one book dealer, and one cabinetmaker. The three claims from West Virginia were filed by planters. Of the six claimants from Texas, three were planters and three were ranchers.

The planters, who represented 82 per cent of these claimants, did not, of course, show their real status as property owners by the amount of goods listed in their petitions. On the other hand, a claim for quartermaster and commissary stores for $10,000 or over filed by a merchant, a craftsman, or the owner of a steamboat might represent his total assets. A planter usually listed only items which could be classed as the normal running equipment of his plantation: feed for the livestock, the livestock itself, food for the plantation community, and equipment for planting and harvesting the crops. The value of his cotton and the capital investment represented by his slaves could not, of course, be included.

Of the additional 786 men and women who filed claims in amounts ranging between $5,000 and $10,000, many were planters with large holdings whose losses had not been so extensive or who had filed in smaller amounts because they could not afford, or did not choose, to fulfill the requirement of coming to Washington, with their witnesses, for a full hearing. The hardship imposed by this statutory rule is revealed by the fact that 198 of the claims originally filed for over $10,000 were subsequently reduced, with the permission of the Washington office, in order to avoid this expensive process. Through amended petitions, 32 of the 191 allowed cases were reduced a total of $133,923.89, and 166 of the 511 disallowed cases were reduced a total of $1,793,240.31, for a grand total reduction of $1,937,263.89. These reductions do not appear in the tables at the end of this chapter, however, because the commissioners, as noted before, used the original face value of the claim in their accounting procedures. Possibly this was an attempt

TABLE 4

State	Claims exceeding $10,000			Claims for $5,000 to $10,000		
	Allowed	Disallowed	Totals	Allowed	Disallowed	Totals
Alabama............	10	23	33	16	47	63
Arkansas...........	17	51	68	26	57	83
Florida.............	5	2	7	5	6	11
Georgia.............	8	52	60	16	73	89
Louisiana...........	30	134	164	20	64	84
Mississippi.........	44	108	152	39	126	165
No. Carolina........	4	7	11	5	10	15
So. Carolina........	4	8	12	4	21	25
Tennessee..........	13	52	65	20	69	89
Texas..............	3	3	6	3	3	6
Virginia............	51	69	120	51	77	128
W. Virginia.........	2	1	3	19	9	28
Totals............	191	510	701	224	562	786

to impress Congress with their zealous concern for the public treasury.

A comparison of claims filed in the amount of $5,000 to $10,000 with those in excess of $10,000 is made in table 4, which has been arranged by states.[6]

As table 4 shows, only 191 claimants in the first group could show a Unionism active enough and sustained enough to pass the severe tests of the commissioners. But, again, the true amount of Unionist sentiment in the propertied group is distorted to some extent, because most of the men and women whose cases were disallowed produced evidence of Unionism in varying degrees of completeness. A breakdown of this group suggests that of the total of 510 claims disallowed, only 144 were classified, even by the commissioners, as belonging to active and consistent secessionists. Of the remaining number, 30 cases were filed

---

[6] Tabulated from data assembled from the Register of Claims and, for each claim over $10,000, from the cases themselves.

by men and women who could prove their loyalty but could not establish their right to the property claimed; 50 showed so strong a case of sustained Unionism that the commissioners reached their final decision only after great deliberation; 105 told a story which might be described as "circumstantial" or "interrupted Unionism," as the evidence showed that they had yielded in varying degrees to the community pressure although never completely accepting the cause of the Confederacy; and 34 classified themselves, or were classified by the commission, as "neutral," implying no allegiance to either side.

The case of Patterson Allan, a native of Virginia, gives an example of the technical decisions which disqualified those 50 claimants whose Unionism stood all but one test. Allan had considered himself a Union man during the entire war. He had voted for a Union man as a delegate to the Richmond convention and had refused to vote for secession in the popular election in Virginia. He avoided the first conscription call by furnishing a substitute, the second because he had more than fifteen slaves. He had never served in the Confederate army or purchased Confederate bonds. Chiefly, however, he rested his proof of Unionism on efforts to obtain the release of his wife, who had been imprisoned by the Confederacy as a Union spy. Mrs. Allan was arrested on evidence that she had secretly sent letters north for the information of Major General John A. Dix. She was finally released to her husband on a bail of $100,000, but he was required to renew it monthly. Altogether, Allan estimated, "it cost me $30,000 in property and confederate money to protect my wife from imprisonment, including lawyers' fees, board, medical attendance, nursing, bribes, &c."

But because he had been permitted to pass in and out of Richmond while obtaining his wife's release, on passes issued by General Charles C. Winder of the Confederate forces, his loyalty was questioned. The commissioners finally concluded that Allan's being allowed to "walk the streets of Richmond unmolested," indicated that "the confederate authorities had the strongest assurances that he was at least not unfriendly to their government." There could be no question of his wife's loyalty, they noted, but the property claimed did not belong to her. As for the claimant, he had not, the commissioners concluded, produced satisfactory evidence respecting his own loyalty. He had, for example, put a substitute into the Confederate army, and "this act alone, unless explained by the most satisfactory evidence, is conclusive against him.'"

[7] Summary Report in the case of Patterson Allan, Goochland County, Virginia [claimed $10,600, disallowed in 1871], C. of C. No. 239, Justice Department, National Archives.

TABLE 5

	Ala.	Ark.	Fla.	Ga.	La.	Miss.	N. C.	S. C.	Tenn.	Tex.	Va.	W. Va.	Total
Allowed:													
As "loyal"................	10	17	5	8	30	44	4	4	13	3	51	2	191
Disallowed:													
With evidence of overt loyalty.......	1	6	..	3	9	2	..	..	3	..	6	..	30
Borderline decision........	3	4	1	7	9	13	1	..	2	..	10	..	50
Circumstantial or interrupted Unionism..	6	7	..	8	21	36	2	2	11	..	12	..	105
Neutrals........	2	5	..	4	4	5	1	..	6	1	6	..	34
Disloyal........	5	17	..	13	41	30	..	5	8	..	24	1	144
Without ruling.......	1	1	..	4	4	..	1	..	1	2	..	..	14
On jurisdictional grounds.....	1	1	1	5	10	5	1	1	12	..	4	..	41
Aliens.........	1	2	..	2	6	4	1	..	..	..	2	..	18
Bankrupts.........	2	5	..	3	8	4	..	..	3	..	4	..	29
Fraud.........	..	1	..	3	10	4	..	..	4	..	..	..	22
Nonprosecution........	1	2	..	..	12	5	..	..	2	..	1	..	23

Among the 105 cases here classified as "circumstantial" or "interrupted" Unionism is that of John E. Tunis, of Norfolk County, Virginia. Tunis, they concluded, was "an undemonstrative man," who "was certainly never an enthusiastic secessionist." His widow testified regarding his Union sentiments, adding that he had "frequently called her a 'little fool' for her faith and belief in the confederate cause." Three or four witnesses spoke of him, "in faint language," as a Union man. Tunis had gone to the North after the Federal occupation of Norfolk, and had invested his funds in United States bonds, which seemed to indicate that "he could have had but little faith in the success of the confederacy."

However, the facts that Tunis' clerk, who was in close business relations with him, had never heard him express his sentiments regarding the Confederacy, and that Governor John Letcher had twice offered him a commission as quartermaster, were considered important. In 1879 the commissioners were ready to conclude, in their report to Congress:

Mr. Tunis was not an able-bodied man, yet, if known as a Unionist, it is not probable that Governor Letcher would have offered him a commission. We have endeavored to ascertain the true status of Mr. Tunis, and have learned very little on that subject. Before reporting favorably on the claim, we must be satisfied of his loyalty to the Federal Government throughout the war. The proof is not satisfactory, and the claim is disallowed.[8]

A classification of the degree of loyalty exhibited in the evidence, together with those cases on which no ruling was required since the cases were disallowed on jurisdictional or other grounds, provides an informal poll of the final decisions in these 686 cases, which are again classified by the states from which they were filed.[9] (See table 5.) The various subheadings as to loyalty are derived from expressions commonly used by the commissioners in their Summary Reports, and reflect the conflicting evidence submitted in most cases.

The test prescribed, by their communities and by the commission, for these men and women was, as the cases cited throughout have shown, especially rigorous. Special community pressure had been exerted upon these men and women precisely because of their position of wealth or influence. Extensive property ownership in itself caused them to be singled out for Confederate taxation, the purchase of bonds,

---

[8] Summary Report in the case of Samuel Selden, executor of John E. Tunis of Norfolk County, Virginia [claimed $14,410.29, disallowed in 1879], C. of C. No. 9567, Justice Department, National Archives.

[9] These figures were prepared from an appraisal of the evidence submitted in the 510 cases disallowed by the commission.

and community leadership in the Southern cause. Their slaves represented capital, and their loyalty was severely tested in the loss of property brought about by the Emancipation Proclamation and other economic measures.

The limitations prescribed by statute and the commissioners' rules served to reduce the numbers of Unionist landed gentry who elected to appear before the commission. Some of the restrictions may be noted. To qualify, their property must have been in the path of Federal troops; they must have lived long enough to have filed a claim or have loyal heirs or assignees; they must have filed the claim before Congress acted abruptly to outlaw any further petitions; they must have proved that they had the extensive holdings they described; and they must have met the restrictions with respect to bankruptcy, citizenship, and title which the rule described. In view of these limitations, it is probable that for every man or woman who filed an honest claim, there were at least four who, with equal qualifications of Unionism and property, failed to do so.

Northerners within the Confederacy, as has been seen, became "aliens" by the terms of the Act of Banishment of August 8, 1861, unless they took the oath of allegiance to the Confederacy. Sequestration of their property became effective on August 30 of the same year. Records of these proceedings, involving hundreds of men and women, bear witness to the number of persons affected. If a man retained a home in the North, the case was clear. If, however, he remained in the South and continued to invest his capital in Southern property, he was accepted as a good security risk by the Confederacy.

Obviously any Northerner who had established himself in the South occupied a precarious position. Consequently, feeling that they were under suspicion, those men and women from the North who remained with their property in the South often became the most ardent advocates of the Davis government. Thirty-four claims in the group over $10,000 were filed by men recently from the North, of whom seventeen had returned to the North during the war. Fifteen of the other seventeen "Northerners" who had remained within the Confederacy had their claims disallowed because of their Confederate sympathies. Orren L. Dodd of Baxter County, Arkansas, for example, was described as a "northern man, who inherited land and slaves" in the South. Of him the commissioners wrote, "What his feelings were toward the Union cause and the Army during the war may be inferred from the fact that when the Federal troops had fought their way down to his neighborhood, to the joy of the truly loyal people, he removed himself a hundred miles further into the confederate lines."[10] For some Northerners, then, their decision was swayed by property interests.

Claims presented by foreigners who had not been naturalized were outlawed by the commissioners as aliens did not come within the statutory definition of citizens. Of the 701 claims for amounts of $10,000 and over, twenty-nine were filed by naturalized citizens. Thirteen of these men had been born in Germany, five in Ireland, five in other British dominions, two in Russia, and one each in Norway, Spain, and France. These claimants were usually of the tradesman or artisan class and were consequently (except for certain German claimants in Texas)[11] from urban areas. All the claimants born in the British dominions lived in Louisiana around New Orleans, as did the single naturalized citizen from France and the one from Norway. The French claimant was a cotton broker, and the Norwegian a ship captain.

Of the total of 949 claims for $10,000 and over, 701 were tested in full and reported to Congress, as has been stated above.[12] These larger cases inevitably came from the more prosperous areas of the South, and also, of course, only from those areas which were within the sweep of the Northern armies. In spite of these limitations, the breakdown of cases (see table 6) shows a wide distribution among states and counties.[13]

---

[10] Summary Report in the case of Orren L. Dodd, Baxter County, Arkansas [claimed $6,784, disallowed in 1880], C. of C. No. 9547, Justice Department, National Archives.

[11] Ella Lonn, *Foreigners in the Confederacy*. Miss Lonn stresses the influence of the Pennsylvania Germans, or "Old Germans," on the economy and opinions of Virginia and shows that 23 per cent of the white population of Richmond in 1860 was foreign-born. The German population was sufficiently numerous to support two German newspapers in that city. In the seaport and trade cities, the foreign-born population in 1860 was surprisingly large, representing 30 per cent of the white population in Charleston; 25 per cent in Mobile; 33 per cent in Savannah; and 42 per cent in Memphis. New Orleans had 64,621 persons classified as foreigners in 1860, including 24,398 Irish, 19,752 Germans, 10,564 French, and 4,343 Scotch and British. In Texas, where farm lands had opened up concurrently with the German migrations in the 1840's, 20 per cent of the white population had been born in Germany, most of them were living on farms, and they were almost invariably opposed to slavery. See especially pp. 1–7, 13, 17 of Miss Lonn's book.

[12] For the full accounting for this group, prepared from the Register of Claims, and for the claims themselves, see chap. vii.

[13] Tabulated from the Register of Claims and the cases themselves.

TABLE 6

County	No. of cases	Amount claimed	Amount allowed	No. of cases	Amount claimed and disallowed
		ALABAMA			
Chambers............	1	$10,500.00	$ 4,688.00	1	$ 10,000.00
Colbert..............	2	38,680.35	9,516.00	4	95,591.60
Conecuh.............	..	....	....	1	14,020.00
Dallas..............	2	33,781.85	9,690.00	2	79,775.00
Jackson.............	..	....	....	3	41,385.50
Lauderdale..........	2	33,585.25	8,304.00	2	36,546.50
Lawrence...........	..	....	....	1	12,927.00
Limestone...........	..	....	....	2	25,771.75
Macon..............	..	....	....	2	20,182.00
Madison.............	..	....	....	2	81,550.50
Mobile..............	2	164,200.00	21,666.00	1	47,485.00
Montgomery.........	1	12,700.00	4,265.00	1	10,000.00
Tuscaloosa..........	..	....	....	1	11,800.00
Totals............	10	$293,447.45	$ 58,128.00	23	$487,034.85
		ARKANSAS			
Arkansas............	..	....	....	3	$ 86,965.50
Ashley..............	..	....	....	2	42,707.50
Bradley.............	1	$ 21,036.53	$ 9,750.00	..	....
Carroll.............	..	....	....	1	16,000.00
Drew...............	..	....	....	1	12,971.50
Franklin............	..	....	....	1	50,910.00
Jefferson............	2	21,309.00	10,819.00	4	102,000.00
Johnson.............	..	....	....	1	21,542.00
Mississippi...........	1	52,615.00	1,211.12	1	33,090.00
Phillips.............	5	108,857.00	21,518.00	8	160,628.70
Prairie.............	..	....	....	1	39,285.00
Pulaski.............	3	36,000.00	4,924.00	17	755,581.75
Sebastian...........	2	26,442.80	6,671.05	9	193,188.48
Washington..........	2	21,499.00	5,727.07	..	....
White..............	..	....	....	1	10,000.00
Woodruff............	1	21,692.50	2,540.00	1	10,248.00
Totals............	17	$309,451.83	$ 63,160.24	51	$1,535,118.43

TABLE 6—*Continued*

County	No. of cases	Amount claimed	Amount allowed	No. of cases	Amount claimed and disallowed
		FLORIDA			
Duval..............	1	$ 10,000.00	$ 9,225.00	..	....
Escambia...........	1	14,703.50	12,240.00	..	....
Holmes.............	..	....	....	1	$ 36,000.00
Monroe............	1	10,000.00	1,500.00	..	....
Nassau.............	2	32,050.00	9,615.00	..	....
St. Johns..........	..	....	....	1	72,708.00
Totals...........	5	$ 66,053.50	$ 32,580.00	2	$108,708.00
		GEORGIA			
Bartow.............	..	....	....	1	$ 26,843.00
Bibb...............	..	....	....	2	32,947.50
Bryan..............	1	$ 10,000.00	$ 10,000.00	..	....
Burke..............	..	....	....	1	20,193.50
Chatham...........	1	60,746.60	1,297.00	15	635,602.59
Clayton............	1	15,950.00	4,030.00	1	13,499.00
Cobb...............	..	....	....	2	94,280.00
Coweta.............	..	....	....	1	13,100.00
De Kalb............	..	....	....	1	12,325.00
Floyd..............	..	....	....	5	110,677.69
Fulton.............	1	27,908.00	550.00	17	332,509.65
Gordon............	2	21,072.33	6,096.00	..	....
Macon.............	..	....	....	1	33,305.00
Morgan............	1	44,567.50	2,164.00	1	25,491.75
Newton............	..	....	....	1	11,636.55
Richmond..........	1	34,092.00	6,386.66	..	....
Walker.............	..	....	....	1	16,006.75
Whitfield..........	..	....	....	2	96,257.00
Totals...........	8	$214,336.43	$ 30,523.66	52	$1,474,674.98
		LOUISIANA			
Ascension...........	..	....	....	1	$ 16,430.00
Assumption.........	1	$ 11,315.00	$ 3,980.00	..	....
Caddo..............	1	126,602.00	5,205.00	..	....
Carroll.............	6	347,268.00	87,004.33	6	161,957.00
Concordia..........	1	51,172.00	13,800.00	..	....
De Soto.............	..	....	....	1	27,049.00
E. Baton Rouge......	1	19,558.00	10,930.00	4	108,187.50
E. Feliciana.........	..	....	....	1	25,600.00

TABLE 6—*Continued*

County	No. of cases	Amount claimed	Amount allowed	No. of cases	Amount claimed and disallowed
LOUISIANA—CONTINUED					
Franklin............	..	....	....	2	84,934.20
Grant..............	..	....	....	1	10,000.00
Iberia.............	1	62,699.00	13,300.00	2	65,457.50
Iberville...........	..	....	....	2	46,654.25
Jefferson..........	..	....	....	2	64,289.00
Lafourche..........	..	....	....	10	412,606.70
Madison...........	..	....	....	11	357,573.56
Natchitoches........	1	15,865.00	474.00	5	81,665.00
Orleans............	7	417,053.09	112,049.65	37	2,653,537.80
Ouachita...........	..	....	....	2	42,445.00
Point Coupee.......	..	....	....	10	221,736.50
Rapides............	5	566,671.08	56,024.72	15	1,059,606.93
Richland...........	..	....	....	2	42,230.00
St. Bernard........	1	14,385.00	175.00	..	....
St. Charles.........	..	....	....	1	130,358.50
St. Landry.........	1	33,135.00	15,750.00	6	139,431.50
St. Martin.........	..	....	....	2	26,384.50
St. Mary...........	3	223,508.96	87,452.88	2	32,266.50
St. Tammany.......	..	....	....	1	29,112.00
Tangipahoa........	..	....	....	1	10,404.00
Tensas............	1	20,065.00	12,620.00	3	51,088.05
Terrebonne.........	..	....	....	1	27,475.05
W. Baton Rouge.....	..	....	....	1	79,442.00
W. Feliciana........	..	....	....	1	169,300.00
Winn..............	..	....	....	1	12,950.00
Totals...........	30	$1,909,297.13	$418,765.58	134	$6,190,172.04
MISSISSIPPI					
Adams.............	6	$319,711.92	$ 98,010.25	12	$368,554.10
Amite.............	..	....	....	1	10,360.00
Benton............	1	12,479.00	8,467.00	..	....
Bolivar............	2	42,313.00	4,813.34	1	11,716.00
Claiborne..........	2	47,800.00	10,930.00	15	469,745.20
Clarke............	..	....	....	1	26,111.25
Coahoma..........	..	....	....	1	11,630.00
Copiah............	2	25,980.00	11,520.00	..	....
Hancock...........	..	....	....	1	135,983.00
Harrison...........	..	....	....	1	12,200.00
Hinds.............	6	128,631.50	13,932.68	15	331,150.75
Issaquena..........	1	19,500.00	7,125.00	..	....

TABLE 6—*Continued*

County	No. of cases	Amount claimed	Amount allowed	No. of cases	Amount claimed and disallowed
MISSISSIPPI—CONTINUED					
Jefferson............	1	16,172.75	4,820.00	4	86,860.00
Lafayette...........	1	13,937.00	4,267.00	3	48,985.50
Madison.............	..	....	....	3	68,068.80
Marshall............	4	79,061.00	21,291.77	·.	....
Monroe.............	..	....	....	5	88,851.80
Noxubee............	..	....	....	1	10,000.00
Rankin.............	..	....	....	1	10,032.00
Scott...............	..	....	....	2	24,139.50
Sunflower...........	..	....	....	1	15,000.00
Tishomingo..........	2	27,813.00	5,599.00	3	54,538.75
Tunica..............	1	21,255.00	425.00	1	14,090.00
Warren.............	12	376,064.10	61,765.33	29	672,356.92
Washington.........	3	42,940.00	17,454.90	6	166,167.00
Yazoo..............	..	....	....	1	13,865.00
Totals.............	44	$1,173,658.27	$270,421.27	108	$2,650,404.77
NORTH CAROLINA					
Franklin............	..	....	....	1	$ 18,562.25
Greene.............	1	$ 10,528.00	$ 7,838.00	..	....
Halifax.............	..	....	....	1	16,062.00
New Hanover........	..	....	....	2	23,260.00
Pasquotank..........	2	23,810.00	3,690.00	..	....
Rockingham.........	..	....	....	2	49,379.65
Wake...............	1	10,870.00	3,596.00	..	....
Wayne..............	..	....	....	1	14,762.00
Totals.............	4	$ 45,208.00	$ 15,124.00	7	$122,025.90
SOUTH CAROLINA					
Abbeville...........	1	$ 56,418.75	$ 720.00	..	....
Beaufort............	..	....	....	2	$ 33,009.00
Charleston..........	1	14,564.00	7,067.00	5	517,134.42
Fairfield............	1	18,587.00	4,381.00	..	....
Georgetown.........	1	235,865.00	879.89	1	14,625.00
Totals.............	4	$325,434.75	$ 13,047.89	8	$564,768.42

TABLE 6—Continued

County	No. of cases	Amount claimed	Amount allowed	No. of cases	Amount claimed and disallowed
		TENNESSEE			
Bedford..............	..	....	....	1	$ 10,388.50
Coffee..............	..	....	....	1	16,237.17
Davidson...........	2	$ 51,658.28	$ 11,279.50	13	427,382.13
Dickson.............	..	....	....	1	13,150.00
Fayette.............	1	31,620.00	14,102.77	4	88,903.40
Franklin............	..	....	....	1	30,585.00
Hamilton...........	2	58,720.40	7,849.00	1	36,830.15
Hardeman...........	..	....	....	1	25,544.23
Haywood...........	1	11,475.00	196.00	..	....
McMinn.............	..	....	....	1	100,571.00
Madison.............	..	....	....	1	13,410.00
Marion..............	..	....	....	1	15,710.00
Maury..............	..	....	....	1	14,375.70
Rutherford..........	..	....	....	3	46,540.50
Shelby..............	7	261,574.62	107,891.25	17	589,692.15
Sumner.............	..	....	....	1	20,000.00
Wayne..............	..	....	....	1	10,865.50
Williamson..........	..	....	....	3	37,493.50
Totals.............	13	$415,048.30	$141,318.52	52	$1,497,678.93
		TEXAS			
Cameron............	1	$ 42,579.25	$ 42,579.25	1	$ 10,000.00
Galveston...........	..	....	....	1	24,887.00
Matagordo..........	..	....	....	1	10,960.00
Nueces.............	2	41,520.00	1,995.00	..	....
Totals.............	3	$ 84,099.25	$ 44,574.25	3	$ 45,847.00
		VIRGINIA			
Albemarle...........	..	....	....	2	$ 21,892.00
Alexandria..........	19	$448,584.42	$100,127.50	6	131,301.11
Amelia..............	..	....	....	1	21,065.00
Augusta.............	..	....	....	1	32,587.50
Brunswick..........	1	29,715.00	2,500.00	..	....
Caroline............	1	13,461.50	7,067.00	..	....
Chesterfield.........	..	....	....	1	14,180.00
Clarke..............	1	27,231.00	4,978.00	..	....
Culpeper............	4	65,874.37	24,053.46	5	115,999.61

TABLE 6—*Concluded*

County	No. of cases	Amount claimed	Amount allowed	No. of cases	Amount claimed and disallowed
		VIRGINIA—CONTINUED			
Dinwiddie............	2	31,179.00	10,180.00	2	25,000.00
Elizabeth City.......	1	29,332.00	9,592.00	..	....
Fairfax..............	5	63,679.50	23,561.75	8	619,034.33
Fauquier............	6	126,895.30	33,705.34	4	62,307.00
Frederick...........	..	....	....	4	53,588.77
Goochland..........	..	....	....	1	10,600.00
Hampshire..........	1	22,974.50	2,187.00	..	....
Hanover............	..	....	....	4	63,304.00
Henrico.............	..	....	....	8	223,223.03
James City..........	1	12,560.00	4,680.00	..	....
Lee.................	..	....	....	1	14,073.00
Loudoun............	..	....	....	5	192,590.50
Louisa..............	..	....	....	1	11,190.00
Norfolk.............	..	....	....	3	89,026.83
Patrick.............	..	....	....	1	12,000.00
Prince Edward.......	..	....	....	1	21,968.50
Prince George.......	1	11,820.00	6,840.00	..	....
Prince William......	3	36,104.24	10,959.30	1	12,716.00
Princess Anne.......	..	....	....	1	23,500.00
Rappahannock.......	..	....	....	1	11,816.00
Rockingham.........	..	....	....	1	34,416.69
Spottsylvania.......	..	....	....	1	71,955.50
Stafford............	3	56,123.09	12,620.04	2	31,454.40
Surry...............	1	34,985.00	5,105.00	..	....
Warren.............	1	12,087.50	3,593.00	1	58,767.40
Washington.........	..	....	....	1	11,300.00
York................	..	....	....	1	17,888.00
Totals............	51	$1,022,606.42	$261,749.39	69	$2,008,745.17
		WEST VIRGINIA			
Jefferson............	2	$24,553.01	$ 6,230.00	1	$14,050.00

As the accompanying map shows, the claims filed by Unionists of substantial property came from three general areas. They came from the large plantations in the rich river lands along the Mississippi or in the tidewater areas of Virginia. They arose where the armies had marched, especially as a result of the campaigns in northern Virginia and Sherman's march on Atlanta. And they lay within the last strong-

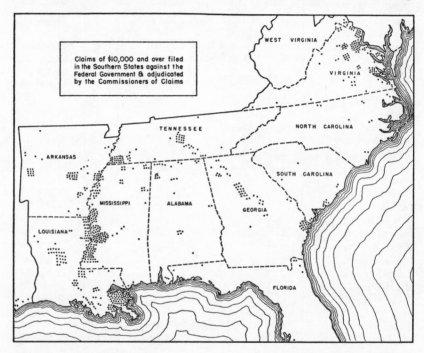

holds of the Henry Clay Whigs, whom Clement Eaton has described as "the most tolerant, the most moderating group in the South."[14] At the same time, the influences of trade with the North and ties with Northern business interests are revealed in the claims clustering about seaport towns and such centers as Memphis, Nashville, and Natchez. Without such centers, the men and women of the interior counties of each state would have had no representation before the commission. Those areas where Unionism was strong but living was sparse—such as the hill country of Mississippi and Alabama, and the Appalachian

---

[14] Clement Eaton, *Freedom of Thought in the Old South*, p. 29. "The moderating influence of the Whig leaders," Eaton concludes, "was due partly to the culture and restraint of the aristocrat, but more directly to a belief that violent attacks on antislavery men and on Northern abolitionists would disrupt the Union" (p. 87).

highlands which bisect Virginia and North Carolina—show no large claims.

A breakdown of the cases according to the amount claimed, which appeared in the third Annual Report, gives an official distribution of the size of the claims:[15]

```
Number of claims under 10,000............................21,347
               10,001–20,000  ...........................   474
               20,001–30,000  ...........................   192
               30,001–40,000  ...........................    84
               40,001–50,000  ...........................    56
               50,001–60,000  ...........................    36
               60,001–70,000  ...........................    21
               70,001–80,000  ...........................    16
               80,001–90,000  ...........................    14
               90,001–100,000  ..........................     8
        [100,000 to a high of 450,001]....................    50
                                                         _____
                                                           22,298
```

Two charts prepared from the materials submitted each year by the commission, for Congressional review, are included here for the information they contain on Southern Unionism as a whole and because they furnish a setting for the large claims. (See tables 7 and 8.) Tennessee and Virginia led in the number of claims filed, whereas comparatively few came from Florida and Texas. But the plantation areas of Louisiana and Mississippi, which appear well down the list with respect to the number of claims, led in the total amounts claimed because most of the large cases came from these areas.[16]

---

[15] 3d Gen. Rept. of C. of C., in *House Misc. Docs.*, 43d Cong., 1st Sess., No. 23, p. 4. The last bracketed entry is a consolidation of the complete report.

[16] Prepared from the tenth Annual Report of the C. of C. in *House Misc. Docs.*, as follows:
(1) Dec. 14, 1871, 42d Cong., 2d Sess., No. 16, p. 7.
(2) Dec. 6, 1872, 42d Cong., 3d Sess., No. 12, p. 2.
(3) Dec. 8, 1873, 43d Cong., 1st Sess., No. 23, pp. 1–4.
(4) Dec. 14, 1874, 43d Cong., 2d Sess., No. 18, p. 1.
(5) Dec. 20, 1875, 44th Cong., 1st Sess., No. 13, p. 5.
(6) Dec. 4, 1876, 44th Cong., 2d Sess., No. 4, pp. 1–2.
(7) Dec. 5, 1877, 45th Cong., 2d Sess., No. 4, p. 3.
(8) Dec. 13, 1878, 45th Cong., 3d Sess., No. 16, pp. 1–2.
(9) Dec. 16, 1879, 46th Cong., 2d Sess., No. 10, pp. 4–5.
(10) March 9, 1880, 46th Cong., 2d Sess., No. 30, p. 1.
To derive the figures in the above tables it is also necessary to consult the case of Marie P. Evans printed separately in *House Misc. Docs.* 44th Cong., 1st Sess., No. 18, Part 2 and a supplement to the 5th Annual Report printed in *House Misc. Docs.*, 44th Cong., 1st Sess., No. 20, Part 2. The total number of cases acted on exceed slightly the number given in the final report of the commissioners, as they did not always deduct modifications ordered by Congress.

TABLE 7

NUMBER OF CLAIMS REPORTED
(By state and by year)

State (In number-order)	1871	1872	1873	1874	1875	1876	1877	1878	1879	1880	Totals
Tennessee	116	397	409	554	242	489	275	275	445	85	3,287
Virginia	262	545	427	475	318	303	292	241	288	46	3,197
Georgia	83	174	262	210	209	211	270	381	402	37	2,239
Alabama	31	345	206	299	205	238	232	186	214	33	1,989
Arkansas	65	184	307	277	187	164	144	114	302	59	1,803
Mississippi	12	213	357	180	151	197	166	102	196	65	1,639
North Carolina	9	272	420	273	128	112	111	147	169	15	1,656
Louisiana	...	27	28	59	57	60	80	36	138	32	517
South Carolina	...	41	30	34	44	59	47	43	74	5	377
West Virginia	...	...	19	32	12	7	26	11	32	1	140
Florida	1	3	8	7	8	17	9	16	19	1	89
Texas	1	8	5	7	...	10	7	7	14	3	62
Totals	580	2,209	2,478	2,407	1,561	1,867	1,659	1,559	2,293	382	16,995

TABLE 8
Number and Amount of Cases Reported Allowed and Disallowed by Year

Year	Cases reported	Wholly disallowed	Allowed in whole or part	Amount claimed	Amount allowed	Amount disallowed
1871.	580	256	324	$ 1,656,357.98	$ 344,168.20	$ 1,312,189.78
1872.	2,209	1,148	1,061	3,850,241.05	806,699.31	3,043,541.74
1873.	2,478	1,386	1,092	4,717,887.29	643,713.04	4,074,174.25
1874.	2,407	1,244	1,163	5,242,706.46	770,711.37	4,471,995.09
1875.	1,561	786	775	4,557,762.42	532,510.50	4,025,251.92
1876.	1,867	891	976	4,264,877.74	474,632.45	3,790,245.29
1877.	1,659	945	714	5,761,106.27	434,638.48	5,326,467.79
1878.	1,559	902	657	2,791,036.66	287,628.44	2,503,408.22
1879.	2,293	1,740	553	8,698,460.56	241,611.22	8,456,849.34
1880.	382	291	91	3,696,566.34	100,607.68	3,595,958.66
Totals.	16,995	9,589	7,406	$45,237,002.77	$ 4,636,920.69	$40,600,082.08

CHAPTER X

THE ISSUE OF SOUTHERN CLAIMS FOR HALF A CENTURY

THE NAST cartoon in which the Republican elephant made its first appearance in 1874 showed the lesser animals stampeding the symbolic elephant into a pit labeled "Southern Claims," "Chaos," and "Rum."[1] By the stroke of his pen, one of the most famous cartoonists of the time thus chose claims from the South as one of the controversial political topics of the 'seventies. Throughout this decade the Republican zealot's aim was to serve those apostles of the "bloody shirt" who thrived on propaganda designed to build up suspicion of the late Confederate states. And as each election year added to the strength of the Democratic party, editorial concern increased over the need to protect the Treasury against what were generally termed "raids from the South."

In October, 1872, a month before the presidential election, an editorial in *The North American Review* reminded its readers that the men of the South were rapidly fulfilling Greeley's prediction that they could "expect to regain as Democrats, through elections, the power they lost as rebels through war." Now that the Liberal Republicans had split the party, in an "anything to beat Grant" campaign, the editorial continued, the Southerners would be able to follow the last public advice of Jefferson Davis, "to wait patiently until they saw their political opponents 'divided and at issue with themselves, and then join the party and support the candidate and the platform that promises a restoration of constitutional liberty.' "[2] Although three thousand troops still remained in the South, thirteen Confederate generals were sitting in Congress, and more Democratic votes in Congress represented the power to pass, or at least persistently to advocate, the private acts covering claims of individual Southerners which could shortly bankrupt the country.[3]

The Northern press charged that these claims, fostered by claim

---

[1] The cartoon, which appeared in *Harper's Weekly*, was recently reprinted, as characteristic of the period, in Roger Butterfield, *The American Past* (New York, 1947), p. 218.

[2] Editorial on the "State of the Union," *The North American Review*, CXV (Oct., 1872), 409. Of the Liberal Republican convention of May 1, the editorial commented, "Here was a revenue-reform convention nominating the most radical and inveterate protectionist in the country; a movement for the purification of politics seized upon and controlled by some of the most desperate political gamesters that even New York City could send to Cincinnati." See *ibid.*, pp. 407–408.

[3] *Ibid.*

agents, were so great in number and so enormous in amount that they dwarfed the national debt, and that all Southern claims were fraudulent. For example, in an editorial headed "More Rebel Claims," the New York *Times* on January 15, 1873, featured a specific claim pending before the Court of Claims in which the Bank of Louisiana asked reimbursement for the $95,000 in specie received from Jefferson Davis. The allowance of such claims, the *Times* warned, must be deplored since they would soon "pay the rebel debt."[4]

Mark Twain, also, chose a particular claim for attack, and then encouraged the controversy his attack provoked. On October 11, 1875, he wrote James G. Blaine, who had been listed as an endorser, that the claimant in this case, one Vaughan, had just written "a marvelously foul & scurrilous letter to the [Hartford] *Courant* in reply to me & they have naturally suppressed the libelous thing. But I am not going to allow any such gem to perish. I shall publish it in the fall, along with my *other* evidence that this beggar is a fraud & a canting hypocrite."[5] Blaine, it should be noted, had already declared himself in the matter in a letter to Twain:

After the late cruel war was over Washington . . . [became] the resort of those suffering patriots from the South who through all Rebel persecutions had been true to the Union and the number was so great that the wonder often was where the Richmond Government found soldiers enough to fill its armies. . . . If the advent of Vaughan teaches you Hartford saints no other lesson, let it deeply impress on your minds a newer, keener, fresher appreciation of the trials & the troubles, the beggars, the swindlers, and the scalawags wherewith the average congressman is evermore afflicted.[6]

This controversy was reflected in the halls of Congress. Commenting on an amendment introduced by Senator George F. Edmunds, in February, 1873, to curb payments to "disloyal" claimants, the worried New York *Times* noted that rejection of this measure in the House marked the fourth time the two houses had collided on this point, and commended the Senate for "always acting to prevent the payment of money

---

[4] The New York *Times*, Jan. 15, 1873, Vol. XXII, No. 6654, p. 1.

[5] Letter from Samuel Langhorne Clemens to James G. Blaine from "Castle Beautiful," Oct. 11 [1875], in Papers of James G. Blaine, Vol. I, Manuscript Division, Library of Congress. In this letter Clemens submitted a draft of his reply which contained the statement that Blaine's " 'real convictions are that Vaughan belongs to that innumerable caravan of dead beats whose headquarters are in Washington.' "

[6] James G. Blaine to Samuel Langhorne Clemens, Augusta, Maine, Oct. 9, 1875, in *ibid.* Blaine explained that Vaughan had appeared in Washington about 1868 or 1869. "His mug was like that of Oliver Twist and he evoked your pity," he wrote, "even if its first of kin, contempt, went along with it.... He fastened on me as his last hope & continually brought me notes of commendation, letters of introduction, & rewards of merit."

to claimants whose treason was notorious, while so many local sufferers by the war are debarred from the possibility of restitution." At
the same time the paper deplored the action of the House which was
"always unwilling to do anything to interfere with payment . . ."[7]

The Southern Claims Commission, however, was generally immune
from attack. The *Times,* in the midst of its war on private claims, took
occasion to commend the commission for its careful and judicious work.
After passage of the appropriation bill for some $870,000 covering
cases allowed in the second Annual Report of the commission, the
paper noted that "ordinarily no such amount could ever get through
. . . but being certified by this commission the bill passed almost unanimously."[8]

As these Annual Reports reached Congress each December during
the 'seventies, the case of the Southern loyalist and his right to compensation was regularly reviewed. The first Annual Report, submitted
on December 11, 1871, was not discussed in the House until May, 1872,
by which time the Committee on Claims had "looked more or less into
every one of the claims allowed and disallowed . . . chiefly . . . to see if
they could depend upon the action of the commission."[9] At the insist-
ence of James Garfield, the bill appropriating a total of $346,990.90
for 324 cases allowed was read paragraph by paragraph. Since each
claimant scheduled for allowance was named in the act alongside the
amount allowed him, this process was a lengthy one. Six of the cases
so reported were deleted by amendment. But on the whole, after some
discussion of the policies outlined by the commission, the House concurred with the estimate of its Committee on War Claims that the
newly constituted board had been "careful, prudent, and just. If it
has been unjust in any respect . . . it has been in giving the benefit of
the doubt always to the Government and against the claimant."[10] In
submitting the bill, the House committee had unanimously recommended that the reports of the commission could be regarded as prima-
facie evidence of loyalty.

In the Senate, by recommendation of its Committee on Claims, five
more cases were deleted by amendment, but the body of the report
was accepted. In conference the House withdrew three of its amendments, the Senate one, and the bill passed both houses and was signed
by the President on June 8, 1872.[11] In general, the annual review fol-

---

[7] New York *Times,* March 1, 1873, Vol. XXII, No. 6693, p. 1.
[8] *Ibid.,* Feb. 9, 1873, Vol. XXII, No. 6675, p. 1.
[9] *Cong. Globe,* 42d Cong., 2d Sess. (May 18, 1872), pp. 3618–3619.
[10] *Ibid.,* p. 3618.
[11] *Ibid.* (June 8, 1872), pp. 4432, 4434, 4460.

lowed this same process. In February, 1873, with the second Annual Report under consideration, the House of Representatives quickly accepted the estimate from Austin Blair of the Claims Committee that "on a careful examination we found that we could not improve the work of the Commission," and the Senate, with a few exceptions, agreed "to stand upon the award of the commission and the approval of the House of Representatives."[12]

An exception occurred in 1875, when Roscoe Conkling and George F. Edmunds questioned whether the commission's report should be accepted as prima-facie evidence, emphasizing the fact that the three-man board was not a judicial tribunal like the Court of Claims, where the government could appear in defense. The function of the commission, they said, was rather to "assemble" ex parte evidence and to preserve testimony.[13] But William Lawrence, chairman of the Claims Committee, pointed out that the claims themselves spoke for the adequacy of the evidence assembled, that the recommendation was in every case unanimous on the part of the three commissioners, that the clerk of the committee had carefully checked each case, and that the committee members themselves had looked into every case in which the amount allowed exceeded $2,000.[14] After this brief flurry the report was accepted as it had been submitted by the commission, with one or two exceptions.[15]

The admiration of William Lawrence for the work of the commission appears in the discussion of a bill which Lawrence introduced on January 28, 1874.[16] Because he considered the commission to be "the best machinery yet devised to secure evenhanded justice" in the matter of war claims, Lawrence's bill proposed to enlarge and perpetuate the board, and to include in its jurisdiction all claims before the Quartermaster and Commissary departments.[17] But on February 4, 1874, President Aldis appeared before the Senate Committee on Appropriations to oppose the bill and suggest that a two-member "Northern Claims Commission" be established to adjudicate the six million claims then pending in the departments. Aldis made it clear at this time that he was concerned with extending the tenure of office of his commission to insure a thorough investigation of the claims already filed.

---

[12] *Ibid.*, 42d Cong., 3d Sess. (Feb. 8, 1873), p. 1202, and (Feb. 26, 1873), p. 1775.
[13] *Ibid.*, 43d Cong., 2d Sess. (March 3, 1875), p. 2192.
[14] *Ibid.*, p. 2267.
[15] *Ibid.*, p. 2275.
[16] *Cong. Record*, 43d Cong., 1st Sess. (Jan. 28, 1874), p. 995.
[17] *Ibid.* (June 3, 1874), pp. 4511–4518.

On December 21, 1874, the Washington *Chronicle* published a scorching editorial attacking the methods by which claims were handled in Congress. The *Chronicle* charged that:

... it is a truth, that the most capable Senators and Representatives of experience will heartily indorse, that a committee of Congress is, in many respects, an unfit and unsafe place for the adjudication of such cases. Unfit because the members of the committees will not all attend and give their attention to the business. The whole work, consequently, devolves on a few persons, who cannot carefully examine all the cases. ...

The laxity of Congress had made it "a sort of axiom at the national capital that no claim presented to Congress can ever be effectually disposed of except by its payment," the paper argued, "while an adverse decision by a court, after a full hearing, would end it forever."[18]

Lawrence wrote an open letter in reply, categorically denying the charge that his committee had been careless, but agreeing that a judicial body of some sort offered the best means for getting at the problem. He reminded the *Chronicle* readers of several bills he had introduced which recognized this problem, and enlarged on his proposal to extend and perpetuate the Southern Claims Commission for this very purpose. A second bill, introduced on June 3, 1874, had proposed to increase the membership of the commission to five, in order to expedite its action on claims without decreasing its efficiency; to strengthen the penalties for perjury in connection with testimony taken; and to transfer all claims from the Quartermaster and Commissary departments to its jurisdiction. Such a solution would, Lawrence pointed out, go far toward withdrawing from Congress the process of "the investigation of the facts," in favor of a more equitable procedure. This bill also proposed an extension of the date for filing claims from March 3, 1873, to March 3, 1875, to provide recourse for those claimants who had been "forever barred" by the summary estoppage act of March 3, 1873.[19]

During the debate on this bill, Lawrence argued on the floor for the continuance of the Claims Commission, as opposed to an alternative suggestion that the same purpose could be accomplished by referring such cases to the Court of Claims. In the first place, he pointed out, the court had already within its limited jurisdiction far more work than it could handle expeditiously. Furthermore, the commissioners of claims had an established and separate jurisdiction, an understanding

---

[18] The Washington *Daily Morning Chronicle*, Dec. 21, 1874, editorial page.
[19] *Cong. Record*, 43d Cong., 1st Sess. (June 16, 1874), p. 5048. This bill passed the House but was not introduced into the Senate.

of the peculiar problems concerned with quartermaster and commissary supplies, and a well-established mode of procedure, and had thoroughly demonstrated their efficiency. An extension of the powers of the commission would, he was convinced, largely eliminate the delay in reaching decisions on claims from the South which had become "a national disgrace."[20]

Lawrence's political motives for such legislation were revealed in his proposal, by a joint resolution, for an amendment to the Constitution which would provide that "no claim against the United States shall be paid unless presented . . . by the claimant within ten years after having the legal right and capacity to do so, or within such less period as may be prescribed by law."[21] The Chicago *Tribune* had commented that his "proposition is a good one," but no amendment to the Constitution was required, since the same purpose could be accomplished by law "and Congress could be bound thereby." On Christmas Day, 1874, Lawrence wrote an open letter addressed to the *Tribune* in which he argued that only an amendment could give assurance against the seeming immortality of claims. An amendment was required, first because the power of investigating claims had been so long exercised by Congress that it had attained the status of an implied constitutional power. Moreover, Congress clearly had the power to appropriate money to pay such claims and, therefore, "whatever theory might be presented as to the duty of Congress to examine and ascertain their amount, Congress will continue to do so . . . especially with the democratic party and the Southern States, so largely interested in claims, fully represented in Congress." As long as the right to file any private claim, without such restrictions, existed in Congress, Lawrence concluded, the status of claims from the South would depend more upon the political complexion of Congress than upon any transitory limiting legislation it could pass. An amendment, therefore, offered the only real remedy for the urgent necessity to "protect the Government against enormous and fraudulent claims, especially those arising in the Southern States and growing out of the war." When the more than thirteen hundred claims then pending in his Committee (asking more than $20,000,000) were added to claims introduced in the Senate "to an enormous amount," it was obvious, he concluded, what raids

[20] *Ibid.* (June 3, 1874), pp. 4510–4517.
[21] The Chicago *Tribune*, Dec. 23, 1874, Vol. XXVIII, No. 123, editorial page. The *Tribune* quotes the resolution in full.

on the Treasury would occur "if the democratic party comes into power."[22]

Meanwhile, on May 1, 1874, the claims commissioners had asked for a ruling regarding numerous petitions for reopening and reëxamining claims they had already disallowed. On May 13 the House committee sent word that "the duty of the Commissions as to each and every claim presented to them . . . is concluded when the same has been reported to Congress, it being understood however, that any additional evidence sent to, or obtained by, the Commissioners after the claim has been reported to Congress, should be forwarded to be filed with such case for the information of the Committee."[23] As a result, Charles F. Benjamin, clerk of the commission, could inform claimants that "the proper & necessary course to pursue & the only course under existing laws is for the claimant to petition Congress for relief." The same ruling applied, of course, to claimants who had failed to file within the two-year period set for receiving claims for the commission.[24]

The effect of such limitations, as soon became obvious, was not to decrease the number of claims being heard but rather to shift the load back to Congress. With the approach of another presidential election, claims from the South again became a featured political issue. In September, 1876, the New York *Tribune* entered wholeheartedly into the campaign against claims, with a charge that the "Bourbon House" had appropriated $485,000 for Southern claimants which, said the *Tribune*, represented a considerable portion of the debt to the United States. Such awards were but a taste of what the country might expect, the writer continued, if the Democrats moved into the White House.[25] The broadside attack became so widespread that the Democratic candi-

---

[22] *Ibid.*, Dec. 28, 1874. Lawrence's letter included a long discussion of the historic right of any citizen to petition the government for a redress of grievances, holding that "where there is a right to petition, there is a corresponding duty to hear and act on the petition." Lawrence continued: "There are two classes of powers; those which are conferred by express provisions of the Constitution and those which are incidental. . . . When our Constitution confers upon Congress, as it does in the very first section of the first article, all legislative powers therein granted, there is given to Congress the incidental power to ascertain every fact necessary to enable it to legislate intelligently on every subject within its constitutional jurisdiction. . . . That power has been exercised from the foundation of the Government up to this time, and it has never been doubted or denied."

[23] Henry H. Smith, clerk, Committee on War Claims, to Commissioners Aldis, Howell, and Ferriss, Washington, May 13, 1874, in Southern Claims Commission, "Miscellaneous Letters Received," Record Group 56, Treasury Department, National Archives.

[24] Letter from Charles F. Benjamin to Amos Payne, Washington, Jan. 22, 1876, in records of the Senate Committee on Claims, 45th Congress, Legislative Department, National Archives.

[25] The New York *Tribune*, Sept. 29, 1876, Vol. XXVI, No. 11077, p. 1.

date, Samuel J. Tilden, in a public letter promised to veto all claims from the South growing out of the war. This statement was immediately labeled by the Republicans as a mere campaign promise designed to impress Northerners, but Southern Democrats understood and endorsed it, since they realized that its real purpose was to win an election.[26]

The New York *Times* commented regarding the Tilden statement: "With a Confederate Congress howling at his heels, and with threats from the leaders who would hold in their hands the success or failure of his administration, he would no more stand by the promise than he would tell the truth about his income tax."[27]

A satirist produced an imaginary bill providing for the Grand Consolidated Rebel War Claims Collection Company of the Solid South which, with the aid of a Democratic President and Congress, would collect from Northerners for "trespassing" in the Confederacy. Named for the board of directors of this mythical company were Jefferson Davis, Robert Toombs, Wade Hampton, Benjamin H. Hill, and General P. G. T. Beauregard. Its chief business was described as obtaining Federal reimbursement for direct taxes, supplies, and rental of buildings during the late war: its aim to obtain a "solid South" and divide the North. Finally, it was explained that it would be open for business and ready to function with a Democratic President and Congress.[28]

In January, 1877, with a lameduck Congress sitting and the outcome of the Hayes-Tilden election still in doubt, the *Times* expressed its impatience over the fact that the House Judiciary Committee had failed to report on a resolution asking for a report on a constitutional amendment which would prohibit payment by the United States of any claims for the use or destruction of property by the Union army during the war. This resolution, which would have called out the amendment within two days, was defeated for lack of a two-thirds vote. The *Times* reminded its readers that, in view of Tilden's promise that claims bills would be vetoed, "the Democratic shuffling with this matter is eminently characteristic. Mr. Tilden's Southern followers do not propose to surrender without a struggle their chance of reimbursing themselves for some of the cost of the rebellion, and a sufficient number

[26] *Ibid.*, Oct. 25, 1876, Vol. XXXVI, No. 11099, p. 2, reprints the letter from Tilden to Abram S. Hewitt. For a sample of selections made by the *Tribune* from editorials in the press of the North and the South commenting on Tilden's promises, see *ibid.*, Nov. 1, 1876, Vol. XXXVI, No. 11105, "Public Opinion," p. 5.

[27] The New York *Times*, Oct. 25, 1876, No. 7836, editorial page.

[28] From the correspondence column in the New York *Tribune*, Nov. 3, 1876, Vol. XXXVI, No. 11107. Even Thurlow Weed had written a letter to the *Tribune* expressing his concern that the South was getting out of hand and, if Tilden was elected, might revolt. See *ibid.*, Nov. 1, 1876, Vol. XXXVI, No. 11105.

of Northern Democrats are in sympathy with the ex-rebels on that point to render the great army of Southern claimants anything but a visionary danger to the National Treasury."[29]

Again four years later, during the Garfield-Hancock campaign, claims were an issue. The New York *Tribune,* which had led in the attack on Southern claims, featured a front-page story titled "Confederate Rapacity," which reviewed its own warnings, and the record of the Democratic party, in the matter of claims. The paper recalled that a series of articles in the summer and fall of 1878 had warned that "a mass of Southern claims were making their appearance in Washington." In October, 1879, another series of articles on claims had caused Democratic statesmen to hasten to declare that "their party as a party was not in favor of the payment of Southern Claims." In view of these promises, the article continued, and especially of Hancock's stand, it seemed remarkable that the Democrats would have the effrontery to present any claims at all, but "the manufacture of Southern Claims as an industry has not ceased."

This broadside attack continued with a review of the series of bills which had been presented to the House within the past year, and then presented an extensive and carefully itemized list of the grand aggregate of the amounts demanded by the "Solid South" for internal improvements, private relief bills, state claims, and refunds on the cotton tax which would, the paper estimated, total $1,390,970,313 in 1880.[30] Hancock's announcement that he would veto all measures for "rebel" claims meant nothing, the *Tribune* insisted: first, because a candidate's letter meant nothing in any case; secondly, because his veto might not be sustained; and thirdly, because the President might die, in which case the Vice-President would be under no commitments. Citing a bill introduced by Congressman William D. Hill of Ohio, which would have removed all claims from the jurisdiction of the Court of Claims and referred them to the appropriate circuit courts, the paper charged that this also was a typical Democratic plot. "The daughters of the horse-leech would not stand before the doors of the White House crying 'Give, give,'" said an editorial. "They would wait at the back-stairs of the courts until Democratic justice, a creature like unto themselves, should come and feed them."[31]

The issue of claims in the 1880 campaign was heightened by the fact that the commissioners of claims had closed their doors early in the

---

[29] The New York *Times,* Jan. 9, 1877, Vol. XXVI, No. 7901, p. 5.
[30] The New York *Tribune,* Sept. 16, 1880, Vol. XL, No. 12359, pp. 1–2.
[31] *Ibid.,* Oct. 8, 1880, Vol. XL, No. 12381, editorial page.

year. Once again, therefore, no regularly established tribunal for the adjudication of claims, except by private acts of Congress, existed. Many claimants argued that the decision as to their disloyalty had rested on a technicality dictated by the restrictive rules of the commission; others felt that the amounts allowed represented mere token payments for the losses they had sustained. In addition, a large number of people, many of whom were appealing to Congress, maintained that the summary act which had, within the single day of March 3, 1873, closed the doors of the commission for the filing of claims, worked a severe hardship. Claimants who had been denied the right to a hearing were held, by this restrictive act, to be barred by reason of their own failure to file claims on time.

It is not surprising, therefore, that a little over nine months after the commisison closed its doors, a bill appeared in Congress making provision for further consideration of claims from the South. The Bowman Act, as it came to be known, was passed two years later, on March 3, 1883, and remained in effect for twenty-eight years, until March 3, 1911. Selwyn Z. Bowman, of Massachusetts, introduced his bill in December, 1881. In his introductory statement he explained that it would provide "that either House of Congress, or any committee of any Department of Government, may (not must or shall, but may) send any claim to the Court of Claims in order that it may not enter judgment, not send an appropriation bill here . . . but find the facts simply and report them to the body which sent the case to them."[32] In effect, he said, it would make the Congress a "supreme court of claims," since the legislative branch of government would occupy a position quite similar to that of the Supreme Court in regard to legal cases.

The ensuing debate occupied two years, as had been the case with the formation of the Southern Claims Commission. And again, like these debates of the previous decade, the whole status of the South was reviewed, with some show of emotion on both sides. Edward S. Bragg, of Wisconsin, charged that "these honest claims which have been spoken of in such pathetic terms [by Bowman] . . . are claims that start from mere nothing and after years and years of talk and conversation . . . become wonderfully large and wonderfully honest. These claims in a great measure are like wine; they grow richer and better and finer-flavored as year after year rolls over them."[33] The bill, he said, should properly have been entitled, "A bill to surrender the Treasury of the United States to the claim agents in Washington."[34]

---

[32] *Cong. Record*, 47th Cong., 1st Sess. (April 21, 1882), p. 3149.
[33] *Ibid.* (April 22, 1882), pp. 3186–3187.
[34] *Ibid.*, p. 3201.

Replying in kind, Bowman charged:

> The gentleman from Wisconsin goes on the assumption . . . that members of Congress are rascals; the Court of Claims are rascals; and the Attorney General is a rascal. . . . I turn in despair to the gentleman from Wisconsin, and hunt like Diogenes with his lantern in vain for an honest man in Congress, in committee, in the Court of Claims, among the judges, in the Attorney-General's Department. I say to him in utter despair, "whom can we trust . . . ?" And that gentleman, pointing with pride to his manly breast, says "Behold me . . . the only monument of honesty in a wicked Congress."[35]

Leonidas C. Houk of Tennessee, who had acted as a special agent for the Southern Claims Commission during its early years, made one of the strongest speeches from the floor favoring the bill. Houk, who served in Congress from 1879 to 1891, rested his argument on the familiar thesis that "Tennessee and for that matter the southern States were never disloyal—rather the individuals or groups thereof were." When Union soldiers like himself were being paid in depreciated greenbacks, he said, loyal Northerners at home were converting their enormous profits into gold-bearing bonds. Meanwhile, the Southern Unionist had been fortunate if he received only a scrap of paper from an army which "had been ordered to forage upon and live off the country as it moved South, giving receipts for supplies as it was impossible to distinguish between loyal and disloyal, and to await eventual payment." Thus, in effect, "the 'war claim' of the Northern man was put in the shape of a bond and the 'war claim' of the Southern Unionist remains an unwritten but equally just obligation of the government."

Houk further warned that the Republican party had better take cognizance of the disaffection in the Border states because of the failure of Republicans to pay just claims. He reviewed the fate of loyal men of Tennessee who had taken advantage of the extension of the act of July 4, 1864, to that state, pointing out that it "was and has been hedged about with so much cumbersome machinery and so many 'red tape' processes . . . originating in the peculiar systems of West Point and the regular Army, that it amounted . . . to an obstruction . . . of the means of reaching justice."[36]

Briefly, the Bowman Act, as it was passed, provided that any committee of either house of Congress, or any of the executive departments having before them any claim which was not "barred by virtue of the provisions of any law of the United States," might refer a claim to the Court of Claims. The court could then, by judicial procedure,

---

[35] *Ibid.*, pp. 3201–3202.
[36] *Ibid.* (April 21, 1882), pp. 3159–3162.

ascertain all the material facts in the case, render judgment, and refer it back to Congress or the department for final decision and indemnification. Section 4 referred to claims for "supplies or stores taken by or furnished to any part of the military or naval forces of the United States," during the war, and required that claimants before the court must show that they did not give "aid or comfort to said rebellion" but were, through the war, loyal to the government of the United States "and the fact of such loyalty shall be a jurisdictional fact," or grounds for dismissal.

This strict limitation respecting loyalty, which harked back to the 1860's, was possible in spite of Supreme Court decisions covering amnesty, because cases filed under the Bowman Act were classified as Congressional cases under the Court of Claims. In such cases the court was endowed only with investigative powers similar to those possessed by the Southern Claims Commission, and the nature of the investigation could, therefore, be specified by the Congress. Section 5 of the Bowman Act was largely concerned with defining the investigative process to be used, and largely accepted the procedure of the court in providing that the attorney general, or his assistants, should always appear for the defendant, the United States, "with the same power to interpose counterclaims, offsets, defenses for fraud practices or attempted to be practiced by claimants, and other defenses . . ."[37]

In its structure, therefore, the Bowman Act was a revamped version of the McDonald amendment which, some twelve years earlier, had sought to extend the limiting act of July 4, 1864, to include claims from the South, with the Court of Claims as the established seat of judgment. According to the court's own interpretation of its jurisdiction under this legislation, "the purpose of the Bowman Act was not to dispense with legal evidence, but to acquire it . . . and when a claim is transmitted by a committee of Congress under the act the purpose is to secure the judicial ascertainment of facts by judicial means, namely, by that which the law defines to be competent evidence."[38] Or, in a more lengthy opinion in the case of *Smith* v. *United States,* this court said regarding the Bowman Act:

The only question presented . . . is whether Congress and its committees and the executive departments shall have the privilege or right, if they deem it advisable, to have the facts in any case before them properly investigated by a tribunal which can ascertain those facts in a legal manner, in the same mode adopted by the courts which have jurisdiction of similar cases, and with the safeguard to the

[37] 22 *U.S. Stat. at L.,* 485.
[38] *Carroll* v. *United States,* 20 Ct. Clms. 431.

Government of the power of cross-examination of witnesses, all of which is impossible to be accomplished by Congress, its committees, or the executive departments.[39]

The key phrase of the act proved to be that part of section 3 which provided that the jurisdiction of the court was limited to cases not "now barred by virtue of the provisions of any law of the United States." For those prospective claimants before the Southern Claims Commission whose right to file had been abrogated with a day's notice on March 3, 1873, the Bowman Act offered no relief. Neither did it apply to the cases barred for nonprosecution under the act of March 3, 1877. Having been "barred forever thereafter" for failure to file or to prosecute a claim within the time specified by these acts, the claimant was subject to the rule of laches. The Bowman Act meant, generally speaking, that the claim must have been previously presented to some officer or tribunal having jurisdiction to entertain it.

Even more important, as the Bowman Act was applied, were those limitations which had been set by the rulings of the commission itself or by the statute creating the commission. For example, those claims of corporations, such as churches, lodges, schools, or hospitals, or claims of persons who had passed through bankruptcy which had been dismissed by the commission as being beyond its jurisdiction, could not be held to come under the Bowman Act, since no other avenue for their review had been opened. Similarly, claims for rent and claims presented by aliens could not be heard under this act. Moreover, the commission's ruling was maintained: that loyalty must be proved, not only by the claimant himself, but—in the event of his death—by every distributee, heir, or creditor. The full effect of these earlier rulings by the commission cannot, of course, be estimated from the number of claims disallowed on jurisdictional grounds, since announcement of such stern rules probably prevented the presentation of many claims, which were therefore not eligible for consideration under the Bowman Act.

As a result of these discriminations maintained by the Bowman Act, the Tucker Act of March 3, 1887, was passed as an extension of the Bowman Act, substantially broadening the jurisdiction of the Court of Claims. By the provisions of the new act, virtually any bill providing for payment of a claim, except a pension, might be referred for review. Many claims were thus admitted for a first hearing almost a quarter of a century after the close of the war. Among the most inter-

---

[39] *Smith* v. *United States*, 19 Ct. Clms. 691.

esting of these cases are the petitions of churches and schools which had waited so long for judicial appraisal.

The distinctions drawn by the Court of Claims between its jurisdiction in the Bowman and in the Tucker acts are set forth in some detail in *Dowdy* v. *United States,* decided on March 16, 1891. The government had argued for dismissal of the case on jurisdictional grounds, resting its case on two main arguments: first, that the court lacked jurisdiction because "the only thing that can be referred under the Tucker Act is 'a bill pending in either House of Congress,'" and second, that, since the Tucker Act really amounted to an amendment of the Bowman Act, claims referred under it fell under the jurisdictional discriminations set by the earlier act. The court's decision, however, overruled the motion of the government's attorneys and held in substance that section 14 of the Tucker Act was "not an amendment of the Bowman Act." The jurisdiction conferred by the Tucker Act was thus "an independent and distinct thing from the jurisdiction conferred by the other," since the wording of the more recent law specified that "any bill may be referred 'except for a pension,' and there is no other restriction upon the jurisdiction of the court."[40]

The court went on to explain that claims for destruction of property by the army or for the occupation of real estate at the seat of war, claims barred by an act of Congress, or even claims of men who had given aid and comfort to the rebellion, were "all within the jurisdiction of the court for the purpose of investigating and reporting the facts," if properly referred under the Tucker Act. Thus almost exactly thirty years after the Supreme Court had held, in the case of *United States* v. *Pargoud* in 1863, that claimants under the Captured and Abandoned Property acts were relieved from "proof of adhesions to the United States during the late civil war," those claimants whose property, as furnished, had consisted of quartermaster and commissary supplies were at last allowed, with respect to loyalty, equal status before the law with the men whose claims came under the act of March 13, 1863.

The true intent of Congress in passing the Tucker Act—as shown by the Dowdy decision—was that under the Bowman Act, the court could not take jurisdiction of a claim barred by any statute. But

---

[40] 26 Ct. Clms. 223. In the opinion, the court censured the House resolution, which had referred the claims under consideration, for referring to them as "claims" rather than as "bills," but concluded, "Nevertheless, the House of Representatives has signified an intent that something pending before it in the nature of a private claim shall be referred to this court for an investigation of the facts, and that the court shall take jurisdiction ... and it is the duty of the court to give effect to the intent of the House if there be any statutory authority for so doing."

under the Tucker Act, the court was "especially directed to report any facts bearing upon the question whether the bar of 'any statute of limitations should be removed by Congress,' or 'which shall be claimed to excuse the claimant for not having resorted to any established legal remedy.' " In conclusion, with reference to use of the term "bill" rather than "claim" in the Tucker Act, the court held that "it is not the original parchment or paper termed a bill which is to be referred to the court.... It is not even its verbal contents. What is intended to be, and what is referred by the statute, is *the subject of legislation described in and represented by the bill.*"⁴¹

The Bowman and Tucker acts were in effect until March 3, 1911, when a law described as "an act to codify, revise, and amend the laws relating to the judiciary," commonly called the Judicial Code, repealed them but provided in section 151 of the code what was practically a reënactment of the Tucker Act, with the additional provisions contained in an act of June 25, 1910, that all cases tried under the Tucker Act must contain in their findings of fact "such conclusions as shall be sufficient to inform Congress of the nature and character of the demand, either as a claim, legal or equitable, or as a gratuity, against the United States and the amount, if any, legally or equitably due from the United States to the claimant."⁴²

Four years later, however, on March 3, 1915, the Crawford amendment to a large Omnibus Claims Bill abruptly withdrew from the Court of Claims all jurisdiction in the matter of Southern war claims. This Omnibus Bill, which was the largest introduced, included allowances for schools and hospitals in the amount of $486,403.28, and for individuals to a total figure of $1,191,368.33. As the names of individual claimants were read, one by one, Senator Coe E. Crawford, of South Dakota, began his own small filibuster on each case. He questioned the rulings of the court on individual cases and charged that the bill itself was "full of driftwood." Finally, in the middle of the monotonous name-by-name review, Crawford proposed his amendment providing that "from and after the passage and approval of this act" the jurisdiction of the Court of Claims could not include any war claims for the destruction of property, for stores and supplies taken or furnished for the use of the army or navy, or, indeed, for "any claim now barred by process of any law of the United States."⁴³

⁴¹ 26 Ct. Clms. 223. In the opinion of the judges, the Court of Claims should take jurisdiction of a private claim referred by the House of Representatives for investigation.

⁴² 36 *U.S. Stat. at L.,* 837.

⁴³ *Cong. Record,* 63d Cong., 3d Sess. (March 3, 1915), p. 5318.

The amendment passed the Senate on a ruling of the presiding officer who, with the consent of Nathan P. Bryan, chairman of the Claims Committee, held that, without motion to the contrary, the amendment would be considered accepted. Only James A. Reed, of Missouri, rose to attack this summary action and to point out that no time had been allowed to consider a bill which would affect hundreds of persons. The bill passed the Senate over Reed's objection; it passed the House with equal speed and, on the following day, had been signed by the President and was in effect." Thus the final curtain on fifty years of claim legislation fell suddenly.

For contrast, the proceedings in the Court of Claims, in those cases which were concerned with a review of decisions rendered by the commissioners of claims, may here be briefly outlined. Reference of a claim to the Court of Claims, under any of the acts previously described, meant only that the claimant had conferred upon him, usually by Congress, the privilege of presenting his claim to the court for a judicial determination of the facts. Under the rules of the court, a sworn petition must have been filed, and witnesses were examined as in chancery practice. Depositions were taken in behalf of the claimant, and his witnesses were subject to cross-examination by counsel representing the government. In addition, lawyers in the service of the Department of Justice made independent investigations of claims, and if any unfavorable facts were found, government witnesses were also called and examined. After the testimony had been taken, counsel for the claimant and for the United States prepared briefs, and usually the cases were argued orally before the court. In every case, an active defense was made by the counsel for the government, employed for that particular purpose, and acting under the direction of an assistant attorney general.

The reports of the assistant attorney general in charge of the defense of cases in the Court of Claims show that beginning with the enactment of the Bowman Act on March 3, 1883, practically two claims out of every three under the jurisdiction of the court were either dismissed or the findings were adverse. Further, with regard to the cases in which allowances were made by the court, the claims were so scaled down by the court that the total of amounts allowed over four decades was only about 8 per cent of the total amounts claimed in all cases considered." These figures may be compared with the ten-year record

⁴⁴ *Ibid.*, pp. 5291–5294; 5303–5312; 5317–5321; and for House action, see pp. 5741–5742.
⁴⁵ 23 Ct. Clms. 463.

of the Southern Claims Commission which showed a total of $4,636,-
920.69 allowed, approximately 7.6 per cent of a total of $60,258,150.44
claimed.[46] Another comparison is offered by the records of the court
covering the awards made under the act of March 13, 1863. By 1888
the Court of Claims had allowed only about twice this amount—or
an estimated $9,864,300.75, for cotton and contraband—to petitioners
from the North as well as from the South.[47]

The following cases give an indication of the court's rulings on those
claims which appeared first before the commission and then were appealed under the Bowman or Tucker acts. In the case of *Nance* v.
United States, the court ruled that findings by the commission that
a claimant was disloyal must stand until his loyalty could be established by competent and sufficient evidence taken since the findings
of the board.[48] Similar rulings in the cases of *Stern* v. *United States*[49]
and *Calhoun* v. *United States*[50] held that a claim rejected by the Southern Claims Commission must also be rejected by the Court of Claims
unless new evidence over and above that considered by the commission
had been included. Again, in *Small* v. *United States*, it was held that
another calling of the same witness for further evidence was insuffi-
cient cause for reopening the case in the court.[51]

Contrasts in procedure between the commission type of examination—as exemplified by the decisions of Aldis, Ferriss, and Howell—
and the clearly judicial type of procedure before the court, appear in
other opinions. In *Dodd* v. *United States*, the court ruled that the
powers of the Southern Claims Commission had not been judicial and
its decisions were not final: that they were, in legal effect, the reports
of a special committee to Congress. At the same time, the appropriation
acts, which provided for the payment of claims recommended by the
commission, were held to have effected a final discharge for claims paid
but of no others.[52] Claims within the jurisdiction of the Southern
Claims Commission but not presented to it were likewise held to be
barred under section 3 of the Bowman Act, even though, as in the
case of *Burwell* v. *United States*, the payment had been accepted under

---

[46] *Cong. Record*, 46th Cong., 3d Sess. (March 3, 1881), pp. 2406–2407, 2431, 2455,
2471.

[47] J. G. Randall, *The Confiscation of Property during the Civil War* (Indianapolis, 1913), p. 50.

[48] *Nance* v. *United States*, 23 Ct. Clms. 463.

[49] *Stern* v. *United States*, 32 Ct. Clms. 533.

[50] *Calhoun* v. *United States*, 24 Ct. Clms. 414.

[51] *Small* v. *United States*, 33 Ct. Clms. 451.

[52] *Dodd* v. *United States*, 21 Ct. Clms. 117.

protest.[53] At the same time, the rules of the court provided that materials assembled by the commission could be submitted as evidence, "subject to such objections to their competency or relevance as might be made if the deponents were examined in open court or their depositions were regularly taken under the rules of this court."[54]

---

[53] *Payne* v. *United States*, 22 Ct. Clms. 144, and *Burwell* v. *United States*, 22 Ct. Clms. 92.

[54] "Additional Rules in the Court of Claims of the United States," term of 1883–84. (Washington, 1884), p. xxx.

CHAPTER XI

THE SOUTHERN UNIONIST JOINS THE SOLID SOUTH: SUMMARY AND CONCLUSIONS

ONE OF THE heaviest penalties the Southern Unionist suffered as a result of the war was that in the half century of sectionalism following the war's conclusion, his real motives, his services, and his very existence within the Southern home front became obscured. One reason for this was his wartime tendency to identify himself with the South, refusing to renounce his section even though he retained his principles. For such men, the cause of the Union was not held to be the exclusive property of the North.

The dichotomy between personal sentiments and abstract convictions is a recurrent theme in the testimony before the commissioners of claims. Ten years after the war, with vitally needed capital at stake, the Unionist almost invariably refused to say that he rejoiced at the liquidation of his section. His purpose seems never to have been to sell out his state but rather to save it from its own folly. Thus Francis A. Owen, of Austin, Mississippi, maintained: "I had no confidence in the success of the South and I did not desire it. I believed it to be an effort to establish an oligarchy, and we would have been a little handful of men just there, and we would have had to have pocketed the insults of the North and every other nation that was disposed to [insult us]." However, "if you want me to say, or expect me to say, that I hate the South because they were at war with the Union, I cannot say it."[1]

Under a similar cross-examination, Augustus F. Hurt, of Fulton County, Georgia, explained, "My sympathies personally were with my friends who were exposed to danger and their homes to desolation, but politically my sympathies were with the country in the efforts to establish peace and restore good government." Mrs. Aaron V. Brown, of Tennessee, in an almost identical phrase, stated, "Whatever sympathies I had with relatives & friends on the Southern side were sentiments of a personal character & not sympathies with the cause in which

---

[1] Testimony of Francis A. Owen, of Austin, Tunica County, Mississippi, before the commissioners, in his own claim [claimed $14,090, disallowed in 1880], C. of C. No. 549, Justice Department, National Archives. The claim was disallowed in spite of the abundant testimony of witnesses as to his loyal reputation. Senator James L. Alcorn, a Mississippi Republican, attested his loyalty with the concluding statement that "the revolution had never received in any way his approbation." Union officers likewise had been convinced of his loyalty.

they were engaged. My sympathies during the war were with the Union cause . . . from the beginning to the end of the war."[2]

Strengthened by such convictions, the Unionist overlooked the epithets of "yankee-lover," "traitor," or "Tory" used by his Confederate neighbors. The doctrine of natural rights inherited from an earlier generation, the classical moderation of a tradition of aristocracy, and the position of almost unquestioned sovereignty occupied by the lord of a plantation all contributed to a sturdy independence on the part of the landed Southerner. Unionism flourished on the very individualism which had helped to produce the Confederacy and which then, in turn, contributed to its disintegration. Even such a stanch revolutionist as Robert Toombs reflected this disintegrating tendency when, on his Georgia plantation in 1864, he defied the Confederate government to impress his goods or to force him to plant grain instead of cotton, by maintaining that the independence of the South would be worthless "unless accompanied by personal liberty."[3]

Data in the records of the Southern Claims Commission pinpoint the diversity as well as the homogeneity of Southern society.[4] The depths of convictions which prompted some Southerners to take their stand for the Union, at the opposite end of the spectrum from Toombs, are graphically revealed in the well-known cases of divided families. Several relatives of James A. Seddon, Confederate secretary of war, appeared before the commission with their claims. His cousin, Dr. Hugh Morson, who had been an assistant surgeon in the United States Navy for ten years before the war, described the breach between the two of them, made by the issue of secession, which had not healed a decade later. "I was more intimate with him than a brother before the war," Morson testified. But he added, "I have not seen him since 1861, when we parted after an intimate talk. . . . Letters pass through my wife when anything comes to the family."[5] Filed as evidence of Morson's claim is a handwritten letter from Seddon, regretting the doctor's persistent Unionist activities within the Confederacy.

---

[2] Testimony of Mrs. Aaron V. Brown, cited in "Summary of testimony for & against loyalty, May, 1879," in her own case [claimed $26,880, allowed $1,869.50 in 1880], C. of C. No. 1613, GAO files.

[3] U. B. Phillips, *The Life of Robert Toombs* (New York, 1913), p. 248.

[4] See especially Clement Eaton, *Freedom of Thought in the Old South;* Ulrich Bonnell Phillips, *The Course of the South to Secession,* edited by E. Merton Coulter (New York, 1939); T. J. Wertenbaker, *Patrician and Plebeian in Virginia* (Charlottesville, Va., 1910); Vernon L. Parrington, *Main Currents in American Thought* (New York, 1927-1930).

[5] Testimony of Hugh Morson before the commission, Washington, Oct. 30, 1872 [claimed $13,461.50, allowed $7,067 in 1872], C. of C. No. 11613, GAO files.

Commodore Edward Middleton, of South Carolina, joint owner of the Hobonny plantation with his brother, served with the United States Navy throughout the war, "though thereby he became estranged from his brother and his family." According to the overseer of the plantation, "All [of the family] except the Commodore were with the South," and the bitterness between the brothers was intensified when Oliver Middleton "lost a son in the war—a very promising young man."[6] The Commodore's loyalty was itself sorely tried, for while he was serving the United States in the Pacific on the U.S.S. *St. Mary,* the Federals under Sherman burned his mansion house and all plantation buildings and carried off large supplies of rice, corn, peas, cattle, sheep, hogs, potatoes, and mules to the troops at Pocataligo.[7] It may be noted, too, that the restrictions against payment of claims to Southerners, even in so obvious a case of loyalty to the Union, had precluded any compensation for his losses until 1873, when he received $12,240 from the Southern Claims Commission.

Mrs. Aaron V. Brown, mentioned above, chose the Union side, because she was the widow of James Buchanan's postmaster general, rather than follow her brother, General Gideon J. Pillow, into the Confederacy. Though her son served on Pillow's staff and she had inherited a large plantation and 120 slaves, her loyalty was readily established. She had acceded to the Emancipation Proclamation and spoken before and during the war of the "inconsistency of the people of the South shouting for liberty and freedom while they themselves held four millions of human beings in severe servitude."[8] Mrs. Brown refused to take an oath to the Confederacy and "regretted the dissolution of the Union and the destruction of the Republic ... and threw my energies, resources, and moral support on the Federal side."

In the final assessment, the Southern Unionist may well have wondered, in the years following Appomattox, whether he had suffered more in the war of weapons or in the debates over his legal rights. He became the chief victim in the clash between the judicial, executive, and legislative branches of the government over the constitutional relation of the defeated Confederacy to the Union. Nevertheless, he pressed his claim in all three branches, demanding that commitments

---

[6] Testimony of Benjamin T. Sellers before the commission, Washington, March 15, 1872, in the case of Edward Middleton, Beaufort, South Carolina [claimed $14,703, allowed $12,240 in 1873], C. of C. No. 10531, GAO files. Sellers described himself as a loyal Confederate.

[7] Summary Report of the commissioners in *ibid.*

[8] Testimony of J. E. Sanders before Special Agent N. M. Fitzgerald, Dec., 1879, in the case of Mrs. Aaron V. Brown [claimed $26,880, allowed $1,869.50 in 1880], C. of C. No. 1613, GAO files.

to his section made by the government of the United States be honored. His supporters used him as a weapon against the whole Radical position. A brief survey of conditions during the late years of the war and the early days of peace suggests that he might have had other uses as well. Many historians maintain that the South was ready, immediately after Appomattox, to accept in good faith its failure to establish the right of secession, to agree to the repudiation of Southern war debts, and to look forward to full reinstatement within the Union in compliance with the armistice terms.[9] Both Grant and Sherman had prescribed terms of surrender which were moderate and directed toward a reunion of the country. Lincoln, throughout his presidency, saw the Southern Unionist as a man of vital importance in the task of effecting a speedy restoration of the Union. As early as November, 1862, he wrote, regarding proper postwar policy, "To send a parcel of Northern men here as Representatives, elected, as would be understood, (and perhaps really so,) at the point of the bayonet, would be disgraceful and outrageous; and were I a member of Congress here, I would vote against admitting any such men to a seat."[10] In 1863 the nucleus of "loyal" citizens, even the one-tenth of the voters upon which Lincoln arbitrarily settled as a sufficient number to establish "loyal" state governments, could, he believed, form a rallying group to act toward resumption of citizenship under the Federal government. Speedy reunion, rather than subjugation, was his immediate goal. The use of Southern leaders seemed to him absolutely necessary. His conditions for state recognition required an oath of allegiance to the United States by a loyal nucleus equal to one-tenth of the votes cast at the presidential election of 1860 by individuals who had pledged themselves to support the acts and proclamations with respect to slavery. In Louisiana, Arkansas, Tennessee, and Virginia the preliminary steps were inaugurated under this plan, though Congress refused to admit the representatives chosen.[11]

The case histories here under review, and an examination of the

---

[9] Recent studies which reveal the extent of this attitude in the South are Lillian Adele Kibler, *Benjamin F. Perry, South Carolina Unionist* (Durham, N.C., 1946), Charles W. Ramsdell, *Behind the Lines in the Southern Confederacy* (Baton Rouge, 1944), James G. Randall, *Lincoln and the South* (Baton Rouge, 1946), and Howard K. Beale, *The Critical Year: A Study of Andrew Johnson and Reconstruction* (New York, 1930).

[10] Abraham Lincoln to Hon. George F. Shepley, military governor of Louisiana, Washington, Nov. 27, 1862, reproduced in J. G. Randall, *The Civil War and Reconstruction* (Boston, 1937), p. 700.

[11] William A. Dunning, *Essays on the Civil War and Reconstruction* (New York, 1904), pp. 76–77, and the section on "Presidential Restoration of the States," pp. 75–87.

recently opened Lincoln manuscripts, not only document the presence of Unionists of wealth, position, and influence in strategic numbers but also demonstrate that their ideas were welcomed by Lincoln and by key political figures North and South. On August 28, 1863, Armistead Burwell of Vicksburg wrote Lincoln, in the hope that his observations as a native Southerner might be of some weight. This letter, from a trained observer familiar with his subject and devoted to his section as well as to the Union, outlined a program which Lincoln, in large measure, followed. Burwell urged the use of Unionist sentiment and rising disaffection to reunite the country into a peaceful whole. He based his program on three premises which may be repeated here as they were written:

1st It is a great error into which ignorant, excited, and prejudiced men are liable to fall, that those who do not come out boldly for the Union are its enemies, or in the modern phrase, *disloyal*. There are thousands in Miss: who desire most ardently the restoration of the United States Government, who yet see no way, in which their sentiments can be safely or beneficially expressed.

2nd The majority of those who have now resolved upon taking sides with the Union when it is safe and expedient to do so, is bitter and unsparing in its denunciation of Jefferson Davis & Co. This is their first step and a long one, upon the return path. If you wish to hear Jeff: Davis, Wigfall, Toombs, Floyd, &c, &c, cursed from the bottom of the heart, & with the whole soul, go disguised to Vicksburg, and converse with the men of Mississippi.

3rd There are many bold and talented men, once men of wealth and influence, who at all hazards were willing to raise the old standard, and follow it to the death.

Burwell made the challenging statement that *"there are more un-conditionally loyal or Union men in that state* [Mississippi], *in proportion to population than in the state of Ohio or New York."* As for the issue of slavery, he pointed out that the advance of the Union army through a slave country had had the effect of settling the problem by abolishing the institution.

There remained, therefore, two sensible courses: Burwell proposed that an overture be made to the people of Mississippi and Louisiana providing that, on renunciation of their state governments and the restoration of their rights under the Federal constitution, "the whole question of Slavery ... be left to the decision of the Judicial tribunals, to be enforced as are all decrees by the power of the United States Government." Lincoln could then "offer free pardon, abandon all thought of criminations, retaliations, forfeiture and punishment." The founding of one good newspaper in Vicksburg to make such a policy known could, Burwell believed, bring about "a revolution ... more damaging to Jeff Davis & Co., than all that can be done by any one Corps of our Army. In four months Union meetings would be held all over the state, and the state & Federal Governments would take the place now occupied by the tyrannical and usurping faction."[12]

On October 27, 1863, Edward Fowler, "a citizen of Montgomery," brought to Lincoln's attention that the August elections in Alabama had sent "a large majority of *Union men*" to the legislature. R. Jameson, the senator elected to replace Yancey was, Fowler reported, "a devoted union man," and Colonel J. J. Sables, probable successor to the ailing C. C. Clay in the Confederate senate, was known to be a man opposed to "the rebellion with all his heart." The Union cause was being strengthened daily, Fowler wrote, and "prominent men who I know well who twelve months ago were bitter rebels are now *secretly* lending all their energies and influence *for* a quick return to the old flag."[13]

From Arkansas, Hon. E. W. Gantt, formerly a colonel in the Confederate army, forwarded a printed copy of his "Address ... to the People of Arkansas on October 7, 1863," urging a return to the Union as the wise course for a people whose "last man is in the field. Half our territory overrun. Our cities gone to wreck—peopled alone by the aged, the lame and halt, and women and children. ... And anarchy and ruin, disappointment and discontent," he added, "tower over all the land." His own earlier course for secession, Gantt stated frankly, was as wrong as was his refusal to take his seat in the United States Congress after an overwhelming victory in 1860. "To those who differed from me in the commencement of this rebellion—the extent and bloodiness of which no mortal could foresee—I must say, that developments show, that you were right and I wrong. But let bygones, be forgotten, and let us all unite to bring about peace, and to lure our

---

[12] A. Burwell to Abraham Lincoln, St. Louis, Aug. 28, 1863, in R. T. Lincoln MSS, Vol. 121, Manuscript Division, Library of Congress. For the account of Burwell's situation in Vicksburg, see the case of Armistead Burwell, Vicksburg, Mississippi [claimed $35,150, allowed $11,248 in 1879], C. of C. No. 111, GAO files. Burwell's loyalty was unquestioned by the commissioners, his Unionism having been established with the assistance of Duff Green as one of many witnesses.

[13] Edward Fowler to Lincoln, New York, Oct. 27, 1863, in R. T. Lincoln MSS, Vol. 129, Manuscript Division, Library of Congress. Fowler had ʻfled to New York in 1862 after serving as surgeon to the Union prisoners in Montgomery. "Being destitute of food I fed them," he wrote, "naked I clothed them—gave them money, and for this act of mercy I had to leave." Col. Sables, he said, had been "compelled by public opinion to command a Confederate regiment for a time," but was "a man of high courage exalted principle and fully to be trusted" who had served the United States as minister to Belgium under Buchanan.

lost Pleiad from her wanderings, that she may again sparkle in our Nation's coronet of Stars!"[14]

From Louisiana, Rev. Thomas Bacon wrote prophetically in 1864 of the effects on a growing Unionist sentiment of the arbitrary action under General Banks with regard to the pending elections, which "turns our Registry of voters into a nullity ... and opens the door ... to the over-powering [of] the voice of the loyal people of Louisiana by that of strangers." Bacon identified himself to President Lincoln as a "thorough-going Union man of Louisiana," who had "conversed with you several times upon the affairs of our State." There was, he wrote, a complete suppression of "real liberty of discussion about our own local affairs among real Union men," who were growing "indignant and anxious" but "have faith in *you*, sir, that you will not suffer a pretended Government to be thrust upon them."[15] General Banks was, he believed, more unpopular in Louisiana than even General Butler had been, since the people "understood what the latter meant and said but what the former thinks conciliation they judge to be only equivocation."[16] As for himself, Bacon concluded, "I for one, have *no fears* of the re-establishment of Slavery. But I have great fears that peaceful loyalty will be postponed for many a day in Louisiana if we are to be loaded with this sort of Lecompton Constitution upon the pretense of any good end whatever."[17]

The Lincoln-Johnson plan of reconstruction met the ideas of these Southern men. It drew upon positive factors within the framework of defeat and was, as Professor James G. Randall has pointed out, "forthright and practical. It included overthrow of the army and government that warred against the United States, abolition of slavery (though some of Lincoln's statements seemed to imply a concession

---

[14] Address of Hon. E. W. Gantt to the people of Arkansas, Oct. 7, 1863, in R. T. Lincoln MSS, Vol. 127, Manuscript Division, Library of Congress. Gantt warned the South against being "deceived with the hope that the United States will abandon the struggle. They can never do it. They have toiled and spent too much to see the solution of the problem, and not foot up the figures. They scarcely feel the war at home. Their cities are more populous and thrifty today than ever. For every man that dies or gets killed in battle, two emigrate to the country.... They could sink their armies to-day, and raise new levies to crush us and not feel it."

[15] Thomas S. Bacon to "His Excellency, the President of the United States," Feb. 5, 1864, in R. T. Lincoln MSS, Vol. 141, Manuscript Division, Library of Congress. Bacon added, "I belong to none of the associations, clubs, parties or cliques which are at war here. I have no personal entanglement or interest—no animosities or attachments to gratify. I speak only from serious conviction and concern." See also the case of Thomas S. Bacon, Alexandria, Louisiana [claimed $13,500, allowed $3,050 in 1874], C. of C. No. 4041, GAO files.

[16] Bacon to Lincoln, March 4, 1864, in R. T. Lincoln MSS, Vol. 146.

[17] Bacon to Lincoln, Feb. 5, 1864, in *ibid.*, Vol. 141.

here), pardon for the past, loyalty for the future, reunion, amnesty for Confederates, return of confiscated property, and home rule for the South."[18] Questions of Negro suffrage and civil rights were deferred, and revolutionary social changes avoided. The program was aimed at restoration instead of reconstruction, the method was conciliation instead of coercion. The principles were acceptable not only to such loyalists as Thomas Bacon, Judge William Sharkey, James Sullivan, and William Bailey, but also to the swelling ranks of disillusioned Confederates.

The Southern Unionists were in a key position to consolidate disaffection to the Confederacy with latent Unionism into an effective movement for the "Union as it was." Accustomed to think in national terms, they had frequently occupied positions of importance before secession and were more concerned about reunion than any other group, south or north. Some of them were experienced in emancipation, having freed their own slaves. All were acutely aware of the evils and problems of slavery. Their views were tempered, however, by the large uneducated minority in their midst, and they could not readily indulge in the bounding absentee morality of the Northern abolitionist. With intelligent support from Washington, but without the arbitrary and often unreal requirements of the radical plan which was eventually superimposed on the South, they might have helped to reëstablish state governments which combined national purpose with permanent improvement in the conditions of the entire Southern community.

In some instances the Unionist did attain office, only to receive orders from Washington which destroyed his influence. Judge Sharkey who, as has been seen, served as military governor of Mississippi following the war, was finally defeated in his battle to obtain from the courts a ruling on the validity of military government in time of peace. Hon. J. Madison Wells, who was elected governor of Louisiana in November, 1865, and who served until the Federal military occupation under Sheridan in April, 1867, is another conspicuous example of a Unionist in office whose administration was as effectively sabotaged by Federal policy as by embittered secessionists or the Ku Klux Klan.

Wells made no secret of his Union sympathies during the war, and, after a careful examination of his record, the claims commissioners were able to conclude that "there is no doubt of his loyal adherence to

[18] James G. Randall, "Lincoln's Peace and Wilson's," *The South Atlantic Quarterly*, XLII (1943), 226.

the govt. of the United States throughout the war."[19] His Unionism was not of the passive type. Although he was one of the largest land-holders in the state, he had emancipated his own slaves before the war. An old-line Whig and later a Douglas man, he voted against secession candidates for the state convention in 1860. During the following year he succeeded in killing any appropriations in his parish for military purposes. "After all peaceable means resorted to . . . were exhausted," Wells told the commissioners, "I then resorted to violence. I fought them wherever I could. Whenever they destroyed my property I would attempt to catch their wagons and wagon trains." A fugitive from Confederate authorities because of his "annoyance to them in the movement of their troops," he organized resistance in the pine woods behind his plantation.[20] To consolidate the dissenting portions of his community, he had circulated the word that he was going to raise the Union flag in the town of Alexandria.[21] When his son, a Confederate conscript, deserted and joined the jayhawkers, Wells was accused of supplying these guerrillas "with the sinews of war."[22] So public were his efforts that he was forced to leave the country, and a purse was made up by his Unionist friends to assist him to escape.[23] With the arrival of the Union army, he returned home to offer his services, and in December, 1863, he went to Washington, where he conferred with Lincoln and Chase.[24]

It is especially to the point as evidence of the possibilities inherent in the Lincoln-Johnson plan that Wells, an active Unionist, was elected to office with the support of Confederate veterans who, under President Johnson's proclamation of amnesty, voted in Louisiana in 1865.[25] His administration as governor (1865 to 1867) was a struggle

---

[19] Summary Report of the commissioners of claims in the case of J. Madison Wells, Rapides, Louisiana, [claimed $450,658.80, allowed $4,080], C. of C. No. 19675, Justice Department, National Archives.

[20] Testimony of J. Madison Wells before the commissioners of claims, Washington, March 24, 1880, in *ibid.*

[21] Testimony of Dr. John P. Davidson, in *ibid.* Davidson said, "Some of his friends feeling very certain that if Wells attempted a feature of that kind he would be killed, sent him word . . . that it would be at the peril of his life if he attempted it."

[22] Testimony of Dr. A. Cockerille, physician and planter, taken in Louisiana by Enos Richmond, special agent, and submitted on Feb. 21, 1880, in *ibid.*

[23] Testimony of Nelson Taylor, keeper of a livery stable and United States mail contractor, Rapides Parish, Louisiana. Taylor himself had contributed to the purse, along with M. R. Ariel, John Bogan, Jr., Thomas McNeil, and H. T. Burgess. See *ibid.*

[24] Summary Report of the commissioners in *ibid.*

[25] For the details of this election, see Roger W. Shugg, *Origins of Class Struggle in Louisiana: A Social History of White Farmers and Laborers During Slavery and After* (University, Louisiana, 1939), pp. 210–212.

with Northern officers of occupation and Southern recalcitrants who were eager to reassert the rights of Southerners. His comment to the commissioners on the Republican policy which had removed him, may be given here for its stark brevity. "We had some difficulty about the levee," he testified on May 26, 1875, in Washington. "I thought that as Governor of the State I had the right to appoint the levee Commission. General Sheridan appointed three gentlemen himself & we differed and he removed me. . . . After his removal of me Congress gave the power to the Commanding General to remove Governors."[26] Perhaps this abrupt dismissal and his wartime experiences account for his questionable conduct as a member of the Louisiana returning board in 1876.

In 1865, as in 1861, that equilibrium of reason and emotion which produces statesmanship was a possibility. Even after Lincoln's death and the consequent increased bitterness, there was widespread approval of a moderate program in the South which was shared, early in 1866, by the majority of Northern political leaders, the outstanding military heroes of the time, and the people at large. The Philadelphia Convention in August was designed to consolidate moderates, in both the North and the South, behind Andrew Johnson. But in the November election, as Professor Howard K. Beale has pointed out in his study of the critical year of 1866, the Radical opponents of the Johnson policy employed "personal defamation, shouts of 'Copperhead' and 'traitor' against political and economic opponents, unreasoning passion, rodomontade—claptrap rather than issues . . ." to win in Congress. As a result, "military rule and negro supremacy supplanted slowly reviving democratic institutions in the South . . . [and] the 'solid South' was created out of political diversity."[27]

Coercion and force became the order of the day. The state governments created under Johnson were dissolved. Military districts were established under armies of occupation. A sweeping new electorate of three-quarters of a million Negroes was enfranchised overnight, and a like number of white voters was disfranchised. Civil courts were ignored, freedom of press and speech invaded, test oaths instituted, and legislatures purged.

[26] Testimony of J. Madison Wells in Washington, May 26, 1875, in his own case, Rapides Parish, Louisiana [claimed $450,658.80, allowed $4,080 in 1880], C. of C. No. 19675, Justice Department, National Archives. Wells was presumably referring to the supplementary reconstruction act of March 23, 1867, which divided the South into five military districts and placed Federal commanders in charge of all political activities.

[27] Beale, *The Critical Year*, pp. vii, 2, 9, and chap. iv, "Moderate Third Party Movement."

Did this vindictive policy toward an entire region, which submerged the Southern Unionist, achieve or delay the fundamental purposes of Radical reconstruction? Despite the ambivalent nature of Northern policy, the perfectionists with their idealistic aims, and the propagandists for the protection of a sectional economy, could not a more realistic *rapprochement* have been effected under a moderate program conducive to the reëmergence of a two-party system? The white rulers of the South were not solid from 1861 to 1866. The war did not allay ante-bellum differences, and frequently it intensified them. It was the specter of black supremacy and the struggle for redemption which finally produced an unstable union between traditional Southern opponents. "The lines of cleavage followed roughly the old seams in the web where the Whigs and Union men of the South had been forcibly joined with the Democrats and Secessionists."[28]

The Whigs were traditionally the custodians of the Federalist legacy in the South. In a renewed two-party strife with the Democrats, political rivalries might have served as a wedge to broaden suffrage and amend inequalities in the state constitutions. Few will now deny that the carpetbag constitutions provided for fundamental and enduring democratic reforms in education, judicial procedure, and franchise, and a broadened concept of governmental responsibility for the welfare of the citizens. But these long-run humanitarian objectives were effectively sabotaged by the short-run means of effecting them. By making the Negro the instrument of Congressional reconstruction, the Radicals may well have delayed his substantive enfranchisement which William A. Dunning has described as "the chief end of the Reconstruction Acts."[29]

The peak period of Radical reconstruction, which brought into full play the doctrine of constructive treason, found dozens of ways of holding the Southern Unionist equally guilty with the most confirmed secessionist. Indeed, in some cases, Unionists were charged with a special responsibility for failing to stop the hasty action of their state. "If they had reflected," reads a House report in 1874, "that secession

---

[28] C. Vann Woodward, *Reunion and Reaction* (Boston, 1951), p. 30.

[29] Dunning, *Essays on the Civil War and Reconstruction*, p. 138. Although the chief contention of the Radicals was that "actual conditions in the South were intolerable, and that military force was needed for the mere maintenance of peace, apart from political reorganization," Dunning concluded that "the weight of evidence pointed to the contrary." Especially reassuring in 1866 were the reports of army commanders and of the commissioners of the Freedmen's Bureau. "The most striking evidence that affairs were assuming a normal condition in the South was afforded by the extent to which military authority and jurisdiction were withdrawn during the year 1866."

and rebellion would stamp them all as *enemies* of the lawful National Government, subject to having their property taken or destroyed, by or in aid of its military operations, or to weaken the power in revolt, without any compensation, it might have induced a vigilance which would have averted the calamity of civil war." In concluding its indictment the report continues, "Their inaction or want of energy in resisting secession brought death and all the woes of war. . . . Their moral guilt was an omission of duty. In the transgression of active secessionists all in legal contemplation transgressed."[30]

The effect, on the Unionist in the South, of such a verdict appears in his testimony before the commission. To Milton Shirk, president of a "literary institution" in Shreveport, Louisiana, his own status in international law, or according to decisions rendered by the Supreme Court or in debates in Congress, was especially confusing as he surveyed his immediate postwar situation. A man of Northern birth, he told the commissioners of claims how, having waited long for the Union army to arrive and liberate him, he freely gave over the keys of his college when that army arrived, so that the buildings might be used as a hospital. But the college was not occupied. Instead, it was burned. "I confess," Shirk testified, "that when my property was destroyed, I felt ugly. . . . I considered that I had been in favor of the Union throughout. . . . It is difficult," he added, "to discriminate between a feeling that would prevail when a man's premises were all on fire, & set on fire by his friends." When he was then subjected to the measures of Congressional reconstruction and his claim for goods furnished the army was repudiated, his loyalty to the government under which he was born received a final blow.[31]

What happened to the Southern Unionist after the war can better be understood in the light of two World Wars and their tragic aftermath. The Civil War, which split such a man's world in two, was followed by a period during which he was suspended in time. The "Union as it was," which he had expected to inherit, had collapsed. His civil and political rights were removed. His potentialities for leadership were limited almost as much by his economic disaster as by his political disfranchisement. The tremendous losses of position and property suf-

---

[30] *House Report No. 134*, 43d Cong., 2d Sess., p. 213.

[31] Testimony of Milton Shirk, Shreveport, Louisiana, taken in Washington, Oct. 25, 1872, in his own case [claimed $126,602, allowed $5,205 in 1872], C. of C. No. 8308, GAO files. Although the commissioners expressed their concern over the great loss sustained by this man of proved Unionism, the steep reduction in the amount claimed and allowed was made because they could not, in line with their policy of ruling out losses due to depredation and destruction, make any allowances for the burning of the college buildings.

fered by these Unionists impoverished them at the moment they were compelled to set up a new labor and wage system for the purposes of restoring production and rebuilding after destruction. By December 20, 1870, Dr. James B. Sullivan, for example, was seeking some $24,-000, a fraction of his total losses, in order that he could once again "put in operation his cotton plantation, now idle, with 160 freedmen who are anxious to do the labor, and to avail themselves of the desire of your petitioner to improve and elevate their condition, in accordance with the view and progress of the Age."[32] His friend William Bailey, likewise stripped of his former prosperity, was also seeking "immediate relief" for the restocking of his plantation, "putting in new crops and thus providing for the support of my Family, including many of my former slaves who are waiting to get employment at wages."[33]

The valiant efforts of Gray W. Smith, of Mississippi, to reëstablish himself during this period were especially noted by Special Agent R. B. Avery in a letter to the commission. Smith owned a plantation of which one thousand acres were in cultivation before the war. During the war years he had put about seven hundred acres in corn, but in his own words, the Union cavalry "were feeding on me every time they came to Holly Springs, and they made 72 raids there."[34] At its close he was in debt to the amount of $32,000 but, the commissioners noted, "like an honest man, determined to pay it without recourse to fraudulent conveyance of lands, or going through bankruptcy." Sending his wife and daughter to live with friends in Memphis, he remained with his son, a Confederate veteran, on the plantation. There they worked the land themselves and cooked their own meals. "Coffee they did not use. In this way they lived for seven years, and the family was not united until the old debts were canceled, by payment in full with

---

[32] Petition of James B. Sullivan "praying for compensation for property," referred to the Committee on Claims, Dec. 20, 1870, thence to the commissioners of claims on March 15, 1871, in his own case [claimed $24,515, allowed $13,563 in 1872], C. of C. No. 250, Justice Department, National Archives.

[33] William Bailey to Edward M. Stanton, secretary of war, dated Nov. 24, 1865, in his own case [claimed $104,492.40, allowed $45,161.72], C. of C. No. 980, GAO files. Action on the payment had been deferred by a special military court on April 4, 1863, and by United States Court in New Orleans in June, 1864. In 1866, Stanton ruled that Bailey could not be paid because of the current construction of the limiting act of July 4, 1864. The case was finally allowed after extended review by the commission and after review by Congress when it reached that body in 1874. See *Cong. Record*, 43d Cong., 1st Sess., pp. 4181–4184; 5141–5152.

[34] Testimony of Gray Smith, Holly Springs, Mississippi, taken at Lamar, Mississippi, Dec. 1, 1877, by Special Agent R. B. Avery, in his own case [claimed $10,000, allowed $7,000 in 1878], C. of C. No. 4686, GAO files.

interest, except one debt due a bank, and upon which the interest was remitted."[35] Immediately after the war, Smith had made out a claim for $66,000 to cover his losses in "mules, horses, hogs, cattle, and other things." But in his own words, "I had no money, and I was in bad health, and I could not go to Washington, and so have had this reduced to $10,000 to enable me to prove it here."[36]

The political and economic liquidation of these individual planter Unionists was a failure in statesmanship. These men had been unwilling to renounce their states in adversity. They had suffered at the hands of their home communities, struggled against wartime inflations and shortages, lost the market for their cash crops, seen their capital in slaves disappear, watched the Union army carry off much of the goods that remained, and had finally been denied their citizenship and their vote as they were indicted with their section. Reconstruction subjected them to harsh measures conceived in the theory that it was good strategy, and often good politics, to maintain that the South had only itself to blame, and that an Old Testament concept of punishing for wrongdoing—the innocent with the guilty—was required.

In Georgia, where prewar Unionism had been powerful and disaffection to the Confederacy marked, the fate of the reviving Unionist party was described by Benjamin H. Hill, who told a Congressional committee in 1871: "We old whigs said, Well you see all the evils of secession that we prophesied have come true; Now we suppose the people will believe us." But in the meantime, "Congress came in, lumped the old Union democrats and whigs together with the secessionists, and said that they would punish us all alike." By that act the best argument of the Union party was nullified since, in Hill's words, it "prevented us from saying to the secession democrats that all they said was untrue; that the northern people had no desire to oppress them, because the acts of Congress proved they [the secessionists] were right."[37]

The bitter opposition to Radical politicians was, moreover, not always limited to native Southerners or former Confederates. One especially violent attack on Washington was written by a veteran of the Union army whose sentiments showed the division in the North at the very moment the solid South was being formed.

[35] Statement of Special Agent R. B. Avery, dated Lamar, Mississippi, Dec. 1, 1877, in *ibid.*
[36] Testimony of Gray Smith, as cited in footnote 34, above.
[37] Statement of Benjamin H. Hill, later senator from Georgia, in the Ku Klux Report, *Annual Cyclopedia* (New York, 1889), pp. 760–762.

You men of the South may rest assured that we, the rank and file of the old Federal Army, who fought you so gallantly, and whom you fought with more than Spartan courage, have no fear of you no more than you have of us. . . . The politicians would hail another war between the North and the South as a special Godsend just now, because they know they have lost the confidence of the masses of the people, and must soon retire to private life, and earn an honest living by honest labors. . . . We know all these hounds. They are scattered all over the North and the South. We are sick unto death of them and are bound to root them out. . . . They never fought in the war. Not they, indeed, except *on paper*. . . . They snuffed the battle from afar, and fired nothing more formidable than general and special orders. War was fun for them. They wept when it closed. It raised some of them from the dunghill of poverty and positive disgrace to the highest stations in the land. They want another war. If they could only get you and me, brethren of the South, by the ears like dogs, they would stand off at a safe distance; as they all did before, and cry "Seek him." But if they cannot involve us in another war, if they can only make the people of the nation believe there is danger of another war, they will accept that as the next best thing. . . . We want no more war. We think you want no more war. . . . Let us be brethren and live at peace forever. But first of all we must take these hounds who are provoking revolution for their selfish purposes and bury them under perfect avalanches of popular indignation and contempt at the ballot box in every State. Crush out all these political harpies and we shall have peace.[38]

By 1877, Professor C. Van Woodward maintains, the Federal support Hill called for became a brief actuality. An alliance between "Southern Conservatives and Northern wealth" was reëstablished, and on this "Whiggish coalition" Hayes based his Southern policy. Within the Whig traditions of compromise dating back to 1820, 1833, 1850, and the efforts of 1861, cabinet posts, withdrawal of the troops, redemption, and internal improvements for the South were to be exchanged for support of Hayes by the electoral commission.[39] Some former Unionists possibly participated in the negotiations. Whatever the high-level policy and behind-the-scenes negotiations may have been, the records of the Southern Claims Commission show they did not benefit individual claimants. Support came too late.

There is no evidence, in the struggles to end Reconstruction, that the Southern Unionists managed to raid the Federal treasury. The

[38] Published in the column "Round about Town," in the New Orleans *Times*, Jan. 29, 1875, Vol. XII, No. 6547, p. 1. The columnist commented, "His language is a little strong but just at the present time we can bear rather vigorous expressions, especially when they come from those whose position in the late conflict exonerates them from the malicious charge of their disloyalty to the Government or chagrin at defeat."

[39] Woodward, *Reunion and Reaction, passim*. A thoughtful and dispassionate new analysis of the impact of Congressional reconstruction on the Negro is presented by George B. Tindall in his work, *South Carolina Negroes, 1877–1900* (Columbia, 1952).

establishment of the Claims Commission had, as a partial aim, the purpose of making some belated restitution to worthy Unionists. But it must also be said that any encouragement to a flickering flame of Unionism which had been inspired when the commission was established, probably died down as the severe testing procedures and the philosophy behind the loyalty test became known. These fundamental concepts of the commissioners were retained unmodified during the decade in which the commission was active, and tended to bury any vestiges of Unionism which may have remained in the 1870's. In the vast mass records of the Southern Claims Commission were preserved the stories of the Unionist's courage and of his betrayal.

APPENDIXES

APPENDIX A

THE EIGHTY questions outlined for the use of the local commissioners by the three-man commission in Washington were revised and reissued on July 1, 1874.* The changes from the original form as presented in the first General Report and as amended in the second were not designed to affect the policy of the commission. Here, then, in its final form, is the questionnaire which had to be answered by each claimant or witness or by every person who gave testimony.

1. What is your name, your age, your residence, and how long has it been such, and your occupation.

2. If you are not the claimant, in what manner, if any, are you related to the claimant or interested in the success of the claim?

The following questions will be put to every claimant, except claimants who were slaves at the beginning of the war:

[NOTE—If the original claimant be dead, these questions are to be answered by each of the heirs or legatees who were not less than sixteen years of age when the war closed.]

3. Where were you born? If not born in the United States, when and where were you naturalized? Produce your naturalization papers, if you can.

4. Where were you residing and what was your business for six months before the outbreak of the rebellion, and where did you reside and what was your business from the beginning to the end of the war? And if you changed your residence or business, state how many times, and why such changes were made.

5. On which side were your sympathies during the war, and were they on the same side from beginning to end?

6. Did you ever do anything or say anything against the Union cause; and if so, what did you do and say, and why?

7. Were you at all times during the war willing and ready to do whatever you could in aid of the Union cause?

8. Did you ever do anything for the Union cause or its advocates or defenders? If so state what you did, giving times, places, names of persons aided, and particulars. Were the persons aided your relations?

9. Had you any near relatives in the Union Army or Navy; if so, in what company and regiment, or on what vessel, when and where did each one enter service, and when and how did he leave service? If he was a son, produce his discharge-paper, in order that its contents may be noted in this deposition, or state why it cannot be produced.

10. Were you in the service or employment of the United States Government at any time during the war; if so, in what service, when, where, or how long, under what officers, and when and how did you leave such service or employment?

11. Did you ever voluntarily contribute money, property, or services to the Union cause; and if so, when, where, to whom and what did you contribute?

* Fourth General Report of the Southern Claims Commission, in *House Misc. Docs.*, 43d Cong., 2d Sess., No. 17, pp. 38–42.

12. Which side did you take while the insurgent States were seceding from the Union in 1860 and 1861, and what did you do to show on which side you stood?

13. Did you adhere to the Union cause after the States had passed into rebellion, or did you go with your State?

14. What were your feelings concerning the battle of Bull Run or Manassas, the capture of New Orleans, the fall of Vicksburgh, and the final surrender of the confederate forces?

15. What favors, privileges, or protections were ever granted you in recognition of your loyalty during the war, when and by whom granted?

16. Have you ever taken the so-called "iron-clad oath" since the war, and when and on what occasions?

17. Who were the leading and best-known Unionists of your vicinity during the war? Are any of them called to testify to your loyalty; and if not, why not?

18. Were you ever threatened with damage or injury to your person, family, or property on account of your Union sentiments, or were you actually molested or injured on account of your Union sentiments? If so, when, where, by whom, and in what particular way were you injured or threatened with injury?

19. Were you ever arrested by any confederate officer, soldier, sailor, or other person professing to act for the confederate government, or for any State in rebellion? If so, when, where, by whom, for what cause; how long were you kept under arrest; how did you obtain your release; did you take any oath or give any bond to effect your release; and if so, what was the nature of the oath or bond?

20. Was any of your property taken by confederate officers or soldiers, or any rebel authority? If so, what property, when, where, by whom; were you ever paid therefor, and did you ever present an account therefor to the confederate government, or any rebel officers?

21. Was any of your property ever confiscated by rebel authority, on the ground that you were an enemy to the rebel cause? If so, give all the particulars, and state if the property was subsequently released or compensation made therefor.

22. Did you ever do anything for the confederate cause, or render any aid or comfort to the rebellion? If so, give the times, places, persons, and other particulars connected with the transaction.

23. What force, compulsion, or influence was used to make you do anything against the Union cause? If any, give all the particulars demanded in the last question.

24. Were you in any service, business, or employment, for the confederacy, or for any rebel authority? If so, give the same particulars as before required.

25. Were you in the civil, military, or naval service of the confederacy, or any rebel State, in any capacity whatsoever? If so, state fully in respect to each occasion and service.

26. Did you ever take any oath to the so-called Confederate States while in any rebel service or employment?

27. Did you ever have charge of any stores, or other property, for the confederacy, or did you ever sell or furnish any supplies to the so-called Confederate States, or any State in rebellion; or did you have any share or interest in contracts?

28. Were you engaged in blockade-running, or running through the lines, or interested in the risks or profits of such ventures?

29. Were you in any way interested in any vessel navigating the waters of the confederacy, or entering or leaving any confederate port? If so, what vessel, when and

where employed, in what business, and had any rebel authority any direct or indirect interest in vessel or cargo?

30. Did you ever subscribe to any loan of the so-called Confederate States, or of any rebel State; or own confederate bonds or securities, or the bonds or securities of any rebel State issued between 1861 and 1865? Did you sell, or agree to sell, cotton or produce to the confederate government; or to any rebel State, or to any rebel officer or agent, and if so, did you receive or agree to receive confederate or State bonds or securities in payment; and if so, to what amount, and for what kind and amount of property?

31. Did you contribute to the raising, equipment, or support of troops, or the building of gunboats in aid of the rebellion; or to military hospitals or invalids, or to relief-funds or subscriptions for the families or persons serving against the United States?

32. Did you ever give information to any person in aid of military or naval operations against the United States?

33. Were you at any time a member of any society or organization for equipping volunteers or conscripts, or for aiding the rebellion in any other manner?

34. Did you ever take an oath of allegiance to the so-called Confederate States? If so, state how often, when, where, for what purpose, and the nature of the oath or affirmation.

35. Did you ever receive a pass from rebel authority? If so, state when, where, for what purpose, on what conditions, and how the pass was used.

36. Had you any near relatives in the confederate army, or in any military or naval service hostile to the United States? If so, give names, ages on entering service, present residence, if living, what influence you exerted, if any, against their entering the service, and in what way you contributed to their outfit and support.

37. Have you been under the disabilities imposed by the fourteenth amendment to the Constitution? Have your disabilities been removed by Congress?

38. Have you been specially pardoned by the President for participation in the rebellion?

39. Did you take any amnesty oath during the war, or after its close? If so, when, where, and why did you take it?

40. Were you ever a prisoner of the United States authorities, or on parole, or under bonds to do nothing against the Union cause? If so, state all the particulars.

41. Were you ever arrested by the authorities of the United States during the war? If so, when, where, by whom, on what grounds, and when and how did you obtain your release?

42. Were any fines or assessments levied upon you by the authorities of the United States because of your supposed sympathy for the rebellion? If so, state all the facts.

43. Was any of your property taken into possession or sold by the United States under the laws relating to confiscation, or to captured and abandoned property?

The following questions will be put to all male claimants or beneficiaries who were not less than sixteen years of age when the war closed:

44. After the presidential election of 1860, if of age, did you vote for any candidate or on any question, during the war, and how did you vote? Did you vote for or against candidates favoring secession? Did you vote for or against their admission?

45. Did you belong to any vigilance committee, or committee of safety, home-guard, or any other form of organization or combination designed to suppress Union sentiment in your vicinity?

46. Were you in the confederate army, State militia, or any military or naval organization hostile to the United States? If so, state when, where, in what organizations, how and why you entered, how long you remained each time, and when and how you left. If you claim that you were conscripted, when and where was it, how did you receive notice, and from whom, and what was the precise manner in which the conscription was enforced against you? If you were never in the rebel army or other hostile organization, explain how you escaped service. If you furnished a substitute, when and why did you furnish one, and what is his name, and his present address, if living?

47. Were you in any way connected with or employed in the confederate quartermaster, commissary, ordnance, engineer, or medical department, or any other department, or employed on any railroad transporting troops or supplies for the confederacy or otherwise engaged in transportation of men and supplies for the confederacy? If so, state how employed, when, where, for how long, under whose direction, and why such employment was not giving "aid and comfort" to the rebellion.

48. Did you at any time have charge of trains, teams, wagons, vessels, boats, or military supplies or property of any kind for the confederate government? If so, give all the particulars of time, place, and nature of service or supplies.

49. Were you employed in saltpeter-works, in tanning or milling for the confederate government, or making clothing, boots, shoes, saddles, harness, arms, ammunition, accouterments, or any other kind of munitions of war for the confederacy? If so, give all the particulars of time, place, and nature of service or supplies.

50. Were you ever engaged in holding in custody, directly or indirectly, any persons taken by the rebel government as prisoners of war, or any person imprisoned or confined by the confederate government, or the authorities of any rebel State, for political causes? If so, when, where, under what circumstances, in what capacity were you engaged, and what was the name and rank of your principal?

51. Were you ever in the Union Army or Navy, or in any service connected therewith? If so, when, where, in what capacity, under whose command or authority, for what period of time, and when and how did you leave service? Produce your discharge-papers so that their contents may be noted herein.

The following questions will be put to every person testifying to the loyalty of claimants or beneficiaries:

52. In whose favor are you here to testify?

53. How long have you known that person altogether, and what part of that time have you intimately known him?

54. Did you live near him during the war, and how far away?

55. Did you meet him often, and about how often, during the war?

56. Did you converse with the claimant about the war, its causes, its purposes, its progress, and its results? If so, try to remember the more important occasions on which you so conversed, beginning with the first occasion, and state with respect to each when it was, where it was, who were present, what caused the conversation, and what the claimant said, in substance, if you cannot remember his words.

57. Do you know of anything done by the claimant that showed him to be loyal to the Union cause during the war? If you do, state what he did, when, where, and what was the particular cause or occasion of his doing it. Give the same information about each thing he did that showed him to be loyal.

58. Do you know of anything said or done by the claimant that was against the Union cause? If so, please state, with respect to each thing said or done, what it was, when it was, where it was, and what particular compulsion or influence caused him to say or do it.

59. If you have heard of anything said or done by the claimant, either for the Union cause or against it, state from whom you heard it, when you heard it, and what you heard.

60. What was the public reputation of the claimant for loyalty or disloyalty to the United States during the war? If you profess to know his public reputation, explain fully how you know it, whom you heard speak of it, and give the names of other persons who were neighbors during the war that could testify to his public reputation.

61. Who were the known and prominent Union people of the neighborhood during the war, and do you know that such persons could testify to the claimant's loyalty?

62. Were you, yourself, an adherent of the Union cause during the war? If so, did the claimant know you to be such, and how did he know it?

63. Do you know of any threats, molestations, or injury inflicted upon the claimant or his family, or his property, on account of his adherence to the Union cause? If so, give all the particulars.

64. Do you know of any act done or language used by the claimant that would have prevented him from establishing his loyalty to the confederacy? If so, what act or what language?

65. Can you state any other facts within your knowledge in proof of the claimant's loyalty during the war? If so, state all the facts and give all the particulars.

The following questions concerning the ownership of property charged in claims will be put to all claimants, or the representatives of deceased claimants.

66. Who was the owner of the property charged in this claim when it was taken, and how did such person become owner?

67. If any of the property was taken from a farm or plantation, where was such farm or plantation situated, what was its size, how much was cultivated, how much was woodland, and how much was wasteland?

68. Has the person who owned the property when taken since filed a petition in bankruptcy, or been declared a bankrupt?

The following questions will be put to female claimants:

69. Are you married or single? If married, when were you married? Was your husband loyal to the cause and Government of the United States throughout the war? Where does he now reside, and why is he not joined with you in the petition? How many children have you? Give their names and ages. Were any of them in the confederate service during the war? If you claim that the property named in your petition is your sole and separate property, state how you came to own it separately from your husband; how your title was derived; when your ownership of it began. Did it ever belong to your husband? If the property for which you ask pay is wood, timber, rails, or the products of a farm, how did you get title to the farm? If by deed, can you file copies of the deeds? If single, have you been married? If a widow, when did your husband die? Was he in the confederate army? Was he in the civil service of the confederacy? Was he loyal to the United States Government throughout the war? Did he leave any children? How many? Are any now living? Give their names and ages. Are they not interested in this claim? If they are not joined in this

petition, why not? State fully how your title to the property specified in the petition was obtained. Did you ever belong to any sewing-society organized to make clothing for confederate soldiers or their families, or did you assist in making any such clothing, or making flags or other military equipments, or preparing or furnishing delicacies or supplies for confederate hospitals or soldiers?

The following questions will be put to colored claimants:

70. Were you a slave or free at the beginning of the war? If ever a slave when did you become free? What business did you follow after obtaining your freedom? Did you own this property before or after you became free? When did you get it? How did you become owner, and from whom did you obtain it? Where did you get the means to pay for it? What was the name and residence of your master, and is he still living? Is he a witness for you; and if not, why not? Are you in his employ now, or do you live on his land or on land bought from him? Are you in his debt? What other person besides yourself has any interest in this claim?

The following questions will be put to all colored witnesses in behalf of white claimants:

71. Were you formerly the slave of the claimant? Are you now in his service or employment? Do you live on his land? Are you in his debt? Are you in any way to share in this claim, if allowed?

The following questions will be put to claimants and witnesses who testify to the taking of property, omitting in the case of each claimant or witness any questions that are clearly unnecessary:

72. Were you present when any of the property charged in this claim was taken? Did you see any actually taken? If so, specify what you saw taken.

73. Was any of the property taken in the night-time, or was any taken secretly, so that you did not know of it at the time?

74. Was any complaint made to any officer of the taking of any of the property? If so, give the name, rank, and regiment of the officer, and state who made the complaint to him; what he said and did in consequence; and what was the result of the complaint.

75. Were any vouchers or receipts asked for or given? If given, where are the vouchers or receipts? If lost, state fully how lost. If asked and not given, by whom were they asked; who was asked to give them, and why were they refused or not given? State very fully in regard to the failure to ask or obtain receipts.

76. Has any payment ever been made for any property charged in this claim? Has any payment been made for any property taken at the same time as the property charged in this claim? Has any payment been made for any property taken from the same claimant during the war; and if so, when, by whom, for what property and to what amount? Had this property, or any part of it, been included in any claim heretofore presented to Congress, or any court, department, or officer of the United States, or to any board of survey, military commission, State commission or officer, or any other authority? If so, when and to what tribunal to which it was presented?

77. Was the property charged in this claim taken by troops encamped in the vicinity, or were they on the march; or were they on a raid or expedition; or had there been any recent battle or skirmish?

78. You will please listen attentively while the list of items, but not the quantities, is read to you, and as each kind of property is called off, say whether you saw any such property taken.

79. Begin now with the first item of property you have just said you saw taken, and give the following information about it: First. Describe its exact condition— as, for instance, if corn whether green or ripe, standing or harvested, in shuck or husked, or shelled; if lumber, whether new or old, in building or piled; if grain, whether growing or cut, &c. Second. State where it was. Third. What was the quantity. Explain fully how you know the quantity; and if estimated, describe your method of making the estimate. Fourth. Describe the quality, to your best judgment. Fifth. State as nearly as you can the market-value of such property at the time in United States money. Sixth. Say when the property was taken. Seventh. Give the name of the detachment, regiment, brigade, division, corps, or army taking the precise property, and the names of any officers belonging to the command. Eighth. Describe the manner in which men, animals, wagons, or other means of transport, were engaged in the removal; how long they were occupied, and to what place they removed the property. Tenth. State if any officers were present; how you knew them to be officers; what they said or did in relation to the property; and give the names of any, if you can. Eleventh. Give any reasons that you may have for believing that the taking of the property was authorized by the proper officers, or that it was for the necessary use of the Army.

80. Now take the next item of property you saw taken, and give the same information, and so proceed to the end of the list of items.

APPENDIX B

REVISED INSTRUCTIONS FOR REPORTS OF SPECIAL AGENTS

THE FOLLOWING instructions appear in the manuscripts in the form of a letter written on April 7, 1875, from Charles F. Benjamin to Special Agent John B. Brownlow. The handwriting is partly that of Benjamin, partly that of President Aldis. The same instructions were forwarded to all special agents in the field. The body of the letter reads:*

...the Commissioners...desire me to communicate to you such instructions as those under which all their agents now operate, and to say that they are to be fully observed by you while in employment, and are not intended to be suspended or changed by any apparently contrary instruction that may be inadvertently given in any single case.

The instructions are as follows, and they are separately paragraphed and numbered for convenience of reference:

1. You are to investigate only such cases as are referred to you for the purpose of investigation, thus confining your services to claims actually under examination and intended for the next report; but this is not to restrain you from sending forward, for future use, any information deemed reliable and important coming into your possession without delay or effort. [Benjamin's writing.]

2. When the investigation of a case is begun, you are to finish it up and send forward your report and evidence as soon as possible, and not leave it to go upon other cases or into other localities, unless you are compelled to postpone it. [Benjamin's writing.]

3. You are to take the depositions of witnesses upon the question of the claimant's loyalty or disloyalty & to establish any other facts requiring the allowance or the disallowance of the claim. [Aldis' writing.]

4. In investigating claims you will act according to your own judgment as to the proper mode of making inquiry and as to the number of witnesses whose depositions you may take; but as your report & the depositions you take will be shown to the claimant or his attorney & will be open to rebuttal, you will of course use much care to have them correct. [Aldis' writing.]

5. You will carefully observe the directions & suggestions sent to you by the Comm'rs and by the Com'r having special charge of the case; and thoroughly examine & report upon those points which he may indicate to you as being important. [Aldis' writing.]

6. If any papers or Exhibits are produced to you send the originals if you can; but if not then send attested copies. [Aldis' writing.]

7. When you have finished taking the evidence in a case then draw up your report. You should state briefly what you have done in investigating the case, the names of the witnesses & a brief summary of your testimony, and such remarks as you deem appropriate as to the appearance & credibility of the witnesses and as to any other facts & matters which in your judgment may affect the decision of the case. [Aldis' writing.]

---

* Charles F. Benjamin to John B. Brownlow, Washington, April 7, 1875, in Southern Claims Commission, "Letters from and about Special Agents," Record Group 56, Treasury Department, National Archives.

8. Confidential or hearsay information may be received by you, but only for the purpose of ascertaining what persons should be examined upon oath, what questions should be put to them to draw out the facts, what other places should be visited in search of evidence, or what steps should be taken by the Commissioners to obtain further evidence for the Government at Washington or elsewhere. [Benjamin's writing.]

9. Your reports are to be in brief, temperate language, exhibiting no personal feeling; each confined to the facts exhibited by the testimony accompanying it, and free from moralizing and generalization. [Benjamin's writing.]

10. The deposition of each witness should begin with a statement of the name, age, residence, and occupation of the witness, whether related to the claimant, whether interested in the claim, and whether his feelings toward the claimant are friendly, unfriendly or neutral. It should be as closely as possible in the words of the witness, confined to the matters under examination and should show how the witness knows the facts, or alleged facts, to which he testifies. [Benjamin's writing.]

11. The Commissioners desire that your earlier investigations should be in the counties of ... [here fourteen Tennessee counties are named as Brownlow's immediate assignment.]

12. At the close of each week, you are to forward for the information of the Commissioners, and to be put on file, a weekly report, showing each day's movement and work and your probable movements for the suceeding week. [Benjamin's writing.]

13. To enable you to administer an oath to a witness and to take his deposition the Commissioners will appoint you a special commissioner, the appointment to be used only for the purposes just stated. [Benjamin's writing.]

APPENDIX C

THE DIGEST OF THE MINOR CASE*

* "Digest of evidence to November 29, 1879," in the claim of Catherine S. Minor, Adams County, Mississippi [claimed $64,155, allowed $13,072 in 1879], C. of C. No. 7960, GAO files. The supplied identification of each witness was taken from the "Alphabetized List of Witnesses," in *ibid*. The conflicting testimony on loyalty is presented in double columns as it was originally briefed by the commissioners. This was their standard practice in the larger cases, and it is interesting to note the number of witnesses involved, the variety of their occupations, and the sharp conflicts in the evidence. For an account of the experiences of this prominent Natchez family of Unionist sentiments, see Frank Wysor Klingberg, "The Case of the Minors: A Unionist Family within the Confederacy," *Journal of Southern History*, XIII (Feb., 1947), 27–45.

How Claimant Acted

Took oath of allegiance soon as Union troops arrived at Natchez (Mrs. *Chotard*). ["distant relative, found loyal by us," for clmt.]

Nursed and supplied Federal sick & wounded; refused to give up carpets to make blankets when demanded by Confederate supply officers (Claimant).

Refused to do anything for the Ladies' Aid Society when solicited; refused to aid witness in getting some clothes thro' lines to her brothers in Confed. army, saying she was a loyal woman (*Mrs. S. A. Jenkins*). ["lady of Natchez," for clmt.]

Had shirts, caps & socks made for Confederate army by witness and Julia Walker & two other women now dead, and boxed up and sent off (*Polly Bell*. wife of Dennis Bell, of whom *infra* Statement denied by oath of claimant and Julia Walker). [Polly Bell, "wife of Dennis & claimant's slave," for govt. Julia Walker not identified.]

Sent socks & cotton bats to rebel hospital (*Dennis Bell*, of whom both claimant and Genl Martin gave very bad accounts as to character. Claimant admits responding in small way to call for socks & bats for hospital partly for humanity & partly for policy, the appeal looking as much humane as political & she having already refused so many calls and opportunities).

Gave provisions to free market for Confed. soldiers families (*Bell & Essig*—claimant says free market was for the poor at large & gave some small contributions from garden for charity). [Essig a "saloon-keeper & shoemaker" and Bell "claimant's slave coachman" both govt. witnesses.]

Gave provisions to Mrs. Elliott, a rebel soldier's wife (*Bell*—Claimant cannot remember so doing but knew Mrs. E. to be wretchedly poor & may have assisted her for that reason alone).

Used to attend the drills of the rebel

company on the bluff & officers used to visit the house. (*LaCoste*—See below for evidence that company was organized at the time of John Brown raid, before the war). [LaCoste, "claimant's slave," and clmt. witness.]

How Claimant Talked

Expressed opposition to secession & rebellion throughout the war—Was opposed to Slavery (Mrs. *Chotard*).

Most violently opposed to the war & in family gatherings would rejoice at Federal victories (Miss *Minor*). ["young sister-in-law," for clmt.]

Heard her give toast to Presdt of U. S. at dinner party in 1864 (*Ault*). ["deputy tax collector," for govt.]

Said she was loyal woman when refusing aid & shelter to witness in 1864, when latter trying to smuggle out clothes to her brothers (*Mrs. Jenkins*).

Often heard her wish for Confederate victories when talking to rebel officers and ladies (*Bell*).

Was an outspoken rebel (*Ford*, concerning whom *infra*.)

Talked like a Confederate (*Essig*, whom Genl Martin says is low saloon-keeper. Claimant says he was a boot-maker who made boots for her husband, but disclaims further acquaintance with him).

Heard her rejoice over Confed. victories when witness dining room servant at Mrs. Chotard's (*Fletcher*—Claimant denies totally and says witness was not at Mrs. Chotard's house, but at Major Chotard's. [Edward Fletcher, "domestic slave, not claimant's" for govt.]

Told her servants would be cruelly treated if went to Yankees (See Scott. Overseer Spain admits that she did say so, but explained to him that it was to keep the negroes [from] running off, to her and their damage, as soon as they learned the Federals were coming. Spain heard her tell them they were free & could go if they would). [Lee Scott was described as "claimant's slave" and testified for her.]

How Claimant Felt

Was an abolitionist in principle—Always hoped Union cause would succeed—Wanted Federal arms to win (claimant).

"Loyal to the flag of the Union throughout the rebellion (*Claimant's application for pardon*).

Reputation of Claimant & Husband

A pre-eminently loyal family. (*Genl McKee*, Pro. Mar. at Natchez).

Received protection papers first eve-

Claimant's family openly disloyal. (Col. *A. K. Johnson*, but Comm'rs did not believe this witness when he testified

ning Federals arrived. Federals told her they knew of them before coming (*Mrs. Rebecca Minor*). [Described as "mother-in-law," C.]

Always protected & favored by Federal commanders (*claimant*).

House a complete resort for the Federal officers (*Organ & Spain*).

[J. R. Organ, "Federal colonel, now planter," and Thos. H. Spain, "former overseer," both for C.]

Was an unfriendly feeling towards them in town (Mrs. *Nutt*). ["lady, found loyal by us," C.]

Found them in bad odor when home on furlough before Fed's came (*Martin*). [Wm. T. Martin, "family lawyer & Confed. genl." C.]

Minor had been extremely popular man before war, but his course made him very unpopular (*Martin*). [C.]

Heard Confed. Genl. York call him "Yankee" in street quarrel after the war (Organ). [C.]

Threats were made against him because he would not join the army (*Claimant*).

Union man, so-called in various forms of phraseology (Adjt. Genl. *Thomas*, Genl. *Gresham*, Colonels *Biddle, Cooley*, & *Davis* in letters on file).

Regarded as decided Union woman (Mrs. *Nutt*). [C.]

Reputation decidedly Union. (Mrs. *Chotard*). [C.]

Reputation that of Union woman (Judge *Winchester*) ["lawyer, ex-judge." C.]

Mrs. Martin, who was her schoolfellow and bosom friend, so that they lived near to each other after both married, in pursuance of an agreement made before, broke off all relations with her because of her course during war & only resumed some six years after broken; on occasion of death in claimant's family (Genl. *Martin*). [C.]

A loyal citizen (Genl [Henry W.] *Farrar*, in pass issued in 1864).

in favor of Andrew Brown's big claim.)

Reputation of claimant and husband both as on Confederate side (*Arrighi*, Mrs. *Crizer, Essig, Fitzhugh, Ford, Forbes, Harper, McClure, March, Scofield, Stewart*. But Mrs. Crizer's husband tried to maintain an unjust suit after Minor's death by subornation, says claimant. Fitzhugh is a negro & was not in position to know what the Minors were or were esteemed to be, says Genl. Martin.

Ford is bitter enemy of Minors says claimant & Martin & has made recent threats, agt claimant and forbidden Minor tenants from coming on his lands. Forbes tried to collect an old bill the third time after it had been paid a second time to make sure, says claimant, and he is an opium-eater and mere wreck of man & scarcely responsible, says Martin.—Never heard of McClure, says Claimant. Scofield is man who got possession of valuable horse of claimant's brother & ordered to give it up by military upon her request, says claimant. Stewart is man who has been trying to collect fraudulent bill & is trying to keep it alive by presentations every now & then. Essig has been already mentioned and Arrighi, Harper & March not attacked.

Mrs. Minor regarded by the Federal officers as disloyal (Capt. *Whitney*). ["Fedl Commissary, now planter." G.]

Never suspected her of Federal sympathies (*Davis*). [Alfred V. Davis "rich-planter, distantly related." G.]

Mr. Minor strong Confederate (*Whitney*). [G.]

How Claimant's Husband Acted

Would not vote at Confederate Presidential election (*claimant*).

When witness undertook to reorganize the cavalry company (raised at time of John Brown scare) for the Confederate service, Minor, who was lieutenant, threw up his commission, accompanying act with strong Union speech (*Martin*). [C.]

When husband of witness got into quarrel about politics at Natchez, Minor, who was present, sided with him & got involved; soon after war began (Mrs. *Nutt*). [C.]

Minor had a uniform & used to drill with rebel company (*Polly Bell*). [G.]

Minor used to drill with Martin's company on bluff, the first year of war, in 1860—Gave two or three horses to company, also big dinner to officers before leaving for Va. He got excused by doctor. Had uniform of gray coat, white vest & white trousers with blue stripe & "Confederate saddle & bridle" (*La-Coste*, but Martin, who was captain says Minor severed from company when it was organized for the war and gave no horses to it). [John LaCoste, "claimant's slave." G.]

Minor gave three horses to Confederate company, one of them to Ham Hatchwood, a member of it (*Bell*—but Martin says no horses given & no Hatchwood in Company). [G.]

Put in a substitute (*Bell*, but claimant asserts necessity as only way of keeping out himself). [G.]

Minor sent a negro to wait upon his overseer Buchanan, who was a private in the cavalry (*Harris*). [Wilson Harris, "claimant's slave." G.]

Minor caused some sick Confederate soldiers to be removed out of range of gunboats fire, when they were expected (*Bell*). [G.]

Minor assisted in burning the cotton of witness because he was a Union man (*Ford*, but Genl Martin says he was of counsel in the suit that followed; that Ford admitted to him that Minor did not burn the cotton; that when Ford sued, he only sued Surget, Minor's brother-in-law; that the Pro' Marshall ordered Minor & Surget to burn the cotton along the river on pain of being sent to the army for refusing: that they demanded a written order before they would act and got it; that Minor warned Ford in ample time to move his cotton back from the river.) [Washington Ford, "planter." G.]

How Claimant's Husband Talked

Always spoke of Federal success as foregone conclusion (claimant).

Said to witness he would not fire a gun while he had a dollar to keep out; that South would be beaten & ruined as the result and that witness should keep out of it (*Spain*). [C.]

Heard Minor, his brother-in-law, Surget, and old Major Benjamin talking together (when by themselves and somewhat under the influence of liquor) about Dick Taylor's success at Berwick's Bay, which they agreed was only temporary & could not affect final result (*Ault*). [Lewis P. Ault, "deputy tax collector." G.]

Made strong Union Speech in giving up lieutenantcy, when company was to be organized for Confederacy (*Martin*). [C.]

Said Confederates bound to succeed & wished them success (*Bell*). [G.]

Would wish that rebels would whip the Yankees. Rejoiced at Bull Run victory (*Smith*, but claimant says this is the negro who testified falsely for the C——s when they sued, after Minor's death for horse feed that he himself had supplied.) [John W. Smith, "colored stable keeper." G.]

Expressed himself as on Confederate side (*Davis*). [G.]

Talked like a Confederate (Mrs. *Crizer, Essig, Fletcher, Forbes, Ford, Smith, Wilkerson*, concerning last of whom claimant says he was overseer, and had trouble in settling accounts & been unfriendly ever since). [All G.]

"Used to say: "Yankees have won" & "Our side has won." (*Polly Bell*). [G.]

Spoke of Federal army as "the enemy," when testifying in court after war (*Ford*). [G.]

BIBLIOGRAPHY

BIBLIOGRAPHY

MANUSCRIPTS

Court of Claims. Court of Claims records consist of printed and typed abstracts and briefs of the arguments for the plaintiff and the government, and the findings of fact for the Captured and Abandoned Property cases and the Southern Claims Commission cases appealed under the Tucker and Bowman acts. They are bound but not published and should not be confused with the Court of Claims *Reports* published annually.

House File Room, House of Representatives. The cases disallowed by the commissioners of claims and not reopened, which were consulted in the House File Room, have now been transferred to the Legislative Department, National Archives.

General Accounting Office, Consolidated File Section. The cases allowed by the commissioners of claims, and paid by the third auditor of the Treasury, were consulted with the permission of the comptroller general.

National Archives. Justice Department.

Record Group 60: General Records of the Department of Justice; Records of the Attorney General; Attorney General's Letter Books; Appointment Papers.

Record Group 123: Records of the United States Court of Claims; Cases before the Commissioners of Claims, allowed and disallowed, which were reopened in the Court of Claims under the Bowman and Tucker acts or for other reasons.

Record Group 205: Records of the Court of Claims Section, Department of Justice; letter books, docket books, and miscellaneous notes.

———. Legislative Department.

Record Group 46: Records of the United States Senate; Files of the Committee on Claims of the Senate for the 41st through the 46th Congresses.

Record Group 233: Records of the House of Representatives; cases disallowed by the commissioners of claims and not reopened or withdrawn.

———. State Department.

Record Group 59: Appointment Papers; Applications and Recommendations.

———. Treasury Department.

Record Group 36: Records of Collector of Customs at New Orleans; New Orleans Manifests.

Record Group 56: General Records of the Department of the Treasury; claims allowed under the special act of May 18, 1872; Cotton and Captured and Abandoned Property cases; Records of the Special Agents; Records of the Appointments Division; Confederate Treasury Department; Restricted Commercial Intercourse and Captured and Abandoned Property acts, general papers; war claims and miscellaneous, Division of Bookkeeping and Warrants; and the Records of the Commissioners of Claims, as follows:

Alphabetical list of claimants: 1 volume, labeled "Claimants under Southern Claims Commission, 1871," gives only name, state, and county of claimant; the other, labeled "Claimants before the Southern Claims Commission, 1873," gives the serial number as well, and each entry is canceled in blue (allowed), green (disallowed), or red (barred for nonprosecution). 2 vols.

[229]

Work book. An unlabeled volume listing claims alphabetically, with brief entries, usually dated, under columns labeled "House," "Sp'l Agt.," and "Archives."

Index to Claims: giving only claimants' names and serial numbers. 5 vols.

Journal of the Commissioners, March 16, 1871–March 9, 1880, and a Rough Journal of the Commissioners, March 16, 1871–Oct. 8, 1872. 3 vols.

Miscellaneous Letters Received, chiefly March 10, 1871–June 29, 1880, including letters received by the commissioners and unattached to specific cases, from claimants, attorneys, informers, Federal officials, and applications for appointment, bills for goods, and fifty-seven summary reports on individual cases. A few letters and papers covering the period March 29, 1864, to approximately April 17, 1900, are also with this group. 6 drawers.

Letters from and about Special Agents R. B. Avery, Liberty Bartlett, John B. Brownlow, S. E. Chamberlain, John D. Edwards, W. M. Fitzgerald, L. C. Houk, H. E. Nelson, W. W. Paine, Theodore W. Parmele, William Richards, Enos Richmond, Ira S. Smith, and George Tucker, chiefly letters of acceptance, and weekly reports covering the period Aug. 8, 1871–Feb. 7, 1880. 3 drawers.

Geographical List of Claims, arranged alphabetically by names of states, thereunder by names of counties, and thereunder by names of claimants, with serial numbers from 1 through 22,298, giving identifying information, the names of attorneys, dates of receipt of depositions, assignment of cases for investigation, filing of attorneyships, dates of oral hearings, and an entry of the date the case was reported to Congress. 40 vols.

Record Group 105: Records on Abandoned Lands.
————. War Department.
Record Group 92: Records of the Quartermaster General's Office; Letter Books, "Claims."
Record Group 109: Sequestration, Confederate Records.
Record Group 192: Records of the Commissary General of Subsistence; Letter Books, "Claims."
Library of Congress, Manuscript Division.
    Papers of the House of Representatives, 44th Cong., 1st and 2d Sessions, including "all complaints and affidavits made to said Commission against the clerk thereof, or any special agent or commissioner appointed by said Board," as required to be turned over to the Committee on War Claims, House of Representatives, by Resolution of May 1, 1876, 44th Cong., 1st Session. 2 boxes.
Confederate State Department Archives
Papers of James G. Blaine
Letters and Papers of Simon Cameron
Letters to Schuyler Colfax
Correspondence of Salmon P. Chase
Papers of Zachariah Chandler

Papers of Hamilton Fish
Papers of U. S. Grant
Papers of Andrew Johnson
R. T. Lincoln Manuscripts
Letters of James M. Mason
Correspondence of Hugh McCulloch
Papers of Thaddeus Stevens

PRINTED GOVERNMENT DOCUMENTS

CONFEDERATE STATES OF AMERICA

Army. Department of Henrico. *Report of Brigadier General John H. Winder, Head-quarters, Department Henrico, Listing the Civilians in Custody, under authority of the War department, in the city of Richmond* [Richmond, 1863]. 8 pp.

Constitution. Texas Convention, 1861. *The Constitution of the State of Texas, as amended in 1861. The Constitution of the Confederate States of America. The Ordinance of the Texas convention; and an Address of the People of Texas.* Austin, 1861. 40 pp.

―――. South Carolina Convention, 1860–1862. *Journal of the Convention of the People of South Carolina, held in 1860, 1861, and 1862, together with the Ordinances, Reports, Resolutions, etc.* Columbia, S.C., 1862. 873 pp.

―――. Mississippi Convention. *Journal of the State Convention and Ordinances and Resolutions adopted in March, 1861.* Jackson, Miss., 1861. 104 pp.

―――. Louisiana Convention, 1861. *Official Journal of the Proceedings of the Convention of the State of Louisiana, By authority.* New Orleans, 1861. 330 pp.

―――. Georgia Convention, 1861. *Journal of the Public and Secret Proceedings of the Convention of the People of Georgia, held in Milledgeville [January 16–25] and Savannah [March 7–23] in 1861. Together with the Ordinance adopted.* Milledgeville, Georgia, 1861. 416 pp.

Congress. 1st Cong., 1st Sess., Feb. 18–April 22, 1862, Vol. 44 [Feb. 18 to March 25] in *Southern Historical Society Papers.* Richmond, Va., 1923―. 1st Cong., 2d Sess., Aug. 18–Oct. 13, 1862, Vol. 46 in *ibid.* 1st Cong., 3d Sess., Jan. 12–May 1, 1863, Vols. 47–48 in *ibid.*

―――. Conference Committees. *Report [of] the Committee of Conference on the disagreeing Votes of the two Houses on the bill (H. R. 9) to Authorize and Regulate the Impressment of Private Property, for the use of the army and other Military Purposes* [Richmond, 1863]. 8 pp.

―――. House of Representatives. Committee on Quartermaster and Commissary Department. *Report of the Committee on Quartermaster and Commissary department* [Richmond, 1864]. 3 pp.

―――. House of Representatives. Special Committee on the Payment of Claims. *Report of the Special Committee on the Payment of Claims* [Richmond, 1864]. 7 pp.

―――. House of Representatives. Special Committee on Impressment. Alabama Legislature. *Joint resolutions of the General Assembly of the State of Alabama in Relation to impressments and the Schedule of prices fixed by Confederate Commissioners* [Richmond, 1864]. 11 pp.

―――. *Journal of the Congress of the Confederate States of America, 1861–1865.* Washington, 1904–1905. 7 vols.

District Courts. Alabama. *Rules of practice under the Sequestration Act for the*

District Courts Confederate States for the District of Alabama. Adopted November, 1861. Mobile, 1861. 10 pp.

————. South Carolina. *The Sequestration Cases before the Hon. A. G. Magrath. Report of Cases under the Sequestration Act of the Confederate States, heard in the District Court for the State of South Carolina, in the city of Charleston. October term, 1861.* Charleston, 1861. 67 pp.

Laws and Statutes. *An Act to alter and amend an act entitled "An Act for the Sequestration of the estates, property and effects of Alien Enemies and for Indemnity of Citizens of the Confederate States, and Persons aiding the same in the existing War with the United States," approved August 30, 1861* [Richmond, 1861]. 11 pp.

————. *A bill to be entitled An Act supplemental to, and amendatory of the several acts for the Sequestration of Estates, Property, and Effects of Alien Enemies, and for Indemnity of Citizens of the Confederate States, and persons aiding the same in the existing war with the United States* [Richmond, 1863]. 4 pp.

————. *A bill to be entitled An Act to Define and Punish Conspiracy against the Confederate States* [Richmond, 1864]. 2 pp.

————. *A bill to be entitled An Act to provide for Sequestrating the Property of Persons liable to military service, who have departed, or shall depart, from the Confederate States without permission* [Richmond, 1864]. 3 pp.

————. *A bill to be entitled An Act to establish the Court for the Investigation of Claims against the Government of the Confederate States* [Richmond, 1863]. 4 pp.

————. *A bill to be entitled An Act providing for the auditing and payment of Properly authenticated claims against the Cotton Bureau in the Trans-Mississippi department* [Richmond, 1865]. 1 p.

Treasury Department. *Message of the President, February 23, 1863 transmitting a Communication from the Secretary of the Treasury and the Attorney General in regard to the Sequestration of Real Estate belonging to alien enemies* [Richmond, 1863]. 7 pp.

————. *Communication from the Secretary of the Treasury Recommending certain changes in the Impressment laws, November 23, 1864* [Richmond, 1864]. 3 pp.

War Department. *Communication of the Secretary of War relative to the "domestic passport system" enforced upon citizens travelling in some parts of the Confederate States outside of the lines of the enemies* [Richmond, 1864]. 9 pp.

————. *Communication of the Secretary of War submitting a report from the Adjutant General relative to the appointments under an act approved June 14, 1864, providing for the establishment and payment of claims for a certain description of property taken or informally impressed for the use of the army, together with a list of commissioners* [Richmond, 1864]. 4 pp.

UNITED STATES

Census Office. 8th Census, 1860. *Population of the United States in 1860; Compiled from the Original Returns of the 8th Census, under direction of the Secretary of the Interior.* Washington, 1864.

————. 9th Census, 1870. *The Statistics of the Population of the United States embracing the Tables of Race, Nationality, Sex, Selected Ages, and Occupations.* Washington, 1872.

————. 10th Census, 1880. *Statistics of the Population of the United States, by*

States, Counties, and Minor Civil Divisions. Compiled from the Returns of the 10th Census. Washington, 1881.

Claims commissioners. *Consolidated Index of Claims Reported to the House of Representatives, 1871–1880.* Washington, 1892.

——. *Summary Reports in All Cases Reported to Congress as Disallowed under the Act of March 3, 1871, reported as follows: 1st General Report, Dec. 11, 1871; 2nd General Report, Dec. 6, 1872; 3rd General Report, Dec. 6, 1873; 4th General Report, Dec. 14, 1874; and Special Report on the Case of Marie P. Evans, Reported Jan. 16, 1875; also including Acts establishing the Commissioners of Claims and Amendatory thereof, and also their 4 General Reports.* Washington, 1876. Vol. I.

——. *5th General Report, Dec. 20, 1875; 6th General Report, Dec. 4, 1876.* Washington, 1877. Vol. II.

——. *7th General Report, Dec. 6, 1877; 8th General Report, Dec. 13, 1878.* Washington, Vol. III.

——. *9th General Report, Dec. 16, 1879; 10th General Report, March 10, 1880.* Washington, 1881. Vol. IV.

——. The ten Annual Reports of the claims commissioners appear in the *House Miscellaneous Documents* as follows:

1st General Report, 1871. 42d Cong., 2d Sess., Vol. I, No. 16.
2d General Report, 1872. 42d Cong., 3d Sess., Vol. I, No. 12.
3d General Report, 1873. 43d Cong., 1st Sess., Vol. I, No. 23.
4th General Report, 1874. 43d Cong., 2d Sess., Vol. I, No. 18.
5th General Report, 1875. 44th Cong., 1st Sess., Vol. I, No. 30.
6th General Report, 1876. 44th Cong., 2d Sess., Vol. I, No. 4.
7th General Report, 1877. 45th Cong., 2d Sess., Vol. I, No. 4.
8th General Report, 1878. 45th Cong., 3d Sess., Vol. I, No. 6.
9th General Report, 1879. 46th Cong., 2d Sess., Vol. I, No. 10.
10th General Report, 1880. 46th Cong., 2d Sess., Vol. II, No. 30.

Congress. *American State Papers*, Vol. IX, "Claims." Washington, 1888.

——. *Biographical Congressional Directory, 1774–1927.* Washington, 1928. 1740 pp.

——. *Claims Referred by Congress to the Court of Claims for a Finding of Fact under the Provisions of the Bowman Act.* Washington, 1909.

——. *Congressional Globe.* 36th Cong., 2d Sess. to 42d Cong., 3d Sess.

——. *Congressional Record.* 43d Cong., Special Sess. to 50th Cong., 2d Sess.

——. *Statutes at Large.* Vols. X to XXXVI.

Court of Claims. *Reports.* Vols. I to XXXVI.

Supreme Court. *Reports.* Vols. LXVI to LXXXVI; Black, 1-2; Wallace, 1–18.

Treasury Department. *An Account of the Receipts and Expenditures of the United States for the Fiscal Year Ending June 30, 1865 ... 1880.* Washington, 1866.

——. *The Accounting System of the United States from 1789 to 1910,* No. 2603. Washington, n.d.

——. *Circular Letter of Instructions to Officers of Treasury Department relative to Commercial Intercourse, Captured, Abandoned, and Confiscable property, Freedmen, etc.* Washington, 1865.

——. *Insurrectionary States. General Regulations for Purchase of Products of Insurrectionary States on Government Account [Sept. 24, 1864, with Executive Orders and General Orders of the War and Navy Departments Relating thereto].* Washington, 1864.

————. *Insurrectionary States, Acts of Congress and Rules and Regulations Prescribed by Secretary of Treasury, in pursuance thereto, with approval of President, concerning Commercial Intercourse with and in States and parts of States declared in Insurrection, Captured, Abandoned, and Confiscable Property, Care of Freedmen, and Purchase of Products of Insurrectionary Districts on Government Account.* Washington, 1868.

————. *Claims. Elementary Manual of Practice. Civil War Claims,* by W. C. Eldridge and L. R. Ginn. No. 2171. Washington, 1900.

————. *Amended Regulations for the Purchase of Products of Insurrectionary States on Government Account, May 9, 1865.* Washington, 1865.

————. *Digest of Decisions and Orders Affecting Settlement of Quartermasters' Accounts in Office of 3d Auditor of Treasury,* compiled by W. P. Dunwoody. Washington, 1866.

BOOKS AND PAMPHLETS

Abel, Annie Heloise. *The American Indian as Slaveholder and Secessionist.* Cleveland, 1915.

Abrams, Alexander St. Clair. *President Davis and his 'Administration.* Atlanta, 1864.

Aldrich, Lewis Cass. *History of Franklin and Grand Isle Counties, Vermont; With Illustrations and Biographical Sketches of the Prominent Men and Pioneers.* New York, 1891.

Ambler, Charles Henry. *Sectionalism in Virginia from 1776 to 1861.* Chicago, 1910.

————. *Francis H. Pierpont, Union War Governor of Virginia and Father of West Virginia.* Chapel Hill, 1937.

Anderson, Charles Carter. *Fighting by Southern Federals in which the Author places the Numerical Strength of the Armies that Fought for the Confederacy at approximately 1,000,000 men and shows that 296,579 White soldiers living in the South, and 137,676 Colored soldiers, and approximately 200,000 Men living in the North that were born in the South, making 634,255 Southern soldiers, fought for the Preservation of the Union.* New York, 1912.

Appleton's Annual Cyclopedia and Register of Important Events . . . Embracing Political, Military, and Ecclesiastical Affairs; Public Documents; Biography, Statistics, Commerce, Finance, Literature, Science, Agriculture, and Mechanical Industry. New York, 1861–1875. 15 vols.

Arnett, Alex Matthews. *The Populist Movement in Georgia: A View of the "Agrarian Crusade" in the Light of Solid South Politics.* New York, 1922.

Arnold, Sir Robert Arthur. *The History of the Cotton 'Famine from the Fall of Sumter to the Passing of the Public Works Act.* London, 1864.

Barnes, William Horatio. *The History of the Forty-first Congress of the United States, 1869–1871.* Washington, 1872.

————. *The History of the Congress of the United States.* New York, 1871.

Beale, Howard Kennedy. *The Critical Year: A Study of Andrew Johnson and Reconstruction.* New York, 1930.

Benton, Elbert Jay. *The Movement for Peace without Victory during the Civil War.* Cleveland, 1918.

Binkley, Wilfred Ellsworth. *American Political Parties, Their Natural History.* New York, 1945.

Borchard, Edwin Montefiore. *Contractual Claims in International Law*. New York, 1913.

Britton, Wiley. *The Civil War on the Border*. New York, 1891–1904. 2 vols.

Brooks, Robert Preston. *Conscription in the Confederate States of America, 1862–1865*. Athens, Ga., 1917.

Buel, Clarence Clough, and Robert Underwood Johnson. *Battles and Leaders of the Civil War*. New York, 1887. 4 vols.

Butterfield, Roger. *The American Past: a History of the United States from Concord to Hiroshima, 1775–1945. Told with the Aid of a Thousand Pictures . . .* New York, 1947.

Capers, Henry Dickson. *The Life and Times of C. G. Mamminger*. Richmond, 1893.

Carpenter, Jesse Thomas. *The South as a Conscious Minority, 1789–1861: A Study in Political Thought*. New York, 1930.

Cheshire, Bishop Joseph Blount. *The Church in the Confederate States: A History of the Protestant Episcopal Church in the Confederate States*. New York, 1912.

Chittenden, Lucius Eugene. *A Report of the Debates and Proceedings in the Secret Session of the Conference Convention for Proposing Amendments to the Constitution of the United States, held at Washington, D.C., in February, 1861*. New York, 1864.

Cleveland, Henry. *Alexander Stephens in Public and Private; with Letters and Speeches, before, during and since the War*. Philadelphia, 1896.

Cole, Arthur Charles. *The Whig Party in the South*. Washington, 1913.

Commons, John Rogers. *Horace Greeley and the Working Class Origins of the Republican Party*. Boston, 1909.

Coulter, Ellis Merton. *The South During Reconstruction. 1865–1877*. Baton Rouge, 1947.

———. *William G. Brownlow, Fighting Parson of the Southern Highlands*. Chapel Hill, 1936.

Craven, Avery Odelle. *The Coming of the Civil War*. New York, 1942.

Curry, J. L. M., *Civil History of the Confederate States, with some Personal Reminiscences*. Richmond, 1901.

Cushman, Robert Eugene. *Leading Constitutional Decisions*. New York, 1946.

Daniel, John Moncure. *Civil History of the Confederate States, with some Personal Reminiscences*. Richmond, 1901.

Davis, Caleb F., comp. *Keokuk Biographical and Historical Sketches*. Keokuk, Iowa, n. d.

Davis, Jefferson. *The Rise and Fall of the Confederate Government*. New York, 1881. 2 vols.

Day, Louis Madison. *The Constitutionality and Legality of Confiscations in Fee under the Act of July 17, 1862*. New Orleans, 1870.

De Forest, John William. *A Union Officer in Reconstruction*. Edited by James H. Croushore and David M. Potter. New Haven, 1948.

Dictionary of American Biography. New York, 1928———. 21 vols.

Dictionary of American History. New York, 1940. 5 vols.

Dodd, William Edward. *The Days of the Cotton Kingdom*. New Haven, 1926.

Dorris, Jonathan T. *Pardon and Amnesty under Lincoln and Johnson*. Chapel Hill, 1953.

Dunning, William Archibald. *Essays on the Civil War and Reconstruction, and Related Topics*. New York, 1904.

Eaton, Clement. *Freedom of Thought in the Old South*. Durham, 1940.

Emerson, Edward Waldo, and Waldo Emerson Forbes, eds. *Journal of Ralph Waldo Emerson with Annotations*. Boston, 1909–1914. 10 vols.

Encyclopedia of Vermont Biography. Edited by Prentiss C. Dodge. Burlington, Vermont, 1912.

Fahrney, Ralph Ray. *Horace Greeley and the Tribune in the Civil War*. Cedar Rapids, Iowa, 1936.

Fish, Carl Russell. *The American Civil War: An Interpretation*. New York, 1937.

Fleming, Walter Lynwood. *Civil War and Reconstruction in Alabama*. New York, 1905.

Flippin, Percy Scott. *Herschel V. Johnson of Georgia, State Rights Unionist*. Richmond, 1931.

Foote, Henry Stuart. *The Bench and Bar of the South and the Southwest*. St. Louis, Mo., 1876.

Goodrich, John Ellsworth. *General Catalogue of the University and State Agricultural School, 1791–1900*. Burlington, Vt., 1901.

Gray, Lewis Cecil. *History of Agriculture in the Southern United States to 1860*. Washington, 1933. 2 vols.

Gray, Wood. *The Hidden Civil War, the story of the Copperheads*. New York, 1942.

Greeley, Horace. *The American Conflict; a History of the Great Rebellion in the United States of America, 1860–65, its Causes, Incidents, and Results; intended to exhibit especially its Moral and Political phases, with the Drift and Progress of American opinion respecting Human Slavery from 1776 to the close of the War for the Union*. Hartford, 1864–1866. 2 vols.

Green, Fletcher Melvin. *Constitutional Development in the South Atlantic States, 1776–1860; a Study in the Evolution of Democracy*. Chapel Hill, 1930.

Gue, Benjamin F. *History of Iowa from the Earliest Times to the beginning of the Twentieth Century*. New York, 1903. 4 vols.

Halleck, Henry Wager. *International Law in Peace and War*. New York, 1861.

Hamilton, Joseph Gregoire de Roulhac, ed. *The Correspondence of Jonathan Worth*. Raleigh, 1909. 2 vols.

Hammond, Matthew Brown. *The Cotton Industry; an Essay in American Economic History*. New York, 1897.

Harlan, Edgar Rubey. *A Narrative History of the People of Iowa, with Special Treatment of the Chief Enterprises in Education, Religion ... Industry, Business, etc.* Chicago, 1931. 5 vols.

Hodgson, Joseph. *The Cradle of the Confederacy or the Times of Troup, Quitman, and Yancey*. Mobile, 1876.

Holden, Austin Wells, and Joel Munsell, eds. *A History of the Town of Queensbury in the State of New York*. Albany, N.Y., 1874.

Holden, J. A. *"In Memoriam" Orange Ferriss, 1814–1894*. Glens Falls, N.Y., 1894.

Holloway, John B. *Laws of the United States and Decisions of the Courts Relating to War Claims*. Washington, 1914.

Howe, Mark Anthony De Wolfe, ed. *Home Letters of General Sherman*. New York, 1909.

Hyman, Harold M. *Era of the Oath*. Philadelphia, 1954.

Johnson, Bradley Tyler. *The Cause of the Confederate States*. Baltimore, 1886.

Jones, John Beauchamp. *A Rebel War Clerk's Diary at the Confederate Capital*. New York, 1935. 2 vols.

Kibler, Lillian Adele. *Benjamin F. Perry, South Carolina Unionist.* Durham, N.C., 1946.

Klingberg, Frank Joseph. *The Anti-Slavery Movement in England: a Study in English Humanitarianism.* New Haven, 1926.

——. *The Tappan Papers; a Sidelight on Anglo-American Relations, 1839–1858, Furnished by the Correspondence of Lewis Tappan and Others with the British and Foreign Anti-Slavery Society.* Washington, 1927.

Laws and Information Relating to Claims against the Government of the United States. Washington, 1866.

Leib, Charles. *Nine months in the Quartermaster's Department; or the Chances for Making a Million.* Cincinnati, 1862.

Lonn, Ella. *Desertion during the Civil War.* New York, 1928.

——. *Foreigners in the Confederacy.* Chapel Hill, 1940.

——. *Reconstruction in Louisiana after 1868.* New York, 1918.

——. *Salt as a Factor in the Confederacy.* New York, 1933.

McHenry, George. *The Cotton Trade: its bearing upon the Property of Great Britain and the Commerce of the American Republics in connection with the System of Negro Slavery in the Confederate States.* London, 1863.

Martin, Bessie. *Desertion of Alabama Troops from the Confederate Army: A Study in Sectionalism.* New York, 1932.

Massey, Mary Elizabeth. *Ersatz in the Confederacy.* Columbia, 1952.

Mathieson, William Law. *Great Britain and the Slave Trade, 1839–1865.* London, 1929.

Milton, George Fort. *Abraham Lincoln and the Fifth Column.* New York, 1942.

Nicolay, John George, and John Hay. *Abraham Lincoln: A History.* New York, 1917. 10 vols.

Nixon, Herman Clarence. *Lower Piedmont Country.* New York, 1946.

Owsley, Frank Lawrence. *State Rights in the Confederacy.* Chicago, 1925.

——. *King Cotton Diplomacy.* Chicago, 1931.

Parrington, Vernon Louis. *Main Currents in American Thought.* New York, 1927–1930. 3 vols.

Paullin, Charles Oscar. *Atlas of the Historical Geography of the United States.* Washington, 1932.

Patrick, Rembert Wallace. *Jefferson Davis and his Cabinet.* Baton Rouge, 1944.

Patton, James Welch. *Unionism and Reconstruction in Tennessee, 1860–1869.* Chapel Hill, 1934.

Pearce, Haywood Jefferson. *Benjamin H. Hill, Secession and Reconstruction.* Chicago, 1928.

Perkins, Howard Cecil. *Northern Editorials on Secession.* New York, 1942. 2 vols.

Phillips, Ulrich Bonnell. *The Life of Robert Toombs.* New York, 1913.

——. *The Course of the South to Secession; an Interpretation.* Edited by E. Merton Coulter. New York, 1939.

——, ed. *The Correspondence of Robert Toombs, Alexander H. Stephens, and Howell Cobb.* Washington, 1913. 2 vols.

Pollard, Edward Alfred. *The Lost Cause: A New Southern History of the War of the Confederates.* New York, 1867.

Portrait and Biographical Album of Lee County, Iowa, containing full page Portraits and Biographical Sketches of Prominent and Representative Citizens of the County, together with Portraits and Biographies of All the Governors of Iowa, and of the Presidents of the United States. Chicago, 1887.

Ramsdell, Charles William. *Behind the Lines in the Southern Confederacy.* Baton Rouge, 1944.

Randall, James Garfield. *The Civil War and Reconstruction.* Boston, 1937.

———. *The Confiscation of Property during the Civil War.* Indianapolis, 1913.

———. *Constitutional Problems under Lincoln.* New York, 1926.

———. *Lincoln and the South.* Baton Rouge, 1946.

———. *Lincoln the President.* New York, 1945. 2 vols.

Richardson, James Daniel, comp. *A Compilation of the Messages and Papers of the Confederacy, Including the Diplomatic Correspondence 1861–1865.* Washington, 1905. 2 vols.

———. *A Compilation of the Messages and Papers of the Presidents.* Washington, 1896–1917. 20 vols.

Rowland, Dunbar, ed. *Jefferson Davis, Constitutionalist: His Letters, Papers and Speeches.* Jackson, Miss., 1923. 10 vols.

Ryle, Walter Harrington. *Missouri: Union or Secession.* Nashville, 1931.

Schwab, John Christopher. *The Confederate States, 1861–1865: A Financial and Industrial History of the South during the War.* New York, 1901.

Shugg, Roger Wallace. *Origins of the Class Struggle in Louisiana: A Social History of White Farmers and Laborers During Slavery and After.* University, La., 1939.

Simkins, Francis Butler, and Roger Hilliard Woody. *South Carolina during Reconstruction.* Chapel Hill, 1932.

Sitterson, J. Carlyle. *The Secession Movement in North Carolina.* Chapel Hill, 1939.

Sowles, Edward Adams. *Memorial Sketch of Hon. Asa Owen Aldis.* Montpelier, Vt., 1904.

Spencer, Cornelia Phillips. *The Last Ninety Days of the War in North Carolina.* New York, 1866.

Stampp, Kenneth M. *And the War Came; the North and the Secession Crisis, 1860–1861.* Baton Rouge, 1950.

Stanwood, Edward. *A History of Presidential Elections.* Boston, 1888.

———. *A History of the Presidency from 1788 to 1897.* Boston, 1912.

Stephenson, Nathaniel Wright. *The Day of the Confederacy: A Chronicle of the Embattled South.* New Haven, 1920.

Stiles, Edward Holcombe. *Recollections and Sketches of Notable Lawyers and Public Men of Early Iowa belonging to the First and Second Generations, with Anecdotes and Incidents Illustrative of the Times.* Des Moines, 1916.

Sumner, Charles. *The Works of Charles Sumner.* Boston, 1900. 20 vols.

Tatum, Georgia Lee. *Disloyalty in the Confederacy.* Chapel Hill, 1934.

Tharin, Robert Seymour Symmes. *Arbitrary Arrests in the South or Scenes from the Experience of an Alabama Unionist.* New York, 1863.

Tindall, George B. *South Carolina Negroes, 1877–1900.* New York, 1952.

Ullery, Jacob G., comp. *Men of Vermont: an Illustrated Biographical History of Vermonters and Sons of Vermont.* Brattleboro, 1894.

Vermont Historical Gazeteer; a Magazine Embracing a History of Each Town, Civil, Ecclesiastical, Biographical and Military. Burlington, Vt., 1868–1891. 5 vols.

Voorhees, Charles Stewart, comp. *Speeches of Daniel W. Voorhees of Indiana,* embracing his most Prominent Forensic, Political, Occasional, and Literary Addresses. Cincinnati, 1875.

War of the Rebellion: a Compilation of the Official Records of the Union and Confederate Armies. Published under the direction of the Secretary of War. Washington, 1880–1901. 128 vols.

Warren, Charles. *The Supreme Court in United States History.* Boston, 1923. 2 vols.

Watts, John. *The Facts of the Cotton Famine.* London, 1866.

Wertenbaker, Thomas Jefferson. *Patrician and Plebeian in Virginia: or the Origin and Development of the Social Classes of the Old Dominion.* Charlottesville, 1910.

Wheaton, Henry. *Elements of International Law.* Boston, 1857.

Whiting, William. *War Powers under the Constitution of the United States. Military Arrests, Reconstruction and Military Government. Also, now first published, War Claims of Aliens. With Notes on the Acts of the Executive and Legislative Departments during our Civil War, and a Collection of Cases Decided in the National Courts.* Boston, 1871.

Wiley, Bell Irvin. *The Life of Johnny Reb, the Common Soldier of the Confederacy.* Indianapolis, 1943.

———. *The Plain People of the Confederacy.* Baton Rouge, 1943.

Williams, Amelia, and Eugene Barker, eds. *The Writings of Samuel Houston, 1813–1863.* Austin, Texas, 1938–1943. 8 vols.

Woodward, C. Vann. *Reunion and Reaction: The Compromise of 1877 and the End of Reconstruction.* Boston, 1951.

Worth, Jonathan. *Correspondence of Jonathan Worth.* [Collected and edited by J. G. de Roulhac Hamilton]. Raleigh, 1909. 2 vols.

Wright, Edward Needles. *Conscientious Objectors in the Civil War.* Philadelphia, 1931.

ARTICLES AND ESSAYS

Beale, Howard K. "On Rewriting Reconstruction History," *American Historical Review,* XLV (1940), 807–827.

Brooks, Robert P. "Conscription in the Confederate States of America, 1862–1865," *Military Historian and Economist,* I (1916), 419–442.

Caldwell, Joshua W. "John Bell of Tennessee: A Chapter of Political History," *American Historical Review,* IV (1899), 651–664.

"Can the South be Starved," *De Bow's Review,* III (1861), 318–319.

Commons, John R. "Horace Greeley and the Working Class Origins of the Republican Party," *Political Science Quarterly,* XXIV (1909), 468–488.

Coulter, E. M. "Commercial Intercourse with the Confederacy in the Mississippi Valley, 1861–1865," *Mississippi Valley Historical Review,* V (1919), 377–405.

De Forest, J. W. "Chivalrous and Semi-Chivalrous Southerners," *Harper's New Monthly Magazine,* XXXVIII (1869), 192–200, 339–347.

Donald, David H. "The Scalawag in Mississippi Reconstruction," *Journal of Southern History,* X (1944), 447–460.

Dunning, W. A. "The Constitution in the Civil War," *Political Science Quarterly,* I (1886), 163–198.

———. "Disloyalty in Two Wars," *Ameircan Historical Review,* XXIV (1919), 625–630.

Dyer, Brainerd. "Francis Lieber and the American Civil War," *Huntington Library Quarterly,* II (1939), 449–465.

Fleming, Walter L. "The Formation of the Union League in Alabama," *Gulf States Historical Magazine,* II (1903), 73–89.

———. "The Peace Movement in Alabama during the Civil War," *South Atlantic Quarterly,* II (1903), 114–124, 246–260.

Ginzberg, Eli. "The Economics of British Neutrality During the American Civil War," *Agricultural History,* X (1936), 147–156.

"Government Claims," *American Law Review,* I (1866–1867), 653–667.

Hamer, Philip M. "The Records of Southern History," *Journal of Southern History,* V (1939), 3–17.

Hesseltine, William B. "Economic Factors in the Abandonment of Reconstruction," *Mississippi Valley Historical Review,* XXII (1935), 191–210.

Hubbard, H. C. " 'Pro-Southern' Influence in the Free West, 1840–1865," *Mississippi Valley Historical Review,* XX (1933), 46–52.

"Indian versus American Cotton," *The London Economist,* XIX (April 13, 1861), 399.

Irvine, Dallas D. "The Fate of Confederate Archives," *American Historical Review,* XLIV (1939), 823–841.

Kendrick, B. B. "The Colonial Status of the South," *Journal of Southern History,* VIII (1942), 3–22.

Klingberg, Frank Wysor. "James Buchanan and the Crisis of the Union," *Journal of Southern History,* IX (1943), 455–474.

———. "The Case of the Minors: A Unionist Family Within the Confederacy," *Journal of Southern History,* XIII (1947), 27–45.

———. "The Southern Claims Commission: A Postwar Agency in Operation," *Mississippi Valley Historical Review,* XXXII (1945), 195–214.

Northrop, L. B. "Memoranda on the Civil War; a Statement from the Confederate Commissary General," *Century Magazine,* IX (1885), 936.

Owsley, Frank L. "Defeatism in the Confederacy," *North Carolina Historical Review,* III (1926), 446–456.

———, and Harriet C. Owsley. "The Economic Basis of Society in the late Ante-Bellum South," *Journal of Southern History,* VI (1940), 24–25.

——— ———. "The Economic Structure of Rural Tennessee, 1850–1860," *Journal of Southern History,* VIII (1943), 161–182.

Rainwater, P. L. "An Analysis of the Secession Controversy in Mississippi," *Mississippi Valley Historical Review,* XXIV (1937), 37–42.

Ramsdell, Charles W. "The Natural Limits of Slavery Expansion," *Mississippi Valley Historical Review,* XVI (1929), 151–171.

Randall, James G. "The Blundering Generation," *Mississippi Valley Historical Review,* XXVII (1940), 3–28.

———. "Lincoln's Peace and Wilson's," *The South Atlantic Quarterly,* XLII (1943), 223–242.

Renick, Edward Ireland. "Assignment of Government Claims, St. Louis, 1890," *American Law Review,* XXIV (1890), 442–456.

Roberts, A. Sellew. "The Federal Government and Confederate Cotton," *American Historical Review,* XXXII (1927), 262–275.

———. "The Peace Movement in North Carolina," *Mississippi Valley Historical Review,* XI (1924), 190–199.

Schell, Herbert S. "Hugh McCulloch and the Treasury Department, 1865–1869," *Mississippi Valley Historical Review*, XVII (1930), 404–421.

Schmidt, Louis B. "The Influence of Wheat and Cotton on Anglo-American Relations during the Civil War," *Iowa Journal of History and Politics*, XVI (1918), 400–439.

Schwab, John C. "Prices in the Confederate States, 1861–65," *Political Science Quarterly*, XIV (1899), 281–304.

Silver, James W. "Propaganda in the Confederacy," *Journal of Southern History*, XI (1945), 487–503.

Sitterson, J. Carlyle. "The William J. Minor Plantations: A Study in Ante-Bellum Absentee Ownership," *Journal of Southern History*, IX (1943), 59–74.

"State of the Union," *The North American Review*, CXV (Oct., 1872), 407–409.

NEWSPAPERS

Atlanta (Georgia) *Constitution*, 1873–1880.

Atlanta (Georgia) *Southern Confederacy*, Feb., 1862–Sept., 1863.

Boston (Massachusetts) *Post*, July, 1864–June, 1868.

Burlington (Vermont) *Free Press*, Jan., 1871–April, 1880; 1891.

Charleston (South Carolina) *Daily Republican*, 1869–July, 1872.

Charleston (South Carolina) *Mercury*, Feb., 1861–1864; 1867.

Chicago (Illinois) *Daily Tribune*, June, 1863–July, 1866; 1871; 1874.

Cincinnati (Ohio) *Enquirer*, 1874.

Fort Smith (Arkansas) *New Era*, 1869–1880.

Glens Falls (New York) *Post-Star*, 1870.

Glens Falls (New York) *Times*, 1871.

Greenville (Tennessee) *New Era*, June, 1865–June, 1877.

Jackson (Mississippi) *Weekly Clarion Ledger*, June, 1867; June, 1873–1880.

Keokuk (Iowa) *Daily Gate City*, 1880.

Keokuk (Iowa) *Weekly Constitution*, 1880.

Knoxville (Tennessee) *Weekly Chronicle*, Jan., 1870–1875. This paper was united with Brownlow's *Whig* to form the *Whig and Chronicle*.

Knoxville (Tennessee) *Whig and Chronicle*, 1875–1882.

Little Rock (Arkansas) *Unconditional Union*, 1864–1865.

Little Rock (Arkansas) *National Democrat*, Sept., 1863–Oct., 1865.

Little Rock (Arkansas) *Arkansas Weekly Republican*, 1867.

Little Rock (Arkansas) *Arkansas Campaign Gazette*, 1867–1868.

Lynchburg (Virginia) *Daily Virginian*, June, 1863–April, 1865.

Montgomery (Alabama) *Advertiser*, May, 1862–March, 1865.

Nashville (Tennessee) *Daily Times and True Union*, Feb., 1864–May, 1865.

Natchez (Mississippi) *Daily Courier*, May, 1861–April, 1863.

New Orleans (Louisiana) *Daily True Delta*, Nov., 1860–1862; 1866.

New Orleans (Louisiana) *Times*, July, 1867–1868; June, 1874–1880.

New York (New York) *Herald*, 1868–1872.

New York (New York) *Daily Tribune*, 1841–1880.

New York (New York) *Weekly Tribune*, 1866–1872.

New York (New York) *Times*, 1861–1880.

Norfolk (Virginia) *Virginian*, 1870–1880.

Philadelphia (Pennsylvania) *Public Ledger*, 1869–1879.

Richmond (Virginia) *Daily Examiner*, Dec., 1860–Nov., 1866.

Richmond (Virginia) *Weekly Enquirer*, July, 1861–Jan., 1867.
Richmond (Virginia) *Southern Opinion*, July, 1867–Nov., 1868.
Savannah (Georgia) *Daily Republican*, July, 1866–1872.
Vicksburg (Mississippi) *Daily Times*, 1873–1875.
Vicksburg (Mississippi) *Weekly Herald*, Sept., 1865–Sept., 1866.
Warren County (New York) *Times*, 1870–1871.
Washington (D.C.) *Daily Morning Chronicle*, 1862–1877.
Washington (D.C.) *Daily National Intelligencer*, 1861–1869.
Washington (D.C.) *Daily Whig*, Feb., 1860; July–Oct., 1861; Jan.–June, 1865; April, 1867–1874; Dec., 1878–1880.

INDEX

INDEX